THE ENGLISH
HISTORICAL TRADITIONAL
SINCE 1850

THE ENGLISH HISTORICAL TRADITION SINCE 1850

CHRISTOPHER PARKER

Principal Lecturer and Head of History
Edge Hill College of Higher Education
Ormskirk · Lancs · UK

JOHN DONALD PUBLISHERS LTD
EDINBURGH

To my mother and father

ISBN 0 85976 293 9

Phototypeset by Bookworm Typesetting Ltd, Edinburgh
Printed and bound by Billing & Sons Ltd, Worcester

Preface

'From what has been said it is also clear that the poet's job is not to report what has happened but what is likely to happen: that is, what is capable of happening according to the rule of probability or necessity. Thus the difference behind the historian and the poet is not in their utterances being in verse or prose . . .; the difference lies in the fact that the historian speaks of what has happened, the poet of the kind of thing that *can* happen. Hence also poetry is a more philosophical and serious business than history; for poetry speaks more of universals, history of particulars. 'Universal' in this case is what kind of person is likely to do or say certain things, according to probability or necessity; that is what poetry aims at, although it gives its persons particular names afterward; while the 'particular' is what Alcibiades did or what happened to him'.

Aristotle, *Poetics*

Need this be so? For history — yes, according to the weight of professional opinion in Britain in the last century and a half. But is the professional majority always right? This book is a critical history of that judgement. Since I started to write it, there have been several publications on related themes, particularly on the Victorian era; noticeably, Rosemary Jann's *The Art and Science of Victorian History* (1985), Peter Slee's *Learning and a Liberal Education: The Study of Modern History in the Universities of Oxford, Cambridge and Manchester, 1800 – 1914* (1986), and Philippa Levine's *The Amateur and the Professional: Antiquarians, Historians and Archaeologists in Victorian England. 1836 – 1886* (1986). Also, individual studies continue to be produced, as with Owen Dudley Edwards's *Macaulay* and Hugh Tulloch's *Acton* in the 'Historians on Historians' series (both in 1988). Tulloch's book is very good, but still fails to convince me of the importance of its subject. As for the rest, whatever their merits, they do not seem to suggest any reasons for modifying my thesis about the individualist English historical tradition.

I would like to thank several people for help in my research: the Archivist of the British Library of Political and Economic Science, at the London School of Economics and Political Science, for permission to quote from the Webster Papers; Mrs Teresa Smith for permission to quote from the Collingwood Papers in the Bodleian Library; the John Rylands Library for use of the Freeman Letters; Balliol College Library for use of the A.L. Smith Papers; the Royal Historical Society Library for use of the Prothero Papers; the Bodleian Library for use of the H.A.L. Fisher Papers; Reading University

Library for access to the Papers of F.M. and D.M. Stenton; and Eastbourne Central Library for the use of the Oscar Browning Papers. I would also like to thank Professor Leff for his very helpful reply to my inquiry. I must also acknowledge my copyright agreement with Wesleyan University in respect to passages approximating to two-thirds of Chapter 2, which have appeared in more or less the same form as an article, 'English Historians and the Opposition to Positivism' in *History and Theory* (1983).

I would also like to thank the Research Committee and the Humanities Department at Bristol Polytechnic for support received whilst I was employed there. In particular I would like to mention Madge Dresser and Michael Stanford, my colleagues in teaching on the Theory and Practice of History course for Bristol Polytechnic's M.A. in Historical Studies: in their different ways they helped to sharpen up my ideas and gave me a lasting belief in the two-way relationship between teaching and research.

Ormskirk, 1990   Christopher Parker

Contents

		Page
Preface		v
1.	Introduction	1
2.	Individualism: A National Tradition and a National Perception	20
3.	The New Liberals: Pluralists and Holists	51
4.	History as a Science — More or Less	83
5.	The Great War and the Revival of Traditional Liberalism	104
6.	Liberalism Besieged	119
7.	History as a Special Form of Knowledge	152
8.	The Marxist Initiative	177
9.	Liberalism Without Liberals	202
Selective Bibliography		245
Index		249

CHAPTER 1

Introduction

The purpose of this book is an elucidation of the main characteristics of the English tradition of history as exemplified by the leading exponents of the art of historical writing since the beginning of the process of institutionalising the subject in the mid-nineteenth century. It is based on the belief that, though the main characteristics of the tradition are generally well known, most explanations of them have been misguided or inadequate. They are misguided when they see the English tradition as dominated by Positivism; and they are inadequate when they fail to treat the history of historiography as the history of historical thinking, which like any other branch of intellectual history cannot be isolated from other intellectual developments or from social and political circumstances. At worst they treat of 'great' historians as discrete individuals, and judge them according to some spurious code of professional practice. In doing this they are, however, confirming, albeit unknowingly, the nature of the tradition.

There are some obvious exceptions to that bold denunciation of previous work, which in two instances at least must be mentioned at once, because their conclusions are important to any understanding of the thesis that will be propounded here. The first of these, *The Liberal Anglican Idea of History*, by Duncan Forbes, is only a partial exception to the rule, because, whilst his analysis of the Liberal Anglicans' idea of history is wholly acceptable, he diminishes the value of his own work by assuming that their influence was brief and limited. It is some years now since the book was published, and it is probably less well known than more recent books that still insist on concentrating on famous 'great historians'. Forbes's Liberal Anglican historians were Whately, Milman, Julius Hare, Thirlwall, Thomas Arnold and A.P. Stanley. With the exception of Arnold of Rugby and, perhaps, his disciple Stanley, these men are now little remembered in comparison with their contemporaries, Carlyle and Macaulay.[1]

Forbes's basic thesis was as follows. Influenced by German Idealism directly and, through Coleridge, indirectly, and deeply concerned about the perceived socio-political crisis in post-1815 Britain, the Liberal Anglicans developed an approach to history that was committed to both a

1

deep understanding of the past and a didactic role serving the present. They were dissatisfied with Utilitarian rationalism and its secular belief in progress. Though they appreciated the depth of the Romantic understanding of the past, they found Romanticism also unsatisfying in terms of historical research and in terms of its flight from the problems of the present into an idealised past. They sought to combine the practical relevance of Utilitarianism and the imaginative understanding of Romanticism in a new philosophy of history. An integral part of this philosophy was the cyclical concept of the biography of nations, which received its fullest expression from the pen of Arnold. Each nation passed from youth, through maturity, to old age; to that extent there was a pattern in history from which could be discerned laws of development; but each nation had its own characteristics and, therefore, responded in its own way to the crises engendered at each transitional stage of its life. Moreover, although the nation had an organic existence, its fate could be influenced by the individual actions of its members who retained independence of action and freedom of will. It was crucially important, therefore, that the educated members of a nation should understand its history and know, as it were, what time it was; only then could they act with wisdom. Arnold was sure that the Britain of his own day was advancing to maturity and that he had to be an 'advancer' rather than a 'conservative', though an advancer who would avoid the false rationalism of a-historical Jacobinism. The similarities between this attitude and what later came to be known as Whig history are obvious. Over and above the biography of nations, the Liberal Anglicans also believed in the general moral and intellectual advance of mankind.[2] However, in the case of Arnold at least, his racialism made him sceptical of much further advance, for he could see no new races capable of picking up the torch of civilization from the Teutonic peoples in the way they had received it from others.[3] This 'presentism' usually seen as typifying Whig history, was typical of all those influenced by the new historical consciousness of the nineteenth century: the past was often seen as leading to the present, but not necessarily beyond it. Watching over the whole historical process, however, was a benevolent Deity. God's Providence could be 'ordinary' when expressed in natural laws and the laws of history, or 'special' when miraculous, as in the Christian revelation, or in direct intervention such as occurred during Napoleon's retreat from Moscow.[4]

This was a fundamentally religious conception of history that had a moral and practical purpose, that was predicated on the assumption of the organic life of nations, yet retained a role for the free individual who made moral choices and affected the course of history, even if the emplotment was God's and the general pattern was established. This religious but liberal conception of history was opposed not only to unhistorical liberal rationalism but to the equally unhistorical Oxford Movement which idealised a particular era in the past and, said Milman, wished to return to a medieval church that had been an integral part of the youth of modern nations but would be totally inappropriate to their manhood; Newman and his associates failed to understand the course of history and the needs of their own age. Though both liberal and practical, the Liberal Anglicans wanted to be non-partisan, to speak for the nation and the age. They held out hope for the future whilst not denying the relevance of the past. They believed in the unity of history and in the generic reality of the nation, yet they also believed in the moral responsibility of the individual to God — a God, who was, however, the ultimate arbiter of the fate of nations and of mankind. Theirs was a typically Idealist philosophy of history in the sense that each national society had its own individual identity, and in the sense that each such society developed that identity, through the development of its own collective mind — an example of such a development being the English constitution. As Forbes stressed, however, the Liberal Anglicans believed in 'the ultimate historical agency of the will of the individual', so they were especially concerned with the role of human character. This could leave them, like their younger contemporary, Marx, hovering uncertainly between determinism and freedom: 'human character, as modifying and modified by circumstances, man controlling and controlled by events, must be the historian's ultimate object', said Hare. Also their Idealism never led them to minimise the significance of empirical research; like Ranke in contemporary Germany they could believe in the historical as opposed to the philosophical method yet retain an Idealist outlook. Because of this they did not take natural science as the model for their empirical work, and they and their disciples were to remain immune from Positivist influence and other forms of scientism. They believed in the unity of history and could never accept the notion of historical facts as atomistic. In many ways they anticipated Dilthey in their assumption that the historical method was unique and based as much on understanding as on knowledge.

The Liberal Anglican position, as described by Forbes, was sophisticated, complex — perhaps too complex, even inconsistent, he suggested. Not that there was a self-conscious Liberal Anglican 'school'; Forbes had to construct their ideas from the implicit as well as the explicit in their works. The striking thing about his description, however, is how familiar it is. For he is describing the characteristics of English historiography far beyond the middle of the nineteenth century. Consider them: an empirical method but a rejection of scientific principles and a belief in historical method *sui generis*; a liberal and individualist approach, based on a belief in free will and moral responsibility; the nation as the prime generic concept; developmental and optimistic; and Christian.

Yet, said Forbes, the Liberal Anglicans ceased to exercise influence by the middle of the nineteenth century; they had been superseded by Positivists. Though they were in some ways more advanced and sophisticated than their successors, their inconsistencies betrayed them; lured by Positivism, historians took a wrong turning into barren territory.[5]

What is to be suggested in the coming pages is that the Liberal Anglicans' idea of history proved more durable than Forbes realised, that his masterly analysis of their work was more important than he himself felt able to claim. Of course, it is always difficult in intellectual history to distinguish between a direct causal relationship linking schools or traditions of thought and a mere sharing of common characteristics. It may well be that the ideas of the Liberal Anglicans reappear in the writings of later historians because all shared a common set of individualist, Christian, yet historicist assumptions. However, in some instances, as we shall see, the causal link is clear or explicit — the influence of Arnold on Freeman,[6] for example, or of Stanley on J.R. Green.[7]

Later historians were also to refer to the influence of those 'great' historians, Carlyle and Macaulay. The latter certainly contributed to a dominant Whig national historiography (about which more later), even though the new generation of historians, especially those that were university-based, were rather sparing in their acknowledgements. Just as the mythical Arthurian 'Matter of Britain' had once fortified the English monarchy, so a new mythology, which we might call the 'Matter of England' fortified the Victorian state. Beginning with Teutonic freedoms and concluding with the Glorious Revolution, it already existed as an intellectual tradition, and the new wave of scholarly historians were, at first, simply going to embellish the stories, then add to them — particularly in the matter of the Empire and the Reformation. All this could be accommodated in the Liberal Anglican tradition, as could the classical studies that were still the starting point in the education of the intelligentsia and, therefore, the initial point of comparison for English history. The biographies of ancient Greece and Rome and the biography of England, embellished by examples of public service, were the stuff of an historical education.

Carlyle, though so idiosyncratic and often intemperate and incoherent, was a more acknowledged inspiration. Above all, his championing of the great man in history and his fierce opposition to Positivism were of great influence, and could also be accommodated within the prevailing tradition. He had written two essays on history for *Fraser's Magazine* (1830, 1833). In the first he had asserted that the future was 'predetermined and inevitable' — there was still enough of the Scots Calvinist in him for this — and the motivation of he who sought historical knowledge derived from his recognition that mankind 'lives between two eternities, and warring against Oblivion, he would fain unite himself in clear conscious relation, as in dim unconscious relation he is already united, with the whole Future and the whole Past'. But in this heroic picture of mankind warring against Oblivion we find an anticipation of the obscurantism that followed: the 'current of human affairs' was 'intricate, perplexed and unfathomable'. Social life was the sum of all the individual lives that constituted society; hence 'History is the essence of innumerable Biographies'; and as such it was far too complex to be fully comprehended. Also 'the inward condition of Life' varied from age to age, and its outward signs were difficult to decipher. So the historian had difficulty in knowing who had been truly influential and wherein lay the true origins of things; it was difficult to penetrate beneath the surface sound and fury of supposedly great events. As for institutions, such as the Law or the Constitution, they were only the houses in which life was lived, not Life itself; and the houses were furnished, not by great men, but by the host of nameless men that constituted the stuff of history. These were perceptive comments and could have led away from the coming predominance of constitutional history and the more superficial forms of narrative political history. But Carlyle wrote, not to advocate a new form of history, simply to warn that the most important part of the past was irrecoverable, and even that which was recorded could never be understood objectively or completely. He warned against a naïve belief that what was observed corresponded exactly to what really occurred. There was always discrepancy. In particular, what occurred simultaneously had to be related in succession — 'the things done were not a series, but a group'. Carlyle had spotted that the historian is predisposed to causal chains, not necessarily because of the nature of reality or because of the evidence that confronts him, but because of his own methods of expression. 'Actual events', he said, were not 'related to each other as parent and offspring are; every single event is the offspring not of one, but of all other events, prior or contemporaneous, and will in turn combine with all others to give birth to new: it is an ever-living,

ever-working Chaos of Being . . .' This Chaos, boundless and 'unfathomable as the souls and destiny of man'. was what the historian depicted so
inadequately in linear form: 'Narrative is *linear*, Action is *solid*. Alas for
our "chains", or chainlets, of "causes and effects" . . .' History was the
unfathomable work of God — to be partially revealed in Time,
but revealed wholly only in Eternity. Carlyle's vision of history was, thus,
a holistic one, but one which denied the possibility of true knowledge of
the whole. This idea that much was unknowable, known only to God, is
one which we will see repeated many times in the following decades. It
survived the opposing view that God's purpose could be discerned and
that patterns in the past were visible, and that, above all, a causal chain
was a valid concept. As we shall see, the causal chain was particularly
vital to Stubbs and to his vision of constitutional history.

Though Carlyle regarded historical knowledge as imperfect he also
thought it vitally important: it was 'the true fountain of knowledge' and 'a
Real Prophetic Manuscript' — though, like other prophetic manuscripts, incapable of full interpretation by man. The true historian, unlike
the narrow 'artisan' specialist, was one who could 'inform and ennoble the
humblest department with an Idea of the Whole'. This went further than
Ranke's belief in Universal History, for that would have consisted of the
history of nations at the times when their individual histories assumed
universal significance; Carlyle's vision required a stronger, and typically
Idealist, concept or Idea of the Whole.[8] Though that concept could only
be realised through the study of history, which made action and judgment
possible: 'Only he who understands what has been, can know what should
be and will be. It is of the last importance that the individual have ascer-
tained his relation to the whole'.[9] There are some obvious similarities to
the Liberal Anglican concept of history and its purpose.

Some years later, however, as is well known, Carlyle was defining
Universal History as the history of Great Men. This is often interpreted
as a change of mind on his part — a change for the worse, which
presaged even worse ideas to come. There is a little truth in this, but not
much. He had, it is true, once seen the nameless multitude as preferable
to great men; but his Great Men of the 'Lectures on Heroes' are not all
conventional heroes, and their role in no way diminishes the holistic
and Divine nature of history, nor even its essential obscurity —
though their study is an aid to a partial solving of the problem of knowing and understanding history. Great men were the model for the mass
and also 'all things that we see standing accomplished in the world are
properly the outer material result, the practical realisation and embodiment, of Thoughts that dwelt in the Great Men sent into the world.'

They were 'the soul of the whole world's history'. The spiritual language employed was not accidental, nor was it when 'divine revelation' was employed to unite Great Men with other men, or when Hero Worship was defined as 'transcendent admiration of a Great Man', for 'the greatest of all Heroes is One — whom we do not name here!' It becomes increasingly apparent that the Hero is God's representative on earth, and that loyalty to the Hero was akin to faith in God. Moreover, society was founded on Hero-worship; and Carlyle indulged in some typical word-play with the terms 'hierarchical' and 'hero-archical'. Graduations of rank, as representative of the distribution of real heroic qualities, were not usually '*in*supportably' inaccurate — when they were, then revolution ensued. Revolution might then produce 'cries of Democracy, Liberty and Equality, and I know not what', but Hero-worship was the necessary basis of all society and, once the revolution had done its work, a new hierarchy would assert itself. The Great Man was 'a free force direct out of God's own hand'. Thus, in every sense world history was 'the biography of Great Men'. The Divine nature of the Great Man's authority was further emphasised by Carlyle's choice of his first Hero — none other than the Norse God, Odin, the first Norse man of genius, an actual figure, claimed Carlyle, who had been deified by posterity. Far from evincing shock at such deification with all its implications for Christianity, he thought it no great disservice to the truth (albeit a primitive rendering), given the divine origin of the Hero's power.[10]

The second of his Heroes was Mahomet, definitely God-inspired though not deified. Deification was a simple-minded error, yet it was difficult to know exactly *what* the Great Man was or how to receive him. This was a typical piece of Carlylean mystification — almost keeping his options open, but avoiding a clear explanation of the actual relationship between Great Men and God. They were messengers 'sent from the Infinite Unknown with tidings to us'. Their utterances were 'revelation'. Each one was a 'portion of the primal reality of things'. Another feature of Carlyle's Great Man thesis was the power of ideas within it. The Great Man was always, at heart, a thinker, whatever form his greatness took in particular circumstances. This was obvious in Mahomet's case, for his ideas created Arab power: 'Belief is great, life-giving'. And 'the Great Man was always as lightning out of Heaven', unpredictable.[11] Since the ages of Gods and Prophets, heroism had had to take other forms, but the poet, a Shakespeare or a Dante, still 'penetrated . . . into the sacred mystery of the Universe', and had rightly been at least 'beatified' or 'canonised'.[12] His next group of heroes were 'priests', Luther and Knox, re-emphasising the sacred role.[13] In the modern age, the age of scientific scepticism, anti-heroic and squalidly rationalist, heroes had been forced into secular roles, as with men of letters like Goethe, Johnson, Rousseau and Burns. Yet they too had power — the power of the printed word moved the world as the prophet once had done; a man like Goethe had a 'Divine Idea of the World' and his life was a 'vision of the inward divine mystery'. The writer, like the lightning strike of the prophet, was 'an accident in society. He wanders like a wild Ishmaelite . . .' The art of writing was 'miraculous' for 'in Books lies the soul of the whole Past Time'. Books lived on like the work of God. 'No magic *Rune* is stronger than a Book. All that Mankind has done, thought, gained or been: it is lying as in magic preservation in the pages of Books!' Carlyle's Idealism was of the strongest kind: Great Men were sent from God, ideas of God, miraculous interventions to serve God's otherwise unknowable purpose. Their ideas changed the world, for human society was the product of man's ideas. London, for example, was 'but a thought' of man, or rather 'millions of Thoughts made into One': 'Not a brick was made but some man had to *think* of the making of that brick'.[14] Incidentally, we can see here that his scepticism about the surface of events and his Idealism have led him to an anticipation of Collingwood, in the sense that the thought behind the action is the 'inside' of the historical event. Lastly, Carlyle turned to what we might think of as the more conventional type of hero — 'The Hero as King', the political and war leader, represented in the typology by Cromwell and Napoleon. Unlike Neitzsche, who Carlyle seems to have anticipated in so many respects, he did not underrate the political leader: such a man was the sum of all the Heroic parts. Carlyle neither chose hereditary monarchs for his 'Kings' nor believed in Divine Hereditary Right, but all rulers either had divine right or were committing a diabolic wrong.[15]

Carlyle assumed that: history was about God's purpose; as such it was largely unknowable; and it was a whole, not in the sense of consisting of a simple causal chain, but in an Idealist or perhaps mystical sense; God's Providence became explicit only when Great Men appeared in order to work His Will through changing the ideas of men; history, though not the biography of nations, was the biography of Great Men. We can see that, though there were clear differences between this set of assumptions and the Liberal Anglican mode, they could be assimilated into a common tradition. Like the Liberal Anglicans, and like later Idealists such as Collingwood and Oakeshott, we find that a holistic assumption that reality was a whole and not to be analyzed into causal factors and consequences did not necessarily lead to an abandoning of individualist assumptions about the role of individuals in society as the motor force of history, or to a flight from empirical evidence.

Though, as we shall see, plenty acknowledged Carlyle's influence in the next generation of historians, one of the most generous tributes to Carlyle's influence was actually from Macaulay's great-nephew and ardent apologist G.M. Trevelyan, in 1899. It well illustrates the extent to which Carlyle's influence could contribute to and emphasise the individualist style of English historiography. Carlyle's greatness, said Trevelyan, rested in his recognition of 'men's inmost motives', which were the 'prime motive force' in society, and in his 'unrivalled instinct' for detecting them. He was able 'to write history from the inside of the actors' by 'sympathy with their feelings'. He never classified men; his method was to describe their individual personalities. Most revealingly, he quoted with approval from *Lectures on Heroes*: when the Puritan resisted Charles I he resisted not ship money but religious persecution, and he responded to his persecutor: 'No, by God's help, no; you may take my purse, but I cannot have my moral self annihilated. The purse is any highwayman's who might meet me with a loaded pistol; but the self is mine and God my Maker's; it is not yours, and I will resist you to the death, and revolt against you . . .'[16] These ringing tones sound down through the years; they could almost be the motto of the English historical tradition. It is interesting to note that when, over half a century later, Trevelyan again wrote about Carlyle, his enthusiasm had waned, particularly in regard to the increasingly authoritarian older Carlyle. Trevelyan rejected the notion that the lineage of the British Fascist movement could be traced back to the sage of Chelsea, but the impact of the political events of the intervening years upon Trevelyan's attitude is quite striking.[17] Carlyle's appeal had been to the individualist in Trevelyan; and it was on individualist grounds that Trevelyan finally came close to rejecting him. The significance of Trevelyan's type of experience will be evident when we look at the twentieth century.

The other major work whose conclusions need to be taken into account is P.B.M. Blaas's *Continuity and Anachronism*. Somewhat heavy-handed, particularly in its treatment of Maitland, Pollard and Tout, it is probably little known to other than specialists, but it does raise important issues. Though his study stresses a discontinuity, the reaction against Victorian Whig history in the forty years after the heyday of Stubbs, Freeman and the rest, Blaas's work contains important clues as to how, in another sense, continuity was maintained. His thesis is as follows. Victorian Whig history, best typified by Stubbs (despite his Toryism), was: developmental, having indeed 'an exaggerated sense of continuity' which was used as 'an ideological weapon against revolution' (and, he might have added, against conservatism or reaction); teleological or 'finalist'; 'presentist', in that the present was seen as the ultimate purpose of the past; and, finally therefore, prone to anachronism because of its search for origins. In contrast, historiography in the twentieth century assumes a fair measure of 'coincidence, irony and heterogeneity' as a result of both 'increasing social and political uncertainty' and professional interest in increased 'detail, specialization and refinement of research'. Though the stereotype of the confident Victorian might be questioned, there is a lot of truth in this characterization of modern historiography. The Whig approach to history had been useful pedagogically but, when reaction against Whiggism set in after 1890, the purpose of history changed diametrically, from linking past and present, to the 'liberation of the present from the burden and pressure of the past', a role of less direct political utility which, therefore, encouraged a more objective, scientific ideal of historical writing. Whig constitutional history had become 'the sole explanation for the development of English history as such' and the inevitable reaction had set in by the turn of the century.[18]

Perhaps we should qualify Blaas here by noting that the strength of continuous English constitutional history, exemplifying undeniably Whig characteristics, was such that, by the end of the period of reaction against it, its pedagogical role had not only survived but had expanded until it dominated the history degrees of very nearly all British universities, old and new, in the 1930s, and it mostly retained and extended this position for thirty years thereafter.[19] That there was a scholarly reaction is, however, clear. Blaas saw Seeley, with his emphasis on the power of the state and power within the state, as opposed to liberal constitutionalism, as a forerunner of the anti-Whig tendency. Then early economic history challenged laissez-faire individualism and provided an economic interpretation of national history instead of the prevailing legal or constitutional one. But it was the development of 'record-history', as opposed to 'chronicle-history', which was fatal to the old Whiggism. Men like J.H. Round played the role of iconoclasts with relish, demolishing the works of men like Freeman, accusing them of ignoring the archives, of inaccuracy, and of 'drum and trumpet' narrative. Also there was abroad a new air of 'conservative realism', totally out of sympathy with tales of evolving freedoms. The teleological generalisations of the older generation disappeared under the microscope of the new specialists. Perhaps this attack was in part the natural iconoclasm of a second generation or even a paradigm shift; it was certainly part of the reaction against Victorian culture in the 1890s and early 1900s; Blaas has chosen to emphasise the adoption of supposedly more professional attitudes along with longer hours in the archives. In practical terms, medievalists like Tout placed more emphasis on administration, especially the centralising Norman monarchy, and less on constitutional freedom, whereas the early modern scholars like Pollard had more interest in strong Tudor administration than in the constitutional struggles of the seventeenth century. This can be seen as typical of growing doubts about traditional parliamentary forms of government and the democratic system; Blaas suggests that 'the cult of parliament' came to an end and was superseded by a 'new realism' and demands for efficiency above tradition. This certainly ties in with the mood of 'national efficiency' prevalent at the time.[20]

The new mood was also associated with what Blaas calls a 'cult of facts'. But though he links this with the influence of the French administrative history of writers like Langlois, which English historians were now prepared to read for comparative purposes because of their reaction against the cult of English constitutional history *sui generis*, he does not see any Positivist influence (so strong in France) behind this passion for facts. Indeed, he detects a lack of interest in any philosophy of knowledge including that of the contemporary Idealists, Bradley, Croce and Oakeshott.[21] Though a distaste for Idealist philosophy or metaphysical speculation might be expected of both Positivists and members of the 'cult of facts', Blaas's assumption will need modifying in terms of the influence of idealism upon holistic attitudes, if not epistemological ones. Along with the cult of facts came a new accidentalist view of history, replacing Whig teleology.[22]

Blaas paid particular attention to Maitland, Pollard and Tout. Maitland initiated the mood of hostility to tradition and the fear of anachronism, criticising English legal histories for 'antedating the emergence of modern ideas'. 'The past', said Blaas, approvingly, 'cannot be viewed objectively while a living tradition still clings to it'. Maitland also preferred administration and institutions to the more 'showy side of the constitution'. He accepted 'that future studies would be ever more fragmented and specialized' — in other words that the old grand syntheses had had their day. Pollard believed that initiative, and freedom itself, could only come from above, from authority. He too stressed the ironic and accidental elements in history.[23] Indeed, if these two aspects of his approach clashed, we might add, it was the latter that dominated, as can be seen in his 1916 *History* article on 'The Growth of an Imperial Parliament' — though the wartime atmosphere may have strengthened that tendency. He was examining proposals for an imperial parliament — proposals which, he said, were based on 'faith in man as the conscious creator of his own political universe'. But peoples had rarely been able to mould their institutions, carry out preconceived plans, or in general determine their own future. We do not now believe, he said rather testily, 'that Britain arose from the waves with Magna Carta in its bosom and that the Englishman was endowed by a special dispensation with a natural thirst for a Parliamentary vote'. Likewise, he regarded heroes and 'supermen' as suited only to history's adolescence; men did not will and implement great changes in society; they could neither foresee nor control events.[24] Tout was also seen as an enemy of presentism and anachronism and an admirer of efficient administration above constitutional liberty.[25] In general, Blaas sympathised with the views of Round, Pollard, Maitland and Tout, claiming that they had advanced the study of history by making it more objective, accurate, and less prone to anachronism and presentism. He called this an 'autonomous' ideal.[26]

If Blaas was right in asserting that a major, and successful, revolt occurred against Victorian historiographical traditions in the period 1890-1930, how does this affect the present study, which is focused quite differently? We are looking at the continuity of certain approaches to the study of history; Blaas claims a major discontinuity. The point is that some of these approaches were little changed by the process that Blaas describes; indeed, in some instances, they actually may have been accentuated. This is not to deny the importance of Blaas's thesis; it advances the study of English historiography from the well-trodden paths of the nineteenth century into the *terra incognita* of the early twentieth century. But consider again some of the essential features of Liberal Anglican history. An empirical method — this was accentuated by the new scholarship, which denied the grander themes of Whig history, whilst challenging the expertise and seriousness of the earlier scholarship. The nation was the prime generic concept — and it remained so. If the new administrative and legal history lacked a role for great men and stressed institutions above people, the ironical and accidental view of history more than made up for this decline of individualism on the human front, for at least the great man had been an instrument of God's purpose, part of the Divine plan, and a glimpse of God's will; now there was no plan. Methodological empiricism, a sense of the accidental, and a new secularism, preserved this new institutionalism from holism or organicism as far as the question of the unity of history was concerned. History was still a mystery — more so now, robbed of God's mysterious purpose and no longer guided by his equally mysterious Providence, but a mystery, of accidents and of complex and confusing details. The era of the grand survey, it was frequently said, was over. Man may have lost his will to alter history or even to keep pace with it, but he was certainly not part of some awful, predestined pattern. He moved in confusion of purpose with unforeseen results. Above all, the future was less knowable than before. The practical purpose of history was now less emphasised, its political relevance denied; a mainly professional or autonomous purpose was served — supposedly so, for the largely conservative implications of the new scepticism are obvious. A.J.P. Taylor once claimed (no doubt tongue in cheek) to have had his erstwhile innocent eyes opened to the truly 'Tory', as opposed to impartial, nature of anti-Whig history by reading Feiling's *A History of England* (1950). He too saw 'Tory' history as emphasising administration, and also 'humdrum personal motives and office routine', and as taking 'the ideas out of history'. Comparing Feiling to a servant of the late Roman Empire, busying himself with office routine while civilization collapsed around him, and seeing Tory history as a product of national decline when nobody believed in Whig progress any longer, Taylor anticipated a 'Byzantine' future.[27] If by that he meant labyrinthine and obscure, perhaps Tory history had already slid into the Byzantine mode. Apart from clarity, perhaps the major losses were the sense of individual moral responsibility, belief in God's Providence, and optimism; there was no pattern in history. The historical industry produced nuts and bolts but did not again assemble finished products, working models. However, this is to accept a total discontinuity; the old perspective continued to compete for influence with the new. Whig history was not dead in 1930. But where the old Whiggery and the new 'realism' had similar implications the impact of these would be strong indeed.

The bibliographical part of this introduction has concentrated on the work of Forbes and Blaas; but brief mention must be made of other important contributions. In particular, J.W. Burrow's *A Liberal Descent* provides important insights into the Whig-Liberal tradition, particularly useful for its analysis of Stubbs's preconceptions.[28] Doris Goldstein's reassessment of Bury is important to any study of what was meant when historians talked about their subject as a science.[29] Several recent studies of Marxists by Marxists are also useful, notably *Making Histories*, a product of the Birmingham University Centre for Contemporary Cultural Studies.[30] There is also a good modern study of Seeley.[31] Though this does not exhaust the stock of useful books on English historiography, probably the main influence on the present work has been some of the studies of other national schools of history, such as Keylor's study of the French historical profession before *Annales*,[32] and Iggers's *The German Conception of History*.[33] The latter, particularly, as a critical account of an historical tradition which placed that tradition within the contexts of both national history and intellectual history, has been, if not a model, an inspiration.

To turn from bibliographical to epistemological and methodological matters: it is evident that the Liberal Anglican, Whig and Carlylean traditions could all be characterised as predominantly individualist in their own ways; and it has been argued that Blaas's 'realist' school could also be described as methodologically individualist despite its emphasis on institutions as opposed to individual persons. It would be best, therefore, to examine the concept of *individualism* before proceeding further. Many different ideas of individualism can be identified,[34] though they often overlap, interrelate, and have a common basic appeal. Many of them will be seen to have had peculiar strength in Victorian England and to have a peculiarly close relationship with the self-image of the English. Some could be described as normative, others are descriptive, and a few purport to both describe actual social tendencies and contain within them an ideal of social behaviour. Some have been described as metaphysical (as in the case of individual free will), others are social, political or economic.

From the point of view of Victorian society, and as historians especially, it is perhaps appropriate to start with religious individualism, for it was certainly regarded as the foundation of all arguments on the subject, just as religion was generally regarded as the starting point for most issues of social concern. The idea of man as not only created by God in His image, but individually responsible to God for his own destiny, was fundamental to the individualism of Liberal Anglicans and their successors, such as Stubbs and Creighton, bishops both, and J.R. Green, also an ordained Anglican clergyman. Anything or anybody that seemed to come between God and man was as suspect as was Catholic dogma or a Catholic priest. From this it was but a short step to the doctrine of free will — what Lukes has called 'autonomy' or 'self-direction, according to which an individual's thought and action is his own, and not determined by agencies or causes outside his control'. Usually regarded as incompatible with determinism or holism, it is often regarded as 'a value central to the morality of modern Western civilization'. It will be seen that there was a special concern with this concept in and around the 1860s, and that this concern resurfaced whenever the concept was threatened. Associated with both these ideas was a belief in the consequent 'dignity' of man as an individual, an idea often associated with Christianity but strengthened by both the humanism of the Renaissance and the Protestant Reformation.

Englishmen prided themselves on their devotion to this principle, even to the point of tolerating eccentricities — at least amongst the wealthy and high born. This closely relates in turn to the idea that privacy was necessary, that there should be in both thought and action an area of life preserved for the private individual. It suggests that there is not, and should not be, a total correlation between man and society. The classic secular version of this is, of course, J.S. Mill's *On Liberty* (1859). Some would relate the idea of private property to this notion, in that it can provide the material basis for a private life. Not surprisingly, this attitude was very strong in mid-Victorian society. Though in Mill it appears as part of an essentially rationalist outlook, we will find it also taking a more obscurantist form in the sense that each individual personality retains an area which is private in that it is unknowable and not subject to rational analysis, which can be at variance with the independent, rational decision-making embodied in the classic free will concept. This, as we shall see, got the proponents of free will into all sorts of difficulties. Closely related to this idea is that of self-development, a Romantic rather than a Utilitarian notion, of man as a creative, self-affirming individual fulfilling his potential. For the Romantics the artist was the ideal type; for Carlyle it was the hero or great man, unpredictable, creative and inspired, not subject to the social laws that bound little men. Lukes sees the idea of the community, *Volk* or state as an organic person, as being a development of this type of individualism; and this could certainly contribute to an 'individualist' historical method, in that each nation, state, or any social organism whatever, could be seen as an individual, sharing no essential qualities with similarly named organisms and requiring, therefore, individual historical interpretation and observation. Such a social organism obeys its own laws, not any generic laws, and therefore prediction, inductive law-making and generalisation are inappropriate. In another sense, however, this is an holistic as opposed to an individualist concept, and quite opposed to the sort of individualism that thrived in England, though itself more favoured on the continent, particularly in Germany. As we shall see, the individual and the nation did at times seem to be antagonistic concepts, but English historians did not feel the need to worry unduly about this.

More closely related to prevailing attitudes in mid-Victorian England, though not unconnected with the presumption of self-development and inherent potential was ethical individualism or egoism — a system of ethics built on the idea of enlightened self-interest. Above all this was a Utilitarian precept, which seems to have been pervasive in Victorian society despite its secular presumption. Because of its secularism, however, it seems to figure little in our historian's world view, which may surprise those who take a blinkered view of what constituted Victorian values. If enlightened self-interest be seen as the ethical basis of economic individualism or laissez-faire, then we find surprisingly little of this either in the Victorian period; later on, however, in the twentieth century we find economic liberalism figuring prominently amongst historians opposed to Marxism, the enlightened self-interest of the entrepreneur often being seen as the real motor force in social and economic development. The closely associated theme of political individualism, with individuals being seen as the only rational centres of consciousness and the best judge of their own interest, fits in much more closely with the Whig view of history, not to mention the Liberal Anglican, and was much strengthened by the democratic presumptions of the twentieth century.

Finally, we come to ontological, epistemological, and methodological individualism. The first of these concerns itself with the individual as an abstraction, not as an ideal; it is concerned with determining what the individual is in terms of needs, purposes, interests and so on. Naturally, as it makes its basic presumption in individualist terms it tends to regard society and the state merely as arrangements for dealing with the needs and purposes of the individual. It is embodied in natural law and social contract theories, always very influential in England. As Lukes points out, the economic and social development of England had, by the early nineteenth century, done much to create an actual society that seemed to approximate to this conception. Epistemological individualism is the idea that the source of knowledge is always the individual — after the manner of Descartes; it is, therefore, an empirical epistemology, the empiricist holding that all knowledge begins in the individual mind as sensory perception and as reflection by the individual mind upon that perception. Those who believe in the myth of Positivist influence upon English history will think of this as the crucial determinant, but in fact, as we hope to show, Positivist influence was slight; the real significance of this form of individualism lies, not in the historian's perception of his own method, but in his perception of knowledge in the societies he studies. He would rule out holistic concepts such as group minds and *Zeitgeist*. Methodological individualism, in contrast therefore, is central to our present concerns. Society is seen as explicable solely in terms of facts about individuals; generalization is not totally avoided but collective concepts are. Thus the anti-Whig 'realist' school, though weakening the individualist traditions of Whiggery in terms of the dignity of man, the autonomy of the individual will, the concept of the abstract individual, and so on, strengthened the methodological individualism of English historiography by its reluctance to generalize, its concern with more and more factual detail and its refusal to see any pattern or course of history. This is not mere word play: its importance lies in the similar and negative relationship that these different forms of individualism have towards any construction of social laws, anything that smacked of determinism, any generic concepts and any holistic tendencies. Thus, as the new conservative realism exerted its power, so history lost its national Whig myths and found nothing with which to replace them. As a positive force in the nation's intellectual life history ceased for the moment to exist, and has rarely exerted much power since. All too often it became no more than a spanner in the works of others' complex machines, a solvent of others' theories, a constant negative, with only one idea of its own — that there were no tenable ideas about the course of history or the dynamic forces of social change or the structure of society. The historian became an interrogator, a professional sceptic, a destroyer. He dealt only with detail, in a spirit of irony.

Against all these different concepts of individualism certain holistic attitudes are sometimes ranged. From the historian's point of view, the two most important forms of *holism* are as follows. Firstly, we have the notion that there are social wholes that are both real social facts and more than the sum of their parts. This is clearly in opposition to many of the forms of individualism we have considered and has implications for many more. It involves the development of generic concepts either naïvely (in the sense of naturally, out of our social experience) and intuitively, or scientifically in the inductive sense, and this latter would involve classification and perhaps the development of social laws. (Politically, this form of holism can justify collectivist policies). However, the former method would not necessarily have these implications and could result in the retention of epistemological individualism (and political individualism). The second form of holism to concern us is the notion that, as all reality is a complex whole, historical phenomena must be part of a complex or ground of factors or relationships that cannot be broken down into causes and effects in any simple hierarchical or linear way, and which cannot be subject to analysis. This form of holism, particularly associated with Idealism, and already exemplified by Carlyle, can also, however, lead back to an epistemological and methodological individualism, for on this argument there can be no inductive generalisations about individual unanalyzable situations. In this sense, one could say that the cards are stacked in favour of historical individualism — and this may explain much of what is described in the following pages.

The historian, therefore, is inclined to strict *nominalism*; this means, that though he may use general words like 'state' or 'nation' or 'class', he does not recognise such generalities as real things or as 'universals'. Only the individual is real. Unlike the scientist, the historian will not seek to classify, regarding such classification as quite arbitrary, and will try to limit his use of generic concepts, particularly in any attempt at causal explanation. As we shall see, numerous attempts have been made to steer away from nominalism, but not always with unchallenged or lasting success.

Finally, with apologies to philosophers, I will use the term *naive realism* in the context of historians' perceptions (developing Blaas's use of the term 'realism', and much as McLennan has used the phrase 'common sense realism'[35]) to indicate the naïve view that not only is the past 'real' but that it consists of discrete events and discrete facts accessible only to an empirical approach, and (going beyond McLennan) that that reality can be not only perceived but recreated. The phrase 'recreating the past' is by no means unknown amongst historians and it is a common presumption that this activity is possible. Though I recognise that in the esoteric world of the philosopher the term has a rather different meaning, and that 'realism' and 'nominalism' can, according to certain definitions, be seen as opposites rather than as bedfellows, the term seems to be so appropriate to the naïve historian's perception that its use cannot be resisted.

NOTES

1.   A point alluded to by Forbes himself. D. Forbes, *The Liberal Anglican Idea of History* (Cambridge, 1952), p.viii.

2.   *Ibid.* pp. 1, 4-15, 20-29, 56-60, 63, 90-91.

3.   T. Arnold, *Introductory Lectures on Modern History with the Inaugural Lecture*, seventh edition (London, 1885), pp. 29-31.

4.   Forbes, *Op.cit.*, pp. 60, 72-73.

5.   *Ibid.* pp. 102-106, 118-121, 123-124, 129-131, 135, 143, 151-152.

6.   W.R.W. Stephens, *The Life and Letters of Edward A. Freeman* (London, 1895), i. 66, 108, 110; E.A. Freeman, 'On the Study of History', *Fortnightly Review*, XXIX (1881), 335.

7.   J.R. Green, *Letters of John Richard Green* ed. L. Stephen (London, 1901), pp. 16-19, 21, 153; J. Bryce, *Studies in Contemporary Biography* (London, 1903), pp. 132, 134.

8.   T. Carlyle, 'On History' (1830), *Critical and Miscellaneous Essays* (London, 1869) ii. 253, 255-262.

9.   T. Carlyle, 'On History' (1833), *Ibid.* iv, 213.

10.   T. Carlyle, 'Lectures on Heroes: Lecture I, The Hero as Divinity', *Sartor Resartus, Lectures on Heroes, Chartism, Past and Present* (copyright edn., London, n.d.), pp. 185-186, 193-195, 200-201.

11.   'Lecture II, The Hero as Prophet', *Ibid.*, pp. 216-217, 219, 242.

12.   'Lecture III, The Hero as Poet,' *Ibid.*, pp. 243-244, 248.

13.   'Lecture IV, The Hero as Priest', *Ibid.*, pp.271-299.

14. 'Lecture V, The Hero as Man of Letters', *Ibid.*, pp. 300-302, 304, 306-308.

15. 'Lecture VI, The Hero as King', *Ibid.*, pp. 332-334.

16. G.M. Trevelyan, 'Carlyle as an Historian', *The Nineteenth Century*, XLVI (1899) 499, 502.

17. G.M. Trevelyan, 'Introduction', *Carlyle, An Anthology* (London, 1953), pp. 1-11.

18. P.B.M. Blaas, *Continuity and Anachronism: Parliamentary and Constitutional Development in Whig Historiography and in the Anti-Whig Reaction Between 1890 and 1930.* (London, 1978), 23-26, 28, 33-34.

19. C.J.W. Parker, 'The Development of History Courses in British Universities, 1850-1975' (Exeter University MA thesis, 1976), especially pp.139-189.

20. P.B.M. Blaas, *Op.cit* pp. 36-39, 43-56, 66-69, 197, 208, 213-220.

21. *Ibid.* pp. 69-71.

22. *Ibid.*, p.227.

23. *Ibid.*, pp 259, 263, 268, 274-344.

24. A.F. Pollard, 'The Growth of an Imperial Parliament', *History*, 1 (1916) pp.129-139, 145.

25. Blaas, *Op.cit.* pp 345-347, 357, 362.

26. *Ibid.* pp 370-371.

27. A.J.P. Taylor, 'Tory History' (1950), *Essays in English History* (London, 1977), pp. 21-22.

28. J.W.Burrow, *A Liberal Descent* (Cambridge, 1981).

29. D.S. Goldstein, 'J.B. Bury's Philosophy of History: A Reappraisal', *American Historical Review*, 82 (1977), 896-919.

30. R. Johnson, G. McLennan, B. Schwarz, D. Sutton, *Making Histories: Studies in History, Writing and Politics* (London, 1982).

31. D. Wormell, *Sir John Seeley and the Uses of History* (Cambridge, 1980).

32. W.R. Keylor, *Academy and Community: the Foundation of the French Historical Profession* (Cambridge, Mass., 1975).

33. G.G. Iggers, *The German Conception of History* (Middletown, CT., 1968).

34. S. Lukes, *Individualism* (Oxford, 1973). Lukes identifies eleven types of individualism; my debt to him is obvious. See especially: pp. 94-98, 52-58, 45-51, 59-66, 67-72, 99-106, 79-87, 88-93, 73-78, 107-109, 110-124.

35. G. McLennan, 'History and Theory'. *Literature and History*, 10 (1984), 140-142. In general, a useful article:139-164.

CHAPTER 2

Individualism: A National Tradition and a National Perception

This mysterious citadel of Will[1]

It would be something of a truism to say that a new academic discipline is a product of the intellectual climate of the times, for it could hardly be self-generating in isolation from its environment. But this is still a point worth stressing, because its evident truth seems to be denied by those who insist that history has always been 'dryasdust' or a merely antiquarian amusement with no serious intellectual substance. Whether or not the discipline can then become self-sustaining, through the extension of its own professional ideal, and consequently isolated from other intellectual developments, is another matter, and one which will be of some concern to this study. Initially, however, the discipline is stamped with the concerns of the age that bore it; whether it retains that imprint, modified perhaps by a growing professionalism (which usually implies an objective idea, a commitment to empirical research, and a commonly-accepted paradigm), or whether it acquires new characteristics, will depend upon the degree of its subsequent isolation from other disciplines and other intellectual developments.

As we have already suggested, the mid-Victorian scholars, such as Stubbs, Freeman and J.R. Green, inherited a Liberal Anglican tradition that stressed the role of the individual and resolutely opposed any deterministic approach. It has been suggested recently that this period was one of exceptional concern with the problem of free will and determinism, which subsequent intellectual developments were soon to make redundant; indeed the term 'silly season for determinism', when 'many arguments' were employed in propagating the concept, has been used to describe the period culminating about 1872. If zany arguments were employed in the cause of determinism then equally unsatisfactory arguments were used to defend free will. Inspired by the work of the statistician, Adolphe Quetelet, from 1828 onwards, a generation had come to believe in, or fear, statistical determinism, arousing alarm about the reality of free will. Without free will, it was argued, there could be no moral order; and with statistical determinism there could be no hope of moral progress, for statistics appeared to show a regular incidence of such immorality as crime, suicide and divorce.[2] Henry Thomas Buckle, who was influenced by Quetelet, and discussed the implications of this statistical method in his *History of Civilization in England* (two volumes, 1856, 1861), sought to use this form of determinism for the writing of scientific history after the Positivist manner.[3] Positivism of the prevalent Comtist school can be seen as an attempt to reconcile social laws with a belief in perfectibility, for the positivists believed in using the inductive method to arrive at social laws, and believed that the use of these laws would result in the achievement of comprehensive, truly scientific knowledge, which would make possible the rational organisation of society. In this respect Positivism is appropriately described as a typical nineteenth-century *ersatz* theology, [4] a substitute for religious certainty, and perhaps a product of the new historical awareness that was such a feature of nineteenth-century thought. That there was a tendency to seek refuge in *ersatz* theology is very true, but equally there was a countervailing tendency, naturally strongest amongst those who remained faithful to their church, to oppose these heresies, particularly those of the intolerant, authoritarian and deterministic sort. It matters not that the subsequent development of probability theory has now undermined determinism as surely as determinism itself appeared to threaten free will and chance. Furthermore, as Hacking put it, probability theory has subjected 'the once unthinkable world of chance . . . to the laws of nature,' and thus by 1900 'chance had been tamed'. We have entered a world of probability instead of one divided into necessity and chance. This process had begun in the 1870s, when statisticians, for the first time, were able to subject 'chance' to mathematical analysis, turning it from the great unknown or incalculable into both 'a tool of inference' and an ingredient in mathematical modelling.[5]

The debates of the 1850s and 1860s, the formative years for the English tradition of history, had, however, left their mark. The historians who had, almost without exception, raised their standard against Positivist determinism, failed to take account of probability as a concept in the 1870s and after, and continued to think (as many continue to do) in terms of free will *versus* determinism, the great crusading issue of the formative years. Positivism, then, appeared as the first major threat to the English historical tradition, one which was seen off with much heat, some light, and much hardening of attitudes.

Buckle and Comte were the original influence upon Positivist historical thinking in England. According to Comte, Positive history had to eschew interpreting the great events of the past as if they were the products of the

actions of individuals, as if legislators had great power over the development of civilization, and should recognise the irresistible forces which
compel men to act. He wrote:

> Generally speaking, when the individual appears to exert a great influence, it is not
> due to his own forces, since these are extremely small. Forces external to him act in
> his favour, according to laws over which he has no control. His whole power lies in
> the intelligent apprehension of these laws through observation, his forecast of their
> effects, and the power which he thus obtains of subordinating them to the desired
> end, provided he employs them in accordance with their nature . . . The effect once
> produced, ignorance of natural laws leads the spectator, and sometimes the actor him-
> self to attribute to the power of man what is really only due to his foresight.[6]

This assertion of the primacy of the hitherto hidden laws of development, of a high degree of determinism, of the observational and, hence,
inductive method, and of the prophetic and utilitarian role of historical
study, was part of a general Positivism which denied the status of knowledge to value judgments and normative statements, and which believed in
the unity of the scientific method.[7] From this last belief stemmed Comte's
determination to reform the sciences and create new methods of thought,
especially a new science of society.

Buckle's desire to extend the scientific method to history has to be seen
as part of this ambition. The inductive method had to be used to discover
the laws governing the development of human society in the same way
as natural science had discovered natural laws or regularities, to the
exclusion of theological and metaphysical theories. The inferior quality
of historians, the complexity of social phenomena, prejudice, and passion
had made history lag behind natural science; but there was, logically, no
reason why social phenomena should be less subject to laws than were
natural phenomena. For Buckle, the prime 'vast question' was: 'Are the
actions of men, and therefore of societies, governed by fixed laws, or
are they the result either of chance or of supernatural interference?'[8]
Comte, of course, had gone further than this with the Law of the Three
Stages, the influence of which is evident in Buckle; but Buckle was less
committed to what Kolakowski has called 'an all-embracing construction
of the philosophy of history, crowned by a Messianic vision all his
own'. This construction, he notes, 'is actually deterministic in character although it renounces metaphysically conceived causality in favour of
phenomenalistically interpreted laws. It also holds out the hope of a total
transformation of the world and the impending advent of the absolute
state thanks to the advance of scientific knowledge'.[9] Though Buckle
did not travel this far, he had gone down the same road. Mandelbaum

has distinguished between 'systematic' and 'critical' Positivism, the one doctrinal and the other sceptical, [10] but such a distinction would be too bald applied to Comte and Buckle. Though J.S. Mill emphasized the difference between the two,[11] and it has even been denied that Buckle was a Positivist or shared many of Comte's ideas, [12] they were clearly of the same school.

After Buckle, the main English exponent of a Positivist approach to history was Frederic Harrison. Two lectures on the meaning of history, delivered and published in 1862, do not in fact give a clear exposition of Positivist history, but the second lecture does give us a clear starting point for an investigation of the reasons why Positivist history was rejected. 'The Connection of History', a sketch of world history, concluded with a paean to the French Revolution: 'The great revolution is not ended. The questions it proposed are not yet solved . . . it yet remains with us to show how the last vestiges of the feudal, hereditary, and aristocratic systems may give place to a genuine, an orderly and permanent republic', how Christianity ('grown useless and retrograde') may be 'removed without injury to the moral, religious, and social instincts' with which it had become entangled, and 'how industry may be organised, and the workman enrolled with full rights of citizenship, a free, a powerful and a cultivated member of the social body'. Such was the task; the facilities and the knowledge existed; all that was needed was a system.[13] This was a classic Positivist programme, openly advocated, with specific political, social and economic, religious and ethical intentions. It is little wonder that such a revolutionary design met stiff and successful opposition; it is little wonder that, when associated with such a dangerous programme, all aspects of Positivism were suspect. This, then, was the Positivism that a generation of English historians reacted against or with.

Almost entirely they reacted against Comte, Buckle and Harrison. They were defending individualism, free will and divine judgment. J.M. Robertson, militant free thinker and friend of Charles Bradlaugh, as an outsider and opponent of the ecclesiastical establishment, saw this when he wrote *Buckle and His Critics* (1895), identifying Stubbs, Goldwin Smith, and Froude as historians opposed to Buckle. To a certain extent Buckle had anticipated their objections, maintaining that his approach to history in no way affected the issue of free will. Claiming to have perceived the origins of the concept of 'chance' in hunter-gatherer cultures and of 'necessity' in agrarian communities, he explained free will, a metaphysical concept, as a development of the former, and predestination, a theological concept, as a product of the latter. He did not judge between the two: neither, he argued, was relevant to the uses of scientific history. The inductive method did not concern itself with theological or metaphysical theory.[14] However, no one doubted that this was the key issue. Mill saw that it was so: the most fundamental objection to the idea that historical facts were subject to scientific laws, he said, was 'grounded on the doctrine of Free Will, or, in other words, on the denial that the law of invariable Causation hold true of human volitions', though he denied that a doctrine of causation need be fatalist.[15] Subsequently, it is true, it has been argued from a very different philosophical position and for a different purpose, that the determinist–free will controversy is an irrelevance when considering the historical mode of experience.[16] Buckle did not, however, disarm his critics.

First off the mark were Acton and Simpson,[17] who reviewed Buckle's *History of Civilization in England* (1857) in two aggressive and scornful articles in *The Rambler* in 1858. Acton, as a Catholic, albeit a liberal one, was not part of the ecclesiastical or university establishment, but his own religious and political views were clearly opposed to the sort of message that Buckle purveyed. History and science were seen as opposing concepts: 'History is a generalised account of the personal actions of men united in bodies for any public purposes whatever; and science is the combination of a great mass of similar facts into the unity of a generalisation, a principle, or a law, which principle or law will enable us to predict with certainty the recurrence of like events under given conditions'. Buckle had not only confused science and history: he had denied moral progress, the significance of good and evil deeds, the absolute nature of moral and religious truths and the importance of 'individual happiness or misery'. He made 'the individual soul of no account', viewing people only 'as bodies in mass' or as machines — not as individuals. It was important to retain an individualist approach because 'it is only to men as persons that free will belongs: look at them in masses, and they become machines; with their personality you abstract their freedom'. Buckle's unbreakable law of Providence was really 'the action of a Personal God upon his personal creatures; warning them, teaching them, judging them'.[18] Buckle had failed to establish that 'the actions of men, and therefore of societies, are governed by fixed laws, and not by free-will'. His chief fallacy lay in that, while his own conception of his work required him to treat of men in the mass, in fact he applied his laws 'to man as a person, as an individual'. In fact, man cannot be added to man, 'soul cannot be mixed with soul; each individual stands apart, or loses his individuality by addition'. Acton was convinced that the 'true historian takes the individual for his centre; he describes the typical man, whom all others more or less resemble; he recounts the adventures of the ruler, to whose will multitudes bow'. Buckle's programme was impossible for 'free-will refuses the inductive process'. Buckle had degraded the history of man because history was 'the dealings of God with man'; Buckle had stripped history of 'its philosophical, of its divine, and even of its human character and interest'.[18]

Many years later, in the first volume of the *English Historical Review*, a publication which supposedly marked the establishment of the historical profession in England, Acton was to assert that 'the marrow of civilized history is ethical' and that 'in the revolt of the last ten years against utilitarians and materialists, the growth of ethical knowledge has become for the first time, the supreme object of history'.[19] Not all of his professional colleagues would have agreed with this assessment of their role, as his dispute with Creighton over the latter's *History of the Papacy* testified, but Acton remained convinced that 'it is the office of historical science to maintain morality as the sole impractical criterion of men and things, and the only one on which honest minds can be made to agree'.[20] As he told Creighton, 'The inflexible integrity of the moral code is to me the secret of the authority, the dignity, the utility of history'.[21] For Acton, then, if history was a science, it was because it acquired scientific objectivity through judgment based on the inflexible integrity of the moral code, not because it could formulate laws of human action.

Hard on the heels of this liberal Catholic rebuttal came Goldwin Smith, a man with a broad church background who, though somewhat unorthodox, held to his Anglican views. He was a controversial if not very profound thinker, who by virtue of his position as Oxford's regius professor of modern history, as well as by temperament, would have felt obliged to deal with the issues raised by Buckle and as a consequence of Buckle, with Comte. Before his Oxford audience, in 1859, he attacked the 'necessarian' approach to historical explanation, the view that 'history is governed by necessary laws', virtually paraphrasing Buckle's arguments to illustrate the necessarian position, though not mentioning Buckle by name. He saw Positivism as a challenge to free will, suggesting that men act as if they choose and have responsibility for their actions because they cannot think or act otherwise; this suggests that free will does exist. Logically, this is a weak argument. He also confused law as regularity with law as prescription. When the lectures were published, in 1861, Fitzjames Stephen picked him up on this point, maintaining that the argument about free will and necessity was irrelevant to the issue of laws in human development. Noting the metaphorical character of the term 'natural law', he anticipated modern attitudes to the laws of natural science, arguing that they were but hypotheses based on the assumption that conditions remained unchanged; they were 'limited and conditional'. If laws of human development were no more than these, then they posed no threat to morality, no threat to the doctrine of free will. It was, nonetheless, perfectly reasonable to attempt to predict the act of a free agent, for it was the freedom of choice that made rational choice possible.[22] Stephen's riposte was, however, unnoticed except by Mill. Perhaps Goldwin Smith's greatest error, though, was to assume that the Law of the Three Stages could be disproved by showing, for example, that contemporaries thought theologically about one subject and positively about another — which of course is just what one would expect if sciences develop at different rates.

Some of his arguments, however, have more substance. He fell back on intuition as an alternative to induction; he posited that the facts of history were drawn from such a small portion of mankind's probable existence on this planet that no conclusions could yet be drawn about the laws governing development, about the future, or about the proximate achievement of a final, Positivist stage of human society; and, like Acton, he assumed certain moral absolutes. He also expounded on the role of the irrational, the influence of great men and the role of accident. For good measure, he rounded on Idealism as well as Positivism. It was a comprehensive, if indiscriminate, attack on attempts to systematize the study of history, to use it in a predictive way, and to rob it of its moral purpose, its individualism and its basis in personal responsibility.[23] Returning to the charge in a later lecture, he asserted that necessary laws would rob us of a sense of moral responsibility, of our God-given sense of good and evil, and would be a barrier between man and God.[24]

Goldwin Smith's popular Cambridge counterpart, Charles Kingsley, lost no time in entering the fray: his inaugural lecture (1860) was entitled 'The Limits of Exact Science as Applied to History'. Though he admired the tendency to extend scientific method to history as an optimistic search for more order, he warned against the 'bigotry' of 'young sciences' which he deliberately compared to young men. He distinguished between 'persons' and 'abstractions', objecting to viewing human beings 'rather as things than as persons' and to investing abstractions with personal qualities. 'Discovering, to our just delight, order and law all around us, in a thousand events that seemed to our fathers fortuitous and arbitrary, we are dazzled just now by the magnificent prospect opening before us, and fall, too often, into more than one serious mistake'.[25] Kingsley may have been right about a natural instinct for order and law: what he represented, however, was a potent fear of order and prediction, a fear of the future, and therefore, of knowledge of the future and of a predetermined future. Knowledge is avoided as often as it is sought. God and God-given morality were verities, but as unknowable as they were unquestionable. This interpretation suggests a psychological explanation of his position — perhaps a psychological weakness, a pessimism that preferred ignorance to knowledge. J.B. Bury, however, was to suggest another psychological explanation for the gulf between the utopian theorist and the individualist. Both were optimists, believers in progress; but whereas the socialist and the Comtist believed in the perfectibility of man and therefore in a specific goal, the individualist believed in continued progress. The goal of one was attainable and society would therefore cease to be dynamic, having attained its ideal state. For the other, 'individual liberty is the motive force, and the corresponding political theory is liberalism'. He contrasted the latter attitude with one 'in which the authority of the state is preponderant, and the individual has little more value than a cog in a well-oiled wheel: his place is assigned; it is not his right to go his own way'.[26] He thought that belief in one type of progress against the other was a matter of temperament.

In this spirit, Kingsley had not felt obliged to argue the case for free will; he simply assumed its existence. In other respects, too, Kingsley's arguments were rather insecurely based. Like Goldwin Smith, he confused the idea of law as an average and law as a predetermining force. He also thought that the irrational element in the human will invalidated social laws; but, more than this, his high-flown rhetoric on the subject of the irrational capacity for good and evil, in which he talked of the 'demoniac factor', seems almost an unconscious celebration of the force for evil. Kingsley, nonetheless, must be taken seriously as a representative figure.[27] He certainly saw himself as part of a trend that recognized the role of the individual, of the genius even, with explicit reference to Mill, 'our greatest living political economist', and his essay *On Liberty*, which had been published the year before.[28] Mill had explicitly denied that he was entering the current debate about free will, with *On Liberty*,[29] but in the climate of the time he could not avoid it. This is hardly surprising from one who identified, as a crucial element in his own youthful mental 'crisis', the fear of the doctrine of 'Philosophical Necessity', which had weighed on his existence 'like an incubus'. He had felt, he said, as if he was 'scientifically proved to be the helpless slave of antecedent circumstances', as if his character had been formed by circumstances beyond his control. It is true that he maintained that he had solved the problem,[30] but the incubus was felt by many in these mid-century years. Kingsley, though perhaps drawing on Mill for his ideas on genius,[31] adopted an obscurantist approach to the subject. There were laws but they were unknowable; and the genius, himself an inexplicable phenomenon, could reshape man's destinies, for good or evil. Thus Kingsley anticipated Nietzsche. As for 'the new science of little men', it could be 'no science at all: because the average man is not the normal man'; rather the great man is the 'norma' or standard to which his fellows aspired. He advised his students to stick to uncovering the facts, 'trusting that if we make ourselves masters of them, some rays of inductive light will be vouchsafed to us from Him who truly comprehends mankind'. Thus Kingsley claimed divine justification for a haphazard historical method. For Kingsley, it was verging on blasphemy to seek full understanding of the laws of God, suggesting that we were no less than He. History was 'God educating Man' but it was an education in morality, for morals were the bases of history; as with the Hebrews of old, the state of the nation depended on the state of its morals. Though he claimed to tread a middle path between superstition and necessitarianism when he advocated studying history as a work of God 'without impertinently demanding of Him a reason for his deeds', even his accompanying welcome for science as divine light thrown on divine works hardly corrects the impression of a man deeply troubled by the prospect of knowing too much. Without a belief in moral order we would go mad, said Kingsley; without a belief in moral progress we would break our hearts. Perhaps he feared to investigate too far his beliefs.[32] Isaiah Berlin was to say of Comte, 'He saw no depth in mere darkness'.[33] Perhaps one could say of Kingsley that he lacked Comte's perspective in this respect.

Four years later another historian entered the lists. Though he eschewed anything but praise for Buckle the man, J.A. Froude was a natural opponent of Positivism. He was, above all, Carlyle's disciple, with all that that implied about the role of the individual and the Great Man in history. His close association with Carlyle and the older man's influence, almost ascendancy, is too well known to need elaboration here. He was also related by marriage to Kingsley, and the two became close friends. An early commitment to individualist ethics and an open commitment to partial history seemed to suit him for the antipositivist role. Like so many of his generation, Froude had been through a period of religious doubt and unorthodoxy, complicated by a clerical family background and his combative brother's involvement in the Oxford Movement; and, as a consequence, he had felt obliged to exclude himself from the university establishment. But, though unorthodox, he was a militant Protestant. His biographer suggested that he had a Calvinist sense of predestination, though added that this was coupled with a possibly incompatible sense of man's moral responsibility.[34] If this was so, it did not significantly alter the grounds of the attack he made: he wrote from an individualist position, and like Kingsley, he evinced a fear of knowing the future. Positivists, it has been said, had a 'hunger for systematic and comprehensive explanation' because they needed a substitute religion, both as a framework for organized worship and as an explanation of the universe.[35] For their opponents a fear of comprehensive knowledge, particularly knowledge of good and evil, may have been as strong. Frederic Harrison, one of the leading Positivists in the fullest sense, drew attention to the nature of Positivism's appeal. He said:

> The age is one of Construction — and Positivism is essentially constructive. Men in these times crave something organic and systematic . . . There is abroad a strange consciousness of doubt, instability, and incoherence; and, withal, a secret yearning after certainty and reorganisation in thought and life.

We have, he said, outgrown the old social and religious beliefs and need something to replace them, despite an apparent preference for the current state of moral and intellectual anarchy.[36] Harrison was aware that every social or intellectual impulse was likely to produce a counter impulse — and the resistance to Positivism may have been on even broader issues then he suggests. Mandelbaum has discoursed on the crucial question of unity and diversity in this period of intellectual history and suggested something between a spirit of the age concept and complete diversity,[37] but it is tempting to suggest that the spirit of an age is characterized by the issues of concern rather than by agreement about those issues. Thus, the impulse to Positivism, acutely recognized by Harrison, involved issues of widespread concern amongst the intelligentsia, which by no means spoke with one voice on those issues. The historians, however, were aligned almost exclusively on one side of the debate.

Froude's major pronouncement was 'The Science of History', a lecture delivered at the Royal Institution in 1864. As we would expect, he was particularly concerned with the role of the individual and the great man, and feared that Buckle's approach to history would threaten the sense of moral obligation and responsibility. Natural laws were always liable to be neutralized 'by what is called volition'. If there was freedom of choice, there could be no science of history; if there was a science of history, there was no free choice and 'praise or blame' were irrelevant. Crucially, 'Mankind are but an aggregate of individuals — History is but the record of individual action'. He, too, was sceptical about the predictive powers of history; the supposedly scientific facts of history, the bases of laws, and therefore of prediction, were filtered through the minds that recorded them, fallible instruments. There was, in fact, only one reliable lesson of history: 'that, in the long run, it is well with the good; in the long run, it is ill with the wicked. But this is no science; it is no more than the old doctrine taught long ago by the Hebrew prophets. The theories of M. Comte and his disciples advance us, after all, not a step beyond trodden and familiar ground', for laws of human behaviour were restricted to the lowest, animal level, and did not impinge upon moral choice, on will.

One of the reasons why Froude felt that Buckle had to be resisted was that he was seen to be extending the principles of Adam Smith's political economy to all human activity. This point had also been taken up by Kingsley. Both men, arguing that there was more to morality than enlightened self-interest, felt a duty to attack such an extension. In another respect Froude echoed Kingsley: prediction was impossible — society would change in quite unforeseeable ways in the hectic future. The lessons of history were: 'draw no horoscope' and 'the moral law is written on the tables of eternity', and sin is punished.[38]

Morley, as editor of *The Fortnightly Review*, reviewed 'The Science of History' when it was published three years later. He maintained that there was nothing amoral about Buckle and nothing utilitarian about Comte's morality, and that 'the proper object matter of the science of history is masses of men'. The business of the scientific historian was to discover the laws of the relations between broad, common social influences. A scientific method existed for doing this; and thus would be discovered 'the various impulses by which a society advances from one general state to another general state'. Froude was wrong to see history as a vehicle for moral judgment or to expect to see wickedness punished. Overall, this was not an especially impressive denunciation of Froude's windy lecture. One particularly unimpressive passage suggested that Froude wished to make man 'the slave of his will, rather than its master'.[39] Though, as T.H. Green's lectures on the principles of political obligation were to show, the precise nature of the freedom of will is worth investigation, Morley's comments were crude and showed no real appreciation of the issues involved. Though Robertson was to reserve his most scathing comments for Froude's lecture, it met with no effective contemporary counter-attack. Generally, though antipositivists talked as if they were fighting a successful and dangerous enemy, Mill seemed very aware of the strength and the nature of the opposition to Positivism. When he assumed the role of publicist for Comte's ideas in 1865, he suggested, disarmingly, that Comtist ideas were easily absorbed into the English empirical tradition going back to Hume, and that they need not involve a rejection of God: 'The Positivist mode of thought is not necessarily a denial of the supernatural; it merely throws back that question to the origin of all things'. Indeed, if the universe had a beginning, its beginning by the very conditions of the case was supernatural; the laws of nature cannot account for their own origin. So long as a man's God was not a capricious God, he could happily believe in both fixed laws and a divine origin for those laws. Mill was well aware of the strength of religious feeling in England, suggesting that Protestant individualism, with its sense of 'a direct responsibility of the individual immediately to God', made a particular demand upon the intelligence, and was thus highly educative.[40] However, this attempt to reconcile the two positions did not work; and Mill's advocacy, ironically, may have done nothing to further the Positivist cause because, though very influential in certain quarters, he was identified with a school of thought which was now under attack.

It could be argued that, though Buckle's detractors appeared to hold the floor, they were either outsiders or birds of passage. Acton and Froude, from their very different religious standpoints, were for the moment excluded from university posts, only attaining their regius chairs, at Cambridge and Oxford respectively, late in their lives (in the 1890s) almost as honorary recognition of their services to history. Goldwin Smith and Kingsley, also unorthodox in their different ways, were hardly committed to the profession of historian, and voluntarily left their chairs within three years of each other in the 1860s. Kingsley, indeed, though the decision was his, was under some pressure to go because it was felt that he fell short of professional standards. What of their supposedly more professional and influential successors, men who might be expected to see, as the initial furore subsided, the advantages of establishing history as a science, rigorous and methodical?

At Oxford, Stubbs was far less inclined than his rumbustious predecessor to speak to the world at large or, despite his holy orders, to preach from the professorial chair. As a worker at history, the doyen of constitutional historians, he was happiest with the minutiae of his own studies; and in the main confined his statutory public lectures, about which he complained inordinately, to proprietorial reports on the state of the Oxford history school. He was the most orthodox of Anglicans and was to find preferment as Bishop of Oxford. He was an establishment figure with no sympathy for the idea of a new intellectual élite and no vision of a new future, despite, or perhaps because of, his own upward social mobility. It is not, therefore, surprising to find that his one brief reference to the historical ideas of Positivism should have been hostile; though the attack was oblique, naming no persons or philosophies, it was influential because of his reputation as the foremost historical scholar in England. The attack came, not in his inaugural lecture in 1867, when the air was still full of Froude's sound and fury, but ten years later. The free agency of the human will, he said, was 'the motive cause of all historical events'; and the human will manifested itself in almost innumerable, and therefore virtually unclassifiable variations. In addition, 'generalizations become obscurer and more useless as they grow wider, and, as they grow narrower and more special, cease to have any value as generalizations at all'. As a consequence, he doubted the validity of a science of history, finding it significant that only theorists, not practising historians, espoused it, and that it appeared, in the hands of the doctrinaire, as a political weapon. History as 'the dealings of human wills, in countless combinations, and circumstances which no theory can ever exhaustively calculate', was 'not the field for dogmatic assumption or for speculative classification. Perhaps you think that I am talking at random, that no people were ever so foolish as to suppose that even an exhaustive knowledge of past history would enable a man to prophesy; for such should be the result of scientific treatment'. As a final gibe, he suggested that sometimes men classify the specimens which other men have collected, and claim the character of philosophers without any direct acquaintance with materials at all.[41] Thus Stubbs delivered his magisterial judgment.

It has been suggested recently that an analysis of Stubbs's imagery betrays an underlying Hegelian metaphysic, not consciously adopted but the result of a pervasive and diffuse influence in Stubbs's England.[42] This may be so; but to Robertson, Stubbs, far more than Goldwin Smith or Froude, typified the conventional Christian university establishment. Robertson railed against the stultifying and censorious effect of men like Stubbs, at his 'nursery philosophy' and 'pulpit' formulas.[43] His pulpit formulas were certainly sincere. Ten years earlier he had almost shocked his friend J.R. Green, when he concluded his inaugural lecture by attributing to history the capacity to bring men 'into a perception of the workings of the Almighty Ruler of the World'.[44] Green thought this quaint: 'very odd it must have seemed to Oxford, as it did even to me, but so true to Stubbs — the old simple lesson that the world's history led up to God, that modern history was but the broadening of His light in Christ. I remember when this was my clue to history once — I am afraid I have lost it without gaining another'.[45] Though Green's doubts were more typical of the 1860s than were the elder man's certainties, and give the lie to Robertson's picture of an impregnable and self-satisfied ecclesiastical establishment, the relationship between the two men well illustrated the sentimental hold that older orthodox churchmen could exercise over their younger contemporaries. Insecurity would sharpen the dispute, not dull the establishment's response.

Elsewhere, the situation certainly seemed less secure, at first sight. Stubbs's counterpart at Cambridge, Seeley, might seem an exception to the antipositivist rule, for his biographer has noted the influence of Positivist ideas upon the young Seeley in 1860s London.[46] According to some accounts, the classic mid-Victorian youthful crisis of faith had turned Seeley to Positivism, to which he still held when appointed Kingsley's successor in 1869. His inaugural lecture has been seen as a deliberate refutation of Kingsley's. According to this interpretation he had breached the ecclesiastical establishment. In fact, Seeley was carefully vetted by Gladstone and Kingsley. Gladstone was much impressed by Seeley's *Ecce Homo*, satisfying himself that its author would oppose atheism in terms that the thinking members of the younger generation would appreciate. It is true that Kingsley, himself oppressed by the apparent prevalence of Comte's ideas, did not find Seeley so reassuring in his attitude to Comte and Positivism: 'Just at present', wrote Seeley, 'Comtism seems so irresistibly triumphant, that I have contented myself with pointing out that it is in a sense a Christian movement and with trying to induce the Church to appropriate what is good in it'.[43] Though not the enthusiastic disciple sometimes portrayed, was he soft on Positivism? Recently, Wormell has suggested that his views were by no means uniformly Positivist, containing an admixture of other opinions, including Christian Socialist ones, and excluding some specific Positivist ideas. In addition, it should be noted, his sense of the irresistibility of Comtism stemmed partly from his own sense of inadequacy at this juncture; and the general strength of Positivism has also been questioned. In any case, despite self-doubt, Seeley emerged as well-suited to combat Positivism on its own terms and, for that reason, was recommended by F.D. Maurice as well as by Kingsley. If the influence of Positivism was still evident in his inaugural lecture, in which he declared that history was the residuum of material left over from scientific study in more advanced areas of knowledge, and from which a new science of politics would be developed, he was also at pains to distance himself from Buckle. His later lectures and writings showed not only the influence of Christian Socialism as well as Positivism, but also the influence of both Ranke and the Liberal Anglican School. If any one influence came to predominate, it would seem to be that of the Liberal Anglicans.[48] Ironically, then, though selected with one eye on the need to combat Positivism and its secular tendency, Seeley was at least ambivalent in his attitude to the Positivists. He was not a whole-hearted advocate, nor a practitioner, of history as a Positivist science. In any case, his influence in the Cambridge school of history was constantly challenged from the time when the reform of the history tripos was first mooted in the mid-1880s.

If Seeley was a partial exception to the rule, Lecky has been seen as a complete exception, described as Buckle's 'most faithful disciple'.[49] Though he held no academic post, he was influential in London literary society, and in 1892 could have had the regius chair of modern history at Oxford in place of Froude. As a young man, he was full of admiration for Buckle, an admiration frequently and even extravagantly expressed. In 1861, for example, he referred to Buckle as 'the very greatest intellect ever applied to history, the very greatest thinker and scholar now living', and claimed to be the greatest authority on Buckle. It is possible to see the influence of Positivist attitudes towards the secularization of society and the Law of the Three Stages in Lecky's early works on intellectual history. Lecky himself said of *The History of Rationalism in Europe* and *The History of European Morals*:

> Both books belong to a very small school of historical writings which began in the seventeenth century with Vico, was continued by Condorcet, Herder, Hegel and Comte, and which found its last great representative in Mr Buckle . . . What characterises these writers is that they try to look at history, not as a series of biographies or accidents or pictures, but, as a great organic whole.

Comte, said Lecky, had influenced the ablest men if not the mass, and had passed on two crucial ideas — the Law of the Three Stages and the hierarchy of sciences; 'he has done more than any previous writer to show that the speculative opinions of any age are phenomena resulting from the totality of the intellectual influences of that age'.[50] It is quite wrong to see Lecky as someone who admired Buckle but repudiated Positivism, as a modern study of Positivism suggests;[51] the situation was more complex, with admiration of Buckle and Positivist influence giving way to a more critical attitude as other intellectual influences came to the fore.

It is tempting to see Lecky's Irish background as bearing upon his early interest in Positivism. He was born into the Protestant Ascendancy, and though he maintained a detached and critical attitude to his countrymen, he also indulged, like many of his generation and class, a staunch if moderate Irish patriotism. Desirous, therefore, of regenerating Ireland and of raising its reputation among the educated English public, he was conscious of a degree of clerical obscurantism among the Irish. 'The great desideratum in Ireland is a lay public opinion', he wrote in 1859; and later he suggested that 'among the Irish generally there is a want of hard intellectuality'.[52] This desire for a rational, secular educated élite in Ireland might well have influenced a young man towards Positivist ideas. The contrast with England is striking. In England the educated élite was more rooted in a national political and religious culture, recruiting from traditional social groups such as the clergy or the other professional classes through the agency of the universities. In Ireland a landed Protestant Ascendancy felt increasingly cut off from the mass of the people and the national culture, and fearful of the influence of an obscurantist Catholic clergy; there was no large middle class to bridge the gap between the landed classes and the peasantry. Secularism and the prospect of a new scientific élite must have been very appealing to a young Protestant gentleman anxious to identify with the land of his birth. Perhaps it is significant that the only other leading historian to have flirted with Positivism in his youth (apart from Seeley, who had his own religious doubts, and doubts about the social role of religion which he had tried to satisfy in *Ecce Homo*), was J.B. Bury, who came from a background similar to Lecky's. This may be further evidence in support of the thesis that the strength of the antipositivists lay in their assumed sociopolitical and religious role in the English universities; the Anglo-Irish proved the rule.

Buckle's influence, however, did not maintain its hold upon Lecky; indeed contemporary assertions of the predominance of Positivism seem to be wildly exaggerated. There were many alternative influences at work even in the 1860s, supposedly the decade of greatest Positivist influence. According to his own account of the formative influences in his life, even while he was still at Trinity College, Dublin, the study of Bishop Butler imbued him with a sense of the importance of individual conscience, and Kant and Butler left him with the idea that duty could override calculations of self-interest. He also claimed to have been influenced by Whately, one of the Liberal Anglicans. In 1865, Dean Milman, another Liberal Anglican, praised the young man's work and compared it favourably to Buckle's, claiming that Lecky shared his own views. Lecky retained great respect for Milman and the other Liberal Anglican historians. Lecky was also to take the view that Darwin's *Origin of Species* (published two years after volume I of Buckle's *History of Civilization in England*), by stressing the supreme importance of 'inborn and hereditary tendencies' (now 'the very central fact of English philosophy'), had quickly underminded the earlier work which had emphasized the power of circumstances. The equally deterministic implications of Darwin's work seem to have been lost on Lecky, who mentioned the *Origin of Species* in the context of an argument about the importance of individuals, 'and even accidents', in 'modifying and deflecting' historical trends. It was on this occasion, too, that Lecky characterized Buckle as having 'many of the distinctive faults of a young writer; of a writer who had mixed little with men, and had formed his mind almost exclusively by solitary, unguided study'.[53] This was undoubtedly an accurate portrait of Buckle; but, consciously or not, may also have been a portrait of his own youth, when he had been such an enthusiast for Buckle; for Lecky was lionised by literary society in London after the success of *The History of Rationalism in Europe*, and had entered a world of multifarious and often direct personal influences, far removed from the sense of alienation that had threatened him in Ireland.

The greatest of the influences on Lecky was the ageing but formidable Carlyle, who henceforth acted as a counterweight to Buckle. The issues that led Lecky from Buckle are immediately recognizable: free will, the role of Great Men and of individuals in history; chance or 'accident' in history, and the consequent difficulty of framing laws; moral judgments in history and the intuitive basis for morals. As early as 1861 he had reserved free will and geographical determinism as areas of disagreement with Buckle. The areas of contention widened as, on long walks, Carlyle railed against Comte, 'the ghastliest algebraic factor that ever was taken for a man'. Ironically, the Utilitarians' welcome for the ideas of Comte and the close association then assumed between Positivists and Utilitarians militated against the influence of the former because of the tide of reaction against the latter. We have seen this with Kingsley and Froude, and it was very evident with Lecky, who expected his *History of European Morals from Augustus to Charlemagne* (1869) to offend the Utilitarians because it was based on an intuitive theory of morals. He said that he detested the moral philosophy of the 'advanced thinkers'. He was, said his wife, 'by nature and by conviction an intuitive philosopher; the belief in an original moral faculty was the keynote of his life'.[54]

The intuitive theory of morals and the concept of a moral faculty were very important to Lecky and to the antipositivist position generally. Henry Sidgwick was one of the most important of the university intellectuals who turned to intuitionism. As a Cambridge 'Apostle' in the 1850s he had, like Seeley a decade later, become concerned to reconstruct religious and social beliefs according to the new fashion for scientific method. Though resistant to agnosticism, his doubts led him to resign his fellowship in 1869. His *Methods of Ethics* (1874) was an attempt to reconcile Utilitarian and intuitionist theories.[55] Two years later he returned to the theme, suggesting that a comparison between 'man's actual moral sentiments' and 'the conclusions of utilitarian calculation' was instructive, so long as 'a theory of the origin of morality' was seen to have no bearing on matters of ethical controversy.[56] Ten years later he dealt more explicitly with historical method. Once again, a study of the evolution of ideas could not tell us what was true or what should be — they were metaphysical questions. Even if history enabled us to predict, it could be no more than a negative guide (in that it was pointless to strive for the impossible); it could not tell us whether or not we should strive to hasten the inevitable. History was not a guide to future action.[53] Thus Sidgwick rejected the Comtist vision. Sidgwick, though not himself an historian, was influential: in particular, as a Fellow of Trinity College, he influenced the undergraduate Maitland, between 1869 and 1872, and financed Maitland's readership in 1884. The two remained close throughout Sidgwick's life.[58] It has been noted that Maitland, supposedly the ideal of the objective historian, was, throughout his career, concerned with the relevance of historical work to the cause of legal reform, and with the didactic role of the legal historian, with ethical judgment, and the historian's need to come to terms with the implications of evolutionary theory[59] — all concerns inherited from his mentor.

The fullest expression in Lecky's own works of the relationship between the intuitionist theory of morals and the concept of free will is *The Map of Life* (1899). Rational analysis of actions and ends does little to promote happiness, asserted Lecky; yet the will was not 'a mere slave to pleasure and pain', or 'imperious desires'. Rather 'the conflict between will and the desires, the reality of self-restraint and the power of Will to modify character, are among the most familiar facts of moral life'. A belief in moral responsibility and in free will was a necessity. 'It is impossible to explain the mystery of free will'; but some beliefs were 'not susceptible of demonstrative proof' and one such belief was in 'the existence of a distinction between right and wrong, different from and higher than the distinction between pleasure and pain'.[60] In this rejection of utilitarian ethics, it might be said, Lecky spoke for his age.

The extent to which Lecky distanced himself from Buckle and Positivism is seen by comparing the approach of *History of Rationalism* (1865) with the attitude adopted in his massive *History of England in the Eighteenth Century* (eight volumes, 1878-90). While preparing the latter, in 1875, he said that in the past he had dealt chiefly with

the power of general causes in dominating individualities and determining the general character of successive ages. In this book I am dealing largely with the accidents of history, and with the many causes in which a very slight change in individual action or in the disposition of circumstances might have altered the whole course of history. I quite think, with Grote, that the master error of Buckle was his absurd underrating of the accidents of history; and Herbert Spencer represents the same tendency in an even more exaggerated form.[61]

Shortly after the appearance of the final volume of his *History of England*, Lecky explicitly divided British historians into two schools — that of Buckle and that of Carlyle. Clearly identifying himself with the latter, he professed his belief that 'individual action and even mere accident' modified the 'regularities and irresistible forces' of history. Man, he said, 'is not a mere passive weed drifting helplessly upon the sea of life, and human wisdom and human folly can do and have done much to modify the condition of his being'. But what sort of historical message, we may ask, resulted from this commitment to individual action and even mere accident? What could Lecky put in place of the Comtist vision or, with recognition of the need to elevate 'mere accident' to a causal role, with what could he replace the progressive Whiggism of his predecessors? His answer to this problem provides us with an early example of what was to become the classic low-key rationale for post-Positivist and post-Whig historiography. Historical study would provide one of the best schools for that kind of reasoning which is most useful in 'practical life', teaching how 'to weigh conflicting probabilities, to estimate degrees of evidence, to form a sound judgment of the value of authorities'. It provided the 'mental discipline' of putting oneself in the shoes of both sides; it expanded horizons, yet through comparative study made one aware that not all institutions (such as the British constitution, for example) were equally suited to all nations. Above all, the 'most precious lessons are moral ones', the morality of a nation being the best guide to its potential success or failure.[62] This is rather weak philosophically and it lacks the confident appeal of Whiggism: but it retains a certain Victorian sense of moral purpose, alongside its rather weary weighing of probabilities and its cautious relativism. The insistence upon individual will and moral responsibility had led to the brink of nihilism. When the sense of moral purpose was shed, perhaps as faith declined, then the picture would be a totally negative one. Fear of pattern and prediction would lead to a rather intellectually lazy and uninspiring acceptance that history's only message was that it had no message, that it dissolved theories and patterns. For the moment this rather depressing result was avoided, if narrowly, by a residual sense of moral purpose in writers like Lecky.

Lecky, of course, had been exposed in particular to Carlyle's influence. In the case of J.R. Green, often thought of as the third member of the trio that constituted the 'Oxford school' (Stubbs and Freeman being the senior members), the Liberal Anglican influence had the most direct impact.

While living the life of a disillusioned, dilettante Oxford undergraduate, he heard by chance one of A.P. Stanley's lectures in 1859, and under his influence, was converted to a life of work, history and Christian vocation. Though he was later to acknowledge other influences, including that of F.D. Maurice and Carlyle, the personal contact with Stanley mattered most.

In Green's account of his conversion, one senses the emotional appeal of the Liberal Anglican and Broad Church tradition, with its sense of duty and work ethic, its broadmindedness, its acceptance of the past without denying ambitions for the future. Green was in the process of losing his High Church faith; others turned to the new faith of Positivism, but the church had many manifestations and the troubled minds of the university youth of the 1850s and 1860s could often find a Christian refuge. It is true that, in Green's case, within five years he was, though in holy orders, once again in a crisis of faith — 'near Deism', he said; and shortly after that he was finding the religious close to Stubbs's inaugural lecture rather quaint.[63] But, in general, the strength of the Liberal Anglican influence was remarkable. Though Forbes, the historian of the Liberal Anglicans' historiography, has referred to 'Buckle's enormous success' as 'damning proof of the backwardness of England in the historical movement at least in the nineteenth century',[64] the characteristics of the Liberal Anglican School as he himself describes them are instantly recognizable. 'The whole object of the Liberal Anglican philosophy of history was to show that progress depends entirely on the efforts of individual men; as such it was a reaction against the logical end of a science of history carried *à outrance*: Determinism'; their philosophy of history, like their theology, was founded on 'that ultimate historical reality: the individual will'. Evidently the Liberal Anglicans fared rather well when they marched against the somewhat sparse spears of the Positivists. They believed in 'a universal standard of morality, free will, divine interposition and progress under God's Providence'. They believed in the ultimate, irreducible reality of the individual mind, and they wanted history to serve an immediate practical purpose as a guide to action in the perceived sociopolitical crisis of contemporary society. These characteristics we have seen again and again surviving into the second half of the nineteenth century. This brings into question Forbes's presumption that, through their own logical inconsistencies and the apparent vindication of utilitarian, rationalist optimism by the material prosperity of the mid-Victorian years, the Liberal Anglicans probably lacked influenced by the middle of the century.[65]

Finally, though this is not the place for an analysis of Bury's thought, which has already been shown to be consistently unlike Positivism, [66] there is some additional evidence that helps us to complete our picture. Bury was very critical of Comte, while recognizing his importance. Comte had failed as a prophet; his lack of historical knowledge had led him to easy generalizations which had taught us little; flying in the face of his own theory of knowledge, he had had a tendency to *a priori* thinking; the Law of the Three Stages was discredited; he was too Eurocentric; he ignored the problem of contingency. In addition, echoing his own comments about the temperamental distinction between liberals and adherents of closed systems of thought, Bury was unhappy about Comte's plans for organizing 'the final state of humanity beyond which there would be no further movement', about 'the authoritarian character' of that régime. 'If sociological laws are positively established as certainly as the law of gravitation', he felt, 'no room is left for opinion; right social conduct is definitely fixed; the proper functions of every member of society of no question; therefore the claim to liberty is perverse and irrational'. While recognizing the limitations of nineteenth-century liberalism, Bury saw that it had represented powerful sentiments about individual freedom and had been an effective opposition to Comte's ideas. He saw, quite clearly, the basis of the great divide among 'progressive' thinkers. In concluding his history of the idea of progress, Bury adopted an extreme relativist position, suggesting that the concept of progress, which had been the necessary intellectual environment in which Comte's and Buckle's ideas (among others) had been formulated, was possibly, like its predecessor, providence, destined to be superseded by some more advanced doctrine. Then he took his scepticism one stage further by wondering if this argument was, itself, 'merely a disconcerting trick of dialectic'.[67]

At the turn of the century, though other historians, like Tout, were championing the cause of scientific history, their scientism was of a very limited kind and represented a new sense of professionalism rather than belief in a Positivist methodology. Those who described them as Positivists were hostile to Positivism and assumed that not only had Positivism triumphed, but also that its inadequacies in practice were being demonstrated by historians who devoted themselves to empirical study without inducing general laws. From this has stemmed much misconceived criticism of the English historiographical tradition.[68]

If that tradition remained determinedly nominalist and, thus, individualist and opposed to law-making, it had, however, encompassed a perception of the English national tradition. As we have seen, the individualism of these historians was individualism in several senses of the term: they certainly believed in the dignity of man, and in the autonomy of the individual; they saw society in terms of atomic individuals and were thus methodological individualists; and associated with these attitudes was a complex of religious, social, economic, ethical and political attitudes. Yet they subscribed to a view of history that placed the nation centre-stage and that ascribed to their own nation distinctive generic characteristics and to its history a distinctive continuous pattern, teleologically determined. This looks to be the antithesis of an individualist approach. Isaiah Berlin has seen individualism as a valuable bulwark against the concept of the social whole and against teleological concepts of manifest destiny.[69] He also believed that at this time 'the writing of history transferred emphasis from the achievements of individuals to the growth and influence of institutions conceived in much less personal terms', citing law and government amongst his examples. For Berlin, of course, these were potentially dangerous developments, a prelude to more alarming tendencies in the twentieth century; and he did not accept, as Blaas has done, that the new history was superior in terms of accuracy or objectivity.[70] Though we might share Berlin's scepticism about the new professional ideal, it is clear that his version of events is much too simple. As we have argued, far from leading to a new holism or teleology, the new administrative and institutional historians brought their own brand of methodological individualism to their work. But, more than that, the old individualism had co-existed with a highly developed sense of the English national character, its historical evolution, its embodiment in certain institutions and its destiny. The rest of this chapter is an exploration of the co-existence of the individualist and the generic in the historiography of the time.

As already noted, one of the ways in which romantic individualism developed in the nineteenth century was in the direction of seeing the community, *Volk* or state as an historical individual or super-person. This is usually regarded as a predominantly German form of individualism, however, and the enemy of English individualism. There was, nonetheless, the Liberal Anglican tradition of national biography which had sought to accommodate free will. Of course, for individualists, the essential characteristics of English national history had been the strong commitment of the nation to freedom and to the individual. How could a strict nominalist explain such a phenomenon? The questions of what exactly it was that caused a nation to act in a particular way and of how that action was constituted, were of great contemporary concern. Hegel, Ranke, Carlyle, Buckle — all had had their own explanations. Tolstoy asked: 'What force moves the nations?' He asked his question on the presumption that, though historians still wrote as if the Great

Man moved the nation, the concept was already defunct because its original basis (that the Great Man was the instrument of God) was itself defunct. Rejecting an Idealist position, his own answer was that nations were moved 'by the activity of *all* the people who participate in the events', adding his famous rider that the irony was that those most directly responsible, the direct participants in the event, appear least responsible, whilst those leaders, the Napoleons of history, who are least directly involved, are credited with the greatest responsibility.[71] So Tolstoy's way out of the dilemma was a populist doctrine of collective action by individuals. How did English historians solve the problem?

Stubbs's work on the constitution is the classic explanation of what moved the English nation. The constitution was an expression of our national distinctiveness, our gift for freedom. In his preface to the first edition of his *Select Charters*, Stubbs wrote as follows:

> The study of Constitutional History is essentially a tracing of causes and consequences; the examination of a distinct growth from a well-defined germ to full maturity: a growth, the particular direction and shaping of which are due to a diversity of causes, but whose life and developing power lies deep in the very nature of the people. It is not then the collection of a multitude of facts and views, but the piecing of the links of a perfect chain.

There was, then, in constitutional history a clear causal chain — although the particular direction taken at any given time could be influenced by contingent factors. The nature of the relationship between cause and effect was, however, to an extent, decided by the 'well-defined germ' and 'developing power' of a life that derived from 'the very nature of the people'. Stubbs intended that his own work should play a role in ensuring that the living constitution should continue to be recognised by the nation as vital to its interests: the 'institution of our forefathers' possessed 'a living interest' for a nation realizing its own identity and their study should be part of 'a regular English education'.[72] This echoed his inaugural lecture, in which he had described modern history as 'the living, working, thinking, growing world of today'. Modern history, he proclaimed, was 'the history of ourselves, of the way in which we came to be as we are, of the education of our nation, of the development of our government, of the fortunes of our fathers, that caused us to be taught and governed and placed as we are, and formed our minds and habits by that teaching, government and position'.[73] Stubbs also believed that the English constitution was a force for good even overseas, but as this was an imperial concept it did not distract him from the national importance of the constitution. Years later, his biographer claimed that Stubbs's work had indeed, in both imperial and national contexts, made 'a great people recognise its kinship and its heritage in the past', promulgating ideas that were 'slowly penetrating into the public mind and finding expression in public life'.[74] The point here is that the life of the nation and the life of the constitution are inseparable; Stubbs's work merely brought them even closer together. The nation did not derive its independent character and its freedom from the constitution; the constitution was the expression of the national capacity for freedom. So Stubbs left us with something of a paradox — a nation with a predetermined, collective capacity for individual freedom! However paradoxical, it has proved to be a potent (and perhaps even beneficial) myth.

Stubbs had defined the 'nature of the people' in racial terms: there was a racial capacity for freedom. The racial purity of the English was naturally matched by the purity of their Teutonic institutions, unmixed with Roman traditions. The continuous development of the constitution towards democracy and freedom had been inherent in the earliest tribal gatherings. Stubbs, ordained clergyman and future Bishop, had little trouble in accommodating those impurities, the Christian religion and the Roman Church, when they arrived in Anglo-Saxon times: 'it was through the church that the nation first learned to realize its unity'. Once royal power had consolidated that unity there was a double threat to the life of the nation: royal power itself might have posed a threat to the nation's freedom, a threat intensified with the Norman Conquest; whilst the opposing, centrifugal force of feudalism might have destroyed the unity of the nation, a tendency begun by Canute's earldoms, temporarily suppressed by the Conqueror, and reaching its apogee in the anarchy of Stephen's reign. But with Henry II came the 'rule of law'. After the vicissitudes of John's reign and the triumph of Magna Carta, 'the long struggle of the constitution for existence' entered its final stage, to reach a glorious conclusion in the reign of Edward I, if not a Great Man, at least a great monarch in a long line of otherwise undistinguished kings of England. According to Stubbs, by Edward I's reign 'the nation may be regarded as reaching its full stature'. It was as yet youthful and uncouth, but it had grown up; 'the people are at full growth. The system is raw and untrained and awkward, but it is complete'. This is now recognised to be completely spurious, of course; but it was true to his belief in growth from a 'well-defined germ' to maturity of *the* national institution, by no means unaffected by contingent factors, including a great king, but with its potential defined from the outset, and its fulfilment explained in a teleological way. The history of the nation and of the constitution, crucially of Parliament, were as one. Though Stubbs frequently referred to the constitution as an 'organism', it has been rightly said of Whig history, and of Stubbs's work in particular, that in it constitutional development was still dependent on individual effort.[76] The Liberal Anglican method of national biography was alive and kicking.

Stubbs's Liberal friend, and his successor as Regius Professor at Oxford, Edward Freeman, whose major works had been based on very similar assumptions, was to develop the racial thesis about the national capacity for freedom even further.[77] In 1870 Freeman was helped in firming up his ideas on race by a quite lengthy correspondence with Max Müller, the German-born, Oxford-based philologist.[78] They sent each other copies of their lectures and essays on the subject, and Freeman came to accept a philologically-based Aryan racism in place of the more intuitive, vaguer Teutonism which he had shared with Stubbs and Thomas Arnold. Within a few years, however, Müller, the leading exponent of philological racialism, renounced his views, leaving Freeman and others bereft of expert leadership and faced with the apparently insoluble problem of the impurity of races. Müller, as his letters to Freeman had made clear, had always doubted the physiological evidence for race.[79] So Freeman, never at a loss, produced his own theory of race, in 1877, in response to the crisis. He accepted that 'physical purity of race' did not exist, but maintained that race could still be the essential ingredient determining the character of a nation: provided the nation contained a racial core that had determined its capacities and institutions, it could 'adopt' members of other races, so long as they did not swamp the original core, or retain their own group identity, or come from non-Aryan races (Freeman developed a vicious hostility to non-Aryans).[80] Within the Aryan race the closest kin belonged to the same linguistically-defined family of nations — in the case of the English this was the Germanic or 'Deutsch' family, of course, especially speakers of low 'Dutch' (to use Freeman's terminology).[81] Though he thought that the 'English' nation still comprised those who lived in the 'three homes' of the English, namely old Saxony, England itself, and 'New England' (by which he meant the whole of the United States), he also came to accept an element of environmental conditioning in that the character of the English of England was in part due to their island home.[82] Throughout Freeman's historical work, however, there is the constant assumption that constitutional freedoms were part of the racial heritage and that the English were particularly fortunate in having first preserved and then developed these freedoms in a manner suited to modern conditions. He proclaimed that 'the earliest institutions of England and other Teutonic lands are not mere matters of curious speculation, but matters closely connected with our present political being', and that we had often found it necessary to fall back 'on the very earliest principles of our race . . . the holders of Liberal principles in modern politics need never shrink from tracing up our political history to its earliest beginnings. As far at least as our race is concerned, freedom is everywhere older than bondage; we may add that toleration is older than intolerance. Our ancient history is the possession of the Liberal, who, as being ever ready to reform, is the true Conservative, not of the self-styled Conservative who, by refusing reform does all he can to bring on destruction.'[83] This could almost have been written by Thomas Arnold, who saw himself as an 'advancer' and who had identified 'race, language, institutions, and religion' as the inter-linked elements of nationality, and whose inaugural lecture had first introduced Freeman to the idea that the Germanic peoples, of which the English were a vital part, were the new standard-bearers of European culture with a special destiny.[84]

It has been said that what gives an historical myth its power is that it provides a sense of continuing identity; and that the enemy of such a myth 'is not truth but individualism, the dissolving of the sense of collective identities and temporal continuities'.[85] This is clearly true, but the strength of the English myth, the matter of England, was that, however paradoxically, it embraced the concept of individualism.

Of course there were other ways in which the peculiarities of the English, and in particular their attachment to individual freedom, were explained, illustrated and invoked. The English Reformation was held to have been both a crucial stage in the evolution of the nation and an illustration of its most striking characteristic. The importance to Protestantism of religious and ethical individualism has already been noted. But the advantage of the racial thesis was that it provided a material and hereditary basis for nationhood, which allowed for a sense of collective identity without a commitment to a holistic or high-falutin Idealist philosophy. Hereditarian beliefs provided an explanation of collective behaviour in a scientific, realist mode, acceptable to an individualist outlook. In the twentieth century, with the decline of racial theories and the destruction of the constitutional myth, an equally materialist assumption, as typical of its own day as hereditarian presumptions were of the Victorian era, has been made about the relationship between individualism and national achievement. The replacement thesis is, of course, an economic one: the individualism of English society is causally linked to the nation's economic success in the industrial revolution, and though this is (as always) a dangerously circular type of argument, *vice versa*. Most recently, purporting to demolish what he describes as a Whig version of English social and economic history, but in a sense reverting to the Stubbs-Freeman thesis about the inherently individualistic nature of English society, Macfarlane has argued that the origin of English individualism can, once more, be pushed back well into what we have for long mistakenly thought of as organic, traditional medieval society. He postulates an early demise for 'peasant' society in England and a consequent emergence of an individualistic society as early as the thirteenth century, and even speculates that English individualism can be traced back to the Anglo-Saxons. In a passage that would have pleased Freeman, he also talks of the English carrying their uniquely individualist, non-peasant culture overseas to Australia, New Zealand, Canada and America. 'When Jefferson wrote, "We hold these truths to be sacred and undeniable; that all men are created equal and independent, that from that equal creation they derive rights inherent and inalienable", he was putting into words a view of the individual and society which had its roots in thirteenth century England or earlier'.[86] In no sense has Macfarlane established a new orthodoxy, indeed it is too politically controversial a thesis in contemporary conditions to be likely to receive other than partisan support, but his account will evoke a strong patriotic response, as did the constitutional historians in the mid-Victorian era.

J.S. Mill, in his essay on Coleridge, had drawn attention to the conditions which, he said, the Germano-Coleridge school of philosophy had identified as necessary for social cohesion without docility, for voluntary but habitual submission to law and government. As an example of the ways in which feelings of loyalty could be attached to national traditions, he cited the feeling of loyalty towards laws and ancient liberties, and, indeed to 'the principles of individual freedom and political and social equality, as realised in institutions which as yet exist nowhere, or exist only in a rudimentary state'. Employing these principles, he said, the Germano-Coleridge school had begun to write history that really contributed to an understanding of society.[87] As a tribute to the Liberal Anglicans (as I take it to be), this was perceptive; and as a tribute to the perceived role of the constitution it was very enlightening. Mill, reared in the classical, rationalist individualism of the Utilitarians, recognised the contribution of nationalist sentiment in creating social cohesion — a sentiment that could, moreover, be directed towards ideas of liberty, whether embodied in ancient rights or anticipating their translation into future ideals.

The role of constitutional history did not stop at national cohesion, however; it gave history itself cohesion. As the young W.J. Ashley, the future economic historian, said of constitutional history in 1886, a few years after getting his first-class at Stubbs's Oxford, it forced one 'to try to discover the *meaning* of institutions, their growth and decay, their relation to one another. And thus one gets into the way of regarding the whole of human history as having a meaning, as not being purposeless, as moving to some goal'. An otherwise individualist history was thus saved from antiquarianism and purposelessness. Though Ashley had criticised one of the lesser lights of the Oxford history school, J.F. Bright, for being too Whiggish in the instruction he had provided in constitutional history, we can surely detect the classic and pervasive Whig teleology in his own account of the exemplar role of constitutional history.[88]

For Freeman, of course, the whole of human history, or at least the whole of European history, was the story of Aryan man, who was 'the same in all ages'. The history of the Aryan nations of Europe, their languages, their institutions, their dealings with one another, all form one long series of cause and effect, no part of which can be rightly understood if it be dealt with as something wholly cut off from, and alien to, any other part'.[89] The need for an organising principle, giving shape to history, was evident in the most individualist historians. Stubbs and Freeman, like most of their contemporaries, were committed, despite Carlyle, to causal chains; but, more than that, their causal chains had to have a final purpose or a unifying theme. This may have been a need for history to have a meaning *per se*. Or it may have been, in part, a product of the artistic needs of the historian. Every work of history is a human construction, not a simple reconstruction of the past, so every work of history is also a work of art — good or bad. It has been rightly said of Whig history that it was 'good art', having 'simplicity, economy and demonstrability'. As good art, it concealed 'improbabilities' and made everything look 'true, natural and inevitable'. Yet its mode of explanation was in terms of individual motivation — normally disruptive of clear patterns and generic trends; that it failed to be so in Whig history was due to the fact that in Whig narrative history 'right actions appear to contain their own motives'. We assume as much in ordinary life; only wrong-doing requires explanation. Given the progressive, optimistic themes of Whig constitutional history, therefore, description is explanation enough. So Whig history was enormously popular because it was a humane study — it believed in taking expressed motives seriously and in judging a man by the benevolent consequences of his actions.[90] However, it examined and condemned the motives of the villains and the unwise, the enemies of national liberty and progress. Thus it was dependent on assumptions about free will and moral responsibility, despite its concern with national and constitutional development.

Historians, then, had no worries about reconciling their individualism with their generic Whiggish nationalism. They had felt threatened by Positivism but retreated behind God's Providence and human free will, comforted by the tradition that the English nation was peculiarly advantaged in both respects.

NOTES

1.   H. Sidgwick, *The Methods of Ethics*, seventh edition, (London 1907), p.63. First published in 1874.

2.   I. Hacking, 'Nineteenth Century Cracks in the Concept of Determinism', *Journal of the History of Ideas*, xliv (1983), 455-475.

3.   H.T. Buckle, *History of Civilization in England* (London, 1902), i. 22-35.

4.   M. Richter, *The Politics of Conscience: T.H. Green and His Age* (London, 1964), p. 33. Richter's list of *ersatz* theologies also includes Idealism, heroic vitalism, social Darwinism, nationalism (liberal and integral), and socialism (utopian and scientific).

5.   Hacking, *Op.cit.*, pp. 455, 474.

6.   A. Comte, 'The Positive Philosophy and the Study of History', in *Theories of History*, ed. P. Gardiner (New York, 1959), pp. 80-81.

7.   L. Kolakowski, *Positivist Philosophy from Hume to the Vienna Circle* (Harmondsworth, 1972), pp. 10-18; see also M. Mandelbaum, *History, Man and Reason: A Study in Nineteenth Century Thought* (Baltimore, 1973), pp. 10-11.

8.   Buckle, *Op.cit.*, pp. 4-8, 20.

9.   Kolakowski, *Op.cit.*, pp. 86.

10.   Mandelbaum, *Op.cit.*, pp. 11-20.

11.   J.S. Mill, *Auguste Comte and Positivism* (Ann Arbor, 1961), pp. 46-47.

12.   W.M. Simon, *European Positivism in the Nineteenth Century: An Essay in Intellectual History* (Ithaca, 1963), pp. 219-220.

13.   F. Harrrison, 'The Connection of History', *The Meaning of History and other Historical Pieces* (London, 1906), pp. 79-80.

14.   Buckle, *Op.cit.*, pp. 9-20.

15.   J.S. Mill, 'Elucidations of a Science of History', selected from *A System of Logic* in Gardiner, *Op.cit.*, pp. 95-99.

16.   M. Oakeshott, *Experience and its Modes* [1933] (Cambridge, 1978) p. 144.

17.   Simpson, a Catholic writer, was co-editor of Acton's *Rambler*.

18.   Lord Acton, *Historical Essays and Studies*, ed. J.N. Figgis and R.V. Laurence (London, 1907), pp. 305-313, 319-322, 342.

19.   *Ibid.*, pp. 362.

20.   *Ibid.*, pp. 437.

21.   L. Creighton, *Life and Letters of Mandell Creighton* (London, 1904), i.371-372.

22.   J. Fitzjames Stephen, 'The Study of History' (1861), originally published anonymously in *Cornhill Magazine*, 3 (1861), 666-680, reprinted in *History and Theory*, 1 (1960), 186-201.

23.   Goldwin Smith, *Lectures on Modern History, Delivered in Oxford 1859-61 [1861]* (Freeport, N.Y., 1972), pp. 9-28.

24.   *Ibid.*, pp. 46-47.

25.   C. Kingsley, *The Limits of Exact Science as Applied to History. An Inaugural Lecture Delivered Before the University of Cambridge* (London, 1860), 17-18.

26.   J.B. Bury, *The Idea of Progress: an Inquiry into its Origin and Growth [1920]* (New York, 1955), pp. 234-237.

27.   For a sympathetic rehabilitation of Kingsley, warts and all, see O. Chadwick, 'Charles Kingsley at Cambridge', *Historical Journal*, 18 (1875), pp. 303-325.

28.   Kingsley, *Op.cit.*, pp. 27-42.

29.   J.S. Mill, *On Liberty* [1859] (Harmondsworth, 1974), p. 59.

30.   J.S. Mill, *Autobiography* [1873] (O.U.P. pbk. edn., London, 1971), pp.101-102.

31.   cf. J.S. Mill, *On Liberty*, pp. 129-134. For Mill's attitude see also: Mill, 'Elucidations of a Science of History', in Gardiner, *Op.cit.*, pp. 94-104.

32.   Kingsley, *Op.cit.*, pp. 43, 49-69.

33.   I. Berlin, 'Historical Inevitability', *Four Essays on Liberty* (pbk. edn., London, 1969), p. 42.

34.   H. Paul, *The Life of Froude* (London, 1905), pp. 54, 38-39, 143-144.

35.   Simon, *Op.cit.*, p. 270.

36.   F. Harrison, 'The Positivist Problem', *The Fortnightly Review*, 35 (N.S.) (1869), pp. 470-476. See also C. Kent, *Brains and Numbers: Elitism, Comtism and Democracy in Mid-Victorian England* (Toronto, 1978), pp. 56-57.

37.   Mandelbaum, *Op.cit.*, pp. ix-xi.

38.   J.A. Froude, *Short Studies on Great Subjects* (London, 1915), ii, 8-22.

39.   'Mr Froude on the Science of History', *Fortnightly Review*, 8 (1867), pp. 226-237.

40.   Mill, *Auguste Comte and Positivism*, pp. 14-15, 112.

41.   W. Stubbs, *Seventeen Lectures on the Study of Medieval and Modern History and Kindred Subjects*, 3rd. edn. (Oxford, 1900), pp. 85, 103-106.

42.   J.W. Burrow, *A Liberal Descent*, pp. 146-148.

43.   J.M. Robertson, *Buckle and his Critics: A Study in Sociology* (London, 1895), pp. 293-200.

44.   Stubbs, *Seventeen Lectures*, p. 27.

45.   J.R. Green, *Letters of John Richard Green*, ed. L. Stephen (London, 1901), p. 176.

46.   D. Wormell, *Sir John Seeley and the Uses of History*, pp. 7, 18, 19, 21-4, 30, 32.

47.   S. Rothblatt, *The Revolution of the Dons* (London, 1968), pp. 153, 166-172, 177.

48.   Wormell, *Op.cit.*, pp. 19-25, 29-31, 110, 122-130. In general, see Wormell for the complex influences that played upon Seeley, and the ambivalent nature of his own influence.

49.   J.W. Thompson and B.J. Holm, *A History of Historical Writing* (New York, 1942), ii, 334.

50.   E. Lecky, *A memoir of the Rt. Hon. William Edward Hartpole Lecky by His Wife* (London, 1909), pp. 25, 54-55; *A Victorian Historian. Private Letters of W.E.H. Lecky, 1859-1878*, ed. H. Montgomery Hyde (London, 1947), pp. 10, 40-42, 53, 58-59, 66, 68.

51.   Simon, *Op.cit..*, p. 220. Simon seems to have been misled by the unrepresentative sample of Lecky's letters in Hyde's edition, and even claims that Lecky's own works contain no material relevant to Positivism.

52.   E. Lecky, *Op.cit.*, p. 13.

53.   W.E.H. Lecky, *Historical and Political Essays*, second edn., (London 1910), pp. 83-87, 92-93, 227-250; E. Lecky, *Op.cit.*, p. 39.

54.   W.E.H Lecky, *Op.cit.*, p. 91; E. Lecky, *Op.cit.*, pp. 30, 54, 57-60; Hyde, *A Victorian Historian*, p. 41.

55.   *Dictionary of National Biography*, XXII, Supplement, pp. 1214-1217.

56.   H. Sidgwick, The Theory of Evolution in its Application to Practice, *Mind*, 1 (1876), 67.

57.   H. Sidgwick, The Historical Method, *Mind*, 11 (1886), 203-219.

58.   F.W. Maitland, *The Letters of Frederick William Maitland*, ed. C.H.S. Fifoot (Cambridge, 1965), pp. 1-2, 186; H.A.L. Fisher, *Frederick William Maitland, Downing Professor of the Law of England, A Biographical Sketch* (Cambridge,1910), pp. 7-9.

59.   C. Harvie, *The Lights of Liberalism: University Liberals and the Challenge of Democracy 1860-1886* (London, 1976), p. 214.

60.   W.E.H. Lecky, *The Map of Life; Conduct and Character* (London, 1899). pp. 1-6.

61.   E. Lecky, *Op.cit.*, p. 106.

62. W.E.H. Lecky, *The Political Value of History* (London, 1892), pp. 26, 32-33, 47-57.

63. J.R. Green, *Op.cit.*, pp. 16-19, 21, 153: J. Bryce, *Studies in Contemporary Biography* (London, 1903), pp. 132, 134.

64. D. Forbes, ' "Historismus" in England', *The Cambridge Journal*, 4 (1951), 400.

65. Forbes, *The Liberal Anglican Idea of History*, pp. 20-62, 118-119, 131, 150-152.

66. D. Goldstein, *Op.cit.*, pp. 896-919.

67. Bury, *The Idea of Progress*, pp. 290, 301-306, 351-352.

68. Much of the foregoing argument about the reaction against Positivism has already appeared in my article 'English Historians and the Opposition to Positivism', *History and Theory*, XXII (1983), 120-145. For a fuller elucidation of the misconceived criticism referred to above, especially the role of Collingwood, see 142-145.

69. Noted by Lukes, *Op.cit.*, pp. 52-58.

70. I. Berlin, 'Political Ideas in the Twentieth Century', *Four Essays on Liberty* (pbk. edn., London, 1969), pp. 2-3.

71. L. Tolstoy, *War and Peace* [1868-9] (trans. L.and A.Maude, one vol. edn., (London, 1941), pp. 493-494, 517.

72. W. Stubbs, *Select Charters and Other Illustrations of English Constitutional History from the Earliest Times to the Reign of Edward the First.* (6th edn.), p. xv-xvi.

73. W. Stubbs, 'Inaugural Lecture', *Seventeen Lectures on the Study of Mediaeval and Modern History and kindred subjects* (Oxford, 1900), pp. 16, 18.

74. W. Hutton, 'William Stubbs, Bishop of Oxford 1825-1901'. From *Letters of William Stubbs* (London, 1906), pp. 236-237.

75. W. Stubbs, *Select Charters*, pp. 1-3, 7-8, 10, 12-29, 35-51.

76. R.W.K. Hinton, 'History Yesterday: Five Points about Whig History', *History Today*, IX (1951), 720. Hutton did, however, go too far in denying that Stubbs and co. write in terms of teleological growth and organicism, and in claiming that they were not presentist, 720-721.

77. For a detailed account of Freeman's racial views see C.J.W. Parker, 'The Failure of Liberal Racialism: The Racial Ideas of E.A. Freeman', *Historical Journal*, 24 (1981), 825-846.

78. John Rylands Library, Freeman Letters: Freeman to Müller, 2 June 1870, 31 July 1870; Müller to Freeman, 1 January (1870), 7 January (1870), 'Saturday' (1870), 30 June (1870), 14 August (1870), 12 November (1870), 11 March (1870).

79. John Rylands Library, Freeman Letters: Müller to Freeman, 1 January (1870).

80. E.A. Freeman, 'Race and Language', *Contemporary Review*, XXIX (March, 1877), 713-732.

81. Freeman. 'Origins of the English Nation'. *Macmillans Magazines* XXI (1870), 419-431.

82. Freeman, 'Alter Orbis', *Contemporary Review* XLI (June 1882) 1041-1060; Freeman, *William the Conqueror* (London, 1888), p. 1; Freeman, *Four Oxford Lectures 1887* (London, 1888), pp. 8-9.

83. Freeman, *The Growth of the English Constitution from the Earliest Times*, 3rd edn., (London, 1876), pp. ix-x.

84. T. Arnold, *Introductory Lectures*, pp. 23-30; Freeman, 'On the study of history', *Fortnightly Review*, XXIX (1881), 335; W.R.W. Stephens, *The Life and Letters of Edward A. Freeman* (London, 1895), i.66, 108, 110.

85. J.W. Burrow, *Op.cit.*, pp. 297-298.

86. A. Macfarlane, *The Origins of English Individualism* (Oxford, 1978), pp. 206, 56-57, 202-203.

87. J.S. Mill, 'On Coleridge' [1840] *Mill on Bentham and Coleridge*, ed. F.R. Leavis (Cambridge, 1980), pp. 121-124, 129-133.

88. A. Ashley, *William James Ashley, A Life* (London, 1932) pp. 32-33, 18-19.

89. Freeman, 'The Unity of History', *Comparative Politics and the Unity of History* (London, 1873), pp. 303-304, 333.

90. Hinton, *Op.cit.*, pp. 721-722, 728.

CHAPTER 3

The New Liberals: Pluralists and Holists

The mere individual is a delusion of theory[1]

The dominant intellectual influence in England from the 1870s onwards was Idealism, and it had more impact upon historians than Positivism had had — as we might expect, given the Liberal Anglican and Carlylean influence. There were two ways in which English Idealism could affect the historians' view of their role. Firstly, from the publication of Bradley's essay on 'The Presuppositions of Critical History' (1874) onwards, there was a potential epistemological influence. This we will consider in the next chapter. Secondly, there was the social holism of T.H. Green, F.H. Bradley and Bernard Bosanquet, which could take both statist and pluralist forms, and was often expressed in organicist terms. We need to look at a few key Idealist texts, partly to see the source of acknowledged influences (as with the lectures of T.H. Green), and partly to look, not so much for 'influences', as for the similarities and differences between the spread of Idealism in the separate spheres of philosophy and history (as with Bosanquet's major work in political thought).

Green's *Lectures on the Principles of Political Obligation* (first delivered in 1879) can be seen as the first key text, both because of their importance in Green's corpus and because of their frequently acknowledged influence amongst undergraduates, though we should remember that the men who had influenced Green himself were the same men who had already influenced many historians — Coleridge, Carlyle, F.D. Maurice and Kingsley, for example. Like them, he saw God revealing Himself through history in the lives of great men and in the institutions of Church and State.[2] 'To ask why I am to submit to the power of the state', said Green, 'is to ask why I am to allow my life to be regulated by that complex of institutions without which I literally should not have a life to call my own, nor should be able to ask for a justification of what I am called on to do'. Only through the state did man become 'a moral agent', substituting 'the freedom of subjection to a self-imposed law' for 'slavery to appetite'. Rights began when duties began. The state was no mere 'aggregation of individuals under a sovereign . . . a state presupposes other forms of community, with the rights that arise out of them, and only exists as sustaining, securing and completing them'.[3] Despite the difference between Stubbs's view of the constitution as a natural, instinctive expression of the nation's capacity for freedom, and Green's view of the state as the rational expression of man's desire to free himself from his 'appetite', there are obvious similarities between the views of the two men as to the close relationship between state or constitution and the moral purpose or capacity of the community. Green, of course, wrote of all states, or at least all true states that did not enslave their citizens nor depart too far from their own ideal, all constitutional states with a rule of law and a sense of equity in effect, whilst Stubbs wrote of the English constitution *sui generis*. But one can quite see why in the society that engendered those attitudes, history, especially the history of the constitution, should be seen as a necessary ingredient in the Cambridge moral sciences tripos and as the natural companion of law at Oxford where the moral education of the ruling classes had long been an established objective.[4] Green had begun his crucial lecture, 'Will, not force, is the basis of the state', by condemning political theories that made 'no inquiry into the development of society and of man through society', and he went on to advocate a broad concern with all forms of communal life and the relationship between them and the state, as opposed to a purely hypothetical individualism.[5] This emphasis on the communal or corporate rights of pre-existing groups or institutions within the state was to develop as a major influence upon historical writing.

Our key text from Bradley's works is *Ethical Studies* (1876), especially his famous 'My Station and its Duties'. But before we look at this essay, we must turn to the first of the studies, 'The Vulgar Notion of Responsibility in Connexion with the Theories of Free-Will and Necessity', for as we have seen these 'vulgar' notions had been much exercised in recent years, and Bradley was challenging conventional wisdom. Bradley recognised that the doctrine of free will 'exists apparently for the purpose of saving moral accountability'. The vulgar notion was that the will was to be identified with the self, 'superior to my desires', and exercising over them 'an independent faculty of choice, wherein lies freedom and with it responsibility'. So the self (or will) was seen as an 'uncaused cause' of which we had intuitive knowledge. The 'I' was pure self, superior to all its contents. But, said Bradley, the conclusion of such an argument could only be: 'Freedom means *chance*; you are free, because there is no reason which will account for your particular acts, because no-one in the world, not even yourself, can possibly say what you will, or will not do next. You are "accountable", in short, because you are a wholly "unaccountable" creature'. He continued: 'The irrational connexion, which the Free-Will doctrine fled from in the shape of external necessity, it has succeeded only in reasserting in the shape of chance'. In order to save the doctrine of moral responsibility, the vulgar notion of free will had created an amoral, *irresponsible* idiot. Had he been gifted with foresight, he might have added that historians could create a patternless, ironic, chancy world, the world of post-Whiggism, for the irresponsible idiot to inhabit. With some insight, perhaps derived from his own reclusive nature, he did add that the plain man also clung to the notion of free will because he objected to the idea that his life was mapped out for him and that the growth of his character had been predicted, freely 'invaded by another, broken up into selfless elements, put together again, mastered and handled, just as a poor dead thing is mastered by man . . . nothing remains which is specially his. The sanctum of his individuality is outraged and profaned; and with that profanation ends the existence that once seemed impenetrably sure. To explain the origin of a man is utterly to annihilate him'. Though at times Bradley could write with all the obfuscation and turgidity that seems to be the natural medium of Idealist philosophers, he could also produce brilliantly insightful and vivid passages like this, shot through with martial, morbid, religious and perhaps sexual imagery — though it was odd that he should do so as devil's advocate, unless as a product of his age, despite himself, his own sympathies were involved. Significantly, he added, it is thought rude to profess to understand all but the closest of friends. But, despite these insights, the essential purpose of his essay on free will was to deny the relevance of the free will–determinism debate to the question of moral responsibility. He regarded English thought on this matter as hopelessly out-of-date and insular, and set out to advertise the holism of Idealist philosophy, as an acceptable alternative to individualism, which avoided the vulgar mistakes of recent disputants.[6]

This brings us to 'My Station and its Duties'. Here Bradley held that the purpose of man's life was self-realisation, but 'the realisation of ourselves as the will which is above ourselves', a will which expresses itself through 'the will of living finite beings'. The superior will was a 'moral organism' which achieved reality through 'the will of its self-conscious members'. The individual member could only find self-realisation in terms of its function 'as part of the whole — to be himself he must go beyond himself'. Thus Bradley claimed to resolve all the apparent contradictions in the relationship between the individual and society and all the vulgar arguments about free will and determinism. Roused again to rhetoric, he described the importance of finding oneself part of the whole: 'I am real in it . . . the fruition of my own personal activity, the accomplished ideal of my life which is happiness . . . self-realisation, duty, and happiness in one — yes, we have found ourselves, when we have found our station and its duties, our function as an organ in the social organism.' The individual was not an original reality that preceded the community. Collective organisms were real social facts, more than the sum of their parts, whereas 'the mere individual is a delusion of theory'. So one was totally dependent on one's 'station' in life, which, willy-nilly, brought duties: 'the organs are always at work for the whole, the whole is at work in the organs. And I am one of the organs.' The individual will existed so that the organ could function. Although there could be a society larger than the state, in practice the state was the largest framework within which society, with its laws and institutions, operated. Communities were objective, organic and moral; they could not be manufactured.

This moral world had an inside and an outside. The inside was the spiritual life of the world and it derived from 'the will of the organs', each of which was the expressed will of the whole, and which, emphasised Bradley, was felt to be (and was) the free personal will of the individual. A strong nation needed 'public spirit', which could only derive from individual wills; without this spirit or 'soul' a moral institution was dead. Public morality depended on personal morality. The outside or body of this moral world, which was thus dependent on private wills, consisted of 'systems and institutions from the family to the nation'.[7] Bradley, writing on ethics, was of course concerned with the soul, the ethical life that gave spirit to the form. One could say that the constitutional historian dealt with at least the statist aspect of the body.

It was the third of our key texts, Bosanquet's *The Philosophical Theory of the State* (1899) which dealt most explicitly and enthusiastically with the state as such, despite its author's well-known support for the Charity Organisation Society and the spirit of self-help for which it was famous, or notorious (though Bosanquet was not the most ardent of its laissez-faire supporters). If Bradley had had few readers and his influence had been indirect, through other philosophers, Bosanquet was not only more widely read (*The Philosophical Theory of the State* was into its fourth edition by 1923) but also more in evidence socially. He could not match Green's personal influence, but he did involve himself in a wide range of educational and social issues.

Like Bradley before him, Bosanquet denied the validity of the free will debate. He challenged the Positivists' search for 'law and cause . . . and scientific prediction', whilst accepting the interdependence of all phenomena, man included.

Undoubtedly man lives the life of his planet, his climate, and his locality, and is the utterance so to speak of the conditions under which his race and his nation have evolved. The only difficulty arises if, by some arbitrary line between man and his environment, the conditions which are the very material of his life come to be treated as alien influences upon it, with the result of representing him as being the slave of his surroundings rather than their concentrated idea and articulate expression . . . The world in which man lives *is* himself', not in the sense that he is determined by it but in the sense that it is mediated by his mind.[8]

Bosanquet's holism extended further, to his approach to history itself; this involved a rejection of the commonly used method of linear cause and effect and the employment of an organic, holistic notion of 'complete ground', which bore some resemblance to Carlyle's concepts.[9]

It followed from all this, as with Green and Bradley, that society was an organism. Traditional studies of law, said Bosanquet, had seen institutions as 'artificial, conventional, contractual', created by will and design; but laws and institutions were expressions of national life. In contrast, historians like Seeley and Freeman (in *Introduction to Political Science*, and *Comparative Politics*, respectively) were praised for their recognition that the study of politics involved the study of communities as well as governments. Bosanquet's state was 'not merely a political fabric'; it included 'the entire hierarchy of institutions by which life is determined, from the family to the trade, and from the trade to the Church and the University' — or, presumably, the Charity Organisation Society! All gave 'life and meaning to the political whole'. The state was 'the operative criticism of all institutions'. Like Green, he saw this role as embodying the real or rational will, obedience to which was the safeguard of our true liberty. But all institutions, as the meeting points of individual minds, were 'social' minds in operation, whether they be the family, property, the district, or the locality which could be organised institutionally for different purposes, such as health, public order, education, the relief of poverty, or worship. Thus Bosanquet sketched the network of bodies responsible for public duties in the late-Victorian state, together with the family and property; in other words, his own state represented the national will. Interestingly, he also thought vocation was crucial in determining one's duty to society; but class had ceased to be a 'political institution'. The greatest political institution, however, was undoubtedly the modern nation state, 'the widest organisation which has the common experience necessary to found a common life'. As such, it had absolute power over the individual, although it was itself influenced by its member institutions such as the family, the district and so on. It was 'an ethical idea', and thus 'a faith or a purpose — we might say a mission, were not the word too narrow and aggressive'. Bosanquet's teleology matched that of Whig history any day! Not that the nation state could not be tested, perhaps to destruction if the national Idea was found wanting. The American Civil War had been a test — and the American state had not been found wanting. France, he said in a footnote dated December 1898, was currently being tested; (he must have been referring to the disturbances arising from the Dreyfus 'affaire'). An addition to the note (dated 1919), in subsequent editions, finds that the French national Idea had maintained itself and had demonstrated that the common life of France had the necessary depth; it had earned the right to survive — presumably in battle.[10]

Conceived in the tradition of Victorian liberal constitutionalism by T.H. Green, but derived from Hegelian Idealism, this sort of statism was going to look dangerously authoritarian if ever a threat to traditional ideas of liberty was discerned. In vain would Idealists reiterate their ideas about positive liberty, and draw distinctions between states that approximated to their ideal and states that betrayed their own principles. The pluralist implications of Idealism did find an immediate echo in the work of historians, but the most statist form, though not without its adherents, was to be tested to breaking point by the First World War. It was not a reaction to the increasingly authoritarian nature of the wartime state that challenged Idealist statism, for wartime controls were largely accepted as a necessary sacrifice in the long-term cause of liberty; the reaction was against any set of ideas that could be identified with the enemy — with authoritarian Germany.

Bosanquet's pre-war remarks on the morality of state action brings us to a crucial issue: for him, there was a clear distinction between the morality of individual action and the morality of state action. Not that the state was amoral — on the contrary, it was a moral instrument: 'the state . . . exists to promote good life, and what it does cannot be morally indifferent; but its actions cannot be identified with the deeds of its agents, or morally judged as private volitions are judged'. The state was, moreover, 'the supreme community' and thus 'the guardian of a whole moral world' and not simply 'a factor within an organised moral world'. Thus: 'a public act which inflicts loss, such as war, confiscation, the repudiation of a debt, is wholly different from murder or theft. It is not the act of a private person. It is not a violation of law'. He accepted that states could be criticised as to the conception of good implied by their acts and as to the appropriateness to the conception of those acts. He accepted that 'the organs which act for the state' could be guilty of narrow selfishness or brutality; in which case they would be judged 'before the tribunal of humanity and of history'. So he did not go as far as Ranke in maintaining that the state could not sin in pursuit of its own true interests. States were open to moral criticism, but their agents' public acts were not.[11]

Here are echoes of Creighton's famous quarrel with Acton, in the 1880s, over the question of moral judgments by historians, particularly concerning men of power. Acton, attacking Creighton's handling of the Renaissance Popes, had insisted on judging men of power by 'the inflexible integrity of the moral code' which was 'the secret of the authority, the dignity, the utility of history'. He would have nothing to do with moral relativism. Creighton, on the other hand, very influenced by Hegelian philosophy, and in particular by Carlyle, Edward Caird (his Merton tutor, though later of Balliol), and especially T.H. Green (godfather to Creighton's eldest son), maintained the distinction between private and public morality. He argued that 'anyone engaged in great affairs occupied a representative position, which required special consideration', and his actions were determined by 'the effective force' behind him, of which he was merely the exponent. Creighton was prepared to assert that: 'society is an organism, and its laws are an expression of the conditions which it considers necessary for its own preservation'. He complained that Acton wanted history to prove 'the immutable righteousness of the ideas of modern Liberalism — tolerance and the supremacy of conscience', ideas specific to Victorian England. Creighton wanted to put himself in the place of men from other times and other places.[12] By the Diamond Jubilee year, in a Royal Institution lecture, he was urging that 'the great object of history' is to trace the continuity of national life, and to discover and estimate the ideas on which that life is founded. 'Individuals', he added, 'are only valuable as they express those ideas and embody that life.' For English history, in particular, there was the task of examining 'those qualities which have created the British Empire'.[13] It is easy to see how the Idealist reaction to Acton's unchanging and universal moral code went first to the moral relativism of regarding states as distinct moral worlds and statesmen as the mere creatures of these worlds, and then to an exaltation of the English moral world, even unto Empire, whilst denying the universality of the virtues of tolerance and individual conscience that Acton claimed to find everywhere appropriate. It has been claimed that Creighton lost interest in Idealism after early exposure to its influence,[14] but these characteristic attitudes can be dated after the supposed loss of enthusiasm.

Creighton was not alone in being influenced by the new Idealism, an influence which in his case had come mainly via T.H. Green and

Balliol contemporaries. Another key figure was Arnold Toynbee, the founder of economic history at Oxford. He was very much a product of Balliol, where he arrived in 1875, to find guidance from Jowett, Green, Nettleship and Ruskin, and where he was to become a tutor in political economy from 1878 until his early death, aged only thirty, in 1883. In his lectures to both undergraduate and 'popular' audiences, his main target was the classical economic theory of Ricardo which had masqueraded as natural law uncontrolled by man, and which, by the misrepresentation of popularisers, had been transmuted from so-called natural law into prescriptive rules. He was fiercely opposed to the individualism of the political economists who saw only 'pecuniary interest', or the 'cash nexus' (shades of Carlyle), binding society together, ignoring the binding role of 'families, associations and nations'. Philosophers, moralists and political leaders had all denounced the dissolvent creed of the economists, seeing in individualism a 'solvent of domestic, political and national union'. However, with truly Victorian optimism, the liberal Toynbee averred that the individualist phase had been a necessary evil, for it had destroyed the old servile relationships, created an independent labour force, and thus prepared the ground for a 'new and higher form of social union, which is based on the voluntary association of free men'. The importance of the historical method in all this was that it showed the laws of political economy to be, not natural laws, but relative to a particular society at a particular time.[15]

Toynbee was also keen that the old competitive laws of political economy should not be superseded by the new law of competition — the evolution of species by the survival of the fittest. The whole point of civilisation was to modify the violence of that struggle,[16] just as economic competition had to be controlled 'by positive laws and institutions'.[17] Toynbee may have had Henry George and Karl Marx as much in his sights as Ricardo. For this purpose he took as his mentor 'not Adam Smith, not Carlyle, great as he was, but Mazzini' and *The Duties of Man*: conflicting rights could be reconciled when we acknowledged our duties. This was the 'gospel' he intended to preach.[18] That he saw his role in this quasi-religious way is of interest, given the strong evangelical background of so many English Idealists.[19]

He had learnt much from Green; the close relationship between Green's *Lectures on the Principles of Political Obligation* and Toynbee's lectures is evident. There is the same desire to subject oneself willingly to social restraints or laws, to control the natural instincts, or modify natural laws through civil society, to abandon the slavery to appetite or to fiercely competitive struggle in favour of a higher, rational imperative.

Rights began when duties began. Society was more than an aggregation of self-interested individuals. Moreover, in Toynbee's lecture on the decay of the yeomanry, he reflected on the paradox that the parliamentary system, presided over and made possible by a large, prosperous and independent landed class, which had 'made us a free people', had created, and indeed been based upon the inequitable distribution of land.[20] This was all in the context of Henry George's ideas for land reforms and the radical response to those ideas, but historians had been concerned about the issue of the sociopolitical role of the landed classes for some years.[21] In effect, Toynbee was saying that freedom under the constitution was not enough if that freedom and that constitution protected the rights of a privileged group that claimed proprietary right to both constitution and land, the one by virtue of the other. He was exercising Green's right of dissent if a ruling group misused its power and led the state too far from its own ideal. He was also moving from a purely negative concept of freedom under the law of the constitution to a more positive notion dependent on freedom from economic exploitation. This involved shifting the historical emphasis from the political history of the constitution to the economic history of society. As ever, his apparent radicalism on this issue had deep-seated conservative aims: he was counselling restraint and the renunciation of all sectional interests, reform based on concepts of duty — all as an alternative not only to individualism but to socialism as well.

Toynbee's counterpart at Cambridge was William Cunningham, who by virtue of longevity and the greater prominence of economic history at Cambridge, was even more influential in the development of his subject. The key influences on the young Cunningham are immediately recognisable: Hegelian philosophy and, amongst contemporaries, Kingsley, Sidgwick, T.H. Green ('his master') and F.D. Maurice. By a process of reaction he was also influenced by the economist, Marshall. The influence of Maurice was crucial: like so many of his contemporaries in England, the serious-minded young Scot found in religion a safe refuge from the intellectual storms of the time. 'It is an awful thing', he wrote during his third year at Edinburgh (1868-1869), 'to feel that you are *making yourself, forming your character*, choosing your school, be it Hegelian or Comtist — and all in the dark . . . I feel drawn on into a whirl of theory and speculation on all sides, with nothing left sure to rest on but faith in God'. He went to Cambridge, so he said, in 1869 in order to make contact with Maurice, who seems to have played at Cambridge a role similar to that of A.P. Stanley at Oxford, though Cunningham does not seem to have had to overcome the sort of religious doubts that Stanley exorcised (albeit temporarily) from J.R. Green. Cunningham was impressed by Maurice's sermons, finding his 'emphasis on the will rather than the intellect . . . wholly congenial', but accepting Maurice's teaching (and Kingsley's in *Alton Locke*) that 'the reform of society could only come as the will of man should conform to the will of God'. He became a permanent disciple of Maurice; and he was ordained in 1873. Compatible with his theologically-conceived notions about the will of man working in conformity with the will of God was the Hegelian belief that the history of society had to be studied as a whole and that it was wrong to try to abstract economic development from the whole. He believed that 'economic history was concerned with growth rather than with mechanism, and that the appropriate conceptions were not to be drawn from the mechanical but from the biological sciences'. Like Toynbee, he did not believe in the universal applicability of the laws of political economy; experience of non-European society on an Indian tour strengthened this attitude, as did study of medieval economic history. Each society clearly had its own rules; abstract political economy was remote from the real life of communities. One of the conclusions that he drew from this was the need for empirical research, the need 'to get down to the facts'. It is important to note that he derived this methodologically individualist conclusion from his Idealist organicism — just as Carlyle, Ranke and the Liberal Anglicans had done. We should also note that his early liberalism gave way in the 1880s to the newly prevalent conservatism, preparing the ground for his subsequent devotion to Protection and the Empire.[22]

Considerable personal antipathy led to Cunningham attacking Marshall's ideas and proclaiming the historical inutility of economic theory, using relativist arguments. In particular, he argued:

> Modern economic science is formulated in terms which apply to the unfettered individual and the play of motives on him; the doctrines are all relative to this view of society. In so far as human conduct is determined by motives which evade the economic calculus and cannot be measured, in so far economic doctrine is irrelevant. In so far as transactions are undertaken by combinations where the play of motive is very different from that in the mind of an individual, modern economic doctrine is inapplicable.[23]

The point here is that two distinct reasons for the inutility of economic theory are introduced: one is the idea that individuals are motivated by other than measurable economic motives; this is not the classical rationalist individualism of Utilitarianism or Ricardian theory, but a belief in the privacy of an unknowable part of the self. The other reason is that 'combinations' have motives quite distinct from individual motives — an ontological holism that suggests something akin to a group mind, a concept we must come back to. Cunningham's major works, such as his pathfinding textbook, *The Growth of English Industry and Commerce* (1882), were monuments to his belief in the relativism of economic theory, the importance of looking at economic development as part of a national whole, and the integrity of the English national and imperial idea. It has been quite incorrectly suggested that Cunningham's 'historist' reaction to political economy was influenced by Comte and Positivism, just as it has always been assumed that mainstream history was Positivist. Naturally, so it has been argued, Cunningham had difficulty in integrating his supposed Positivism with the influence of the German historical school of economics as represented by Schmoller.[24] Of course there was no difficulty because there was no Positivism. Like Toynbee, Cunningham had adopted Idealist notions; his social holism, derived from Idealism, led him to methodological individualism. Until it is realised that an individualist, empirical method can derive from Idealism we are going to find this simplistic error again and again in relation to the supposed influence of Positivism as soon as an empirical method is encountered.

If we look at a later piece by Cunningham (1901), we find that his position was totally anti-Positivist and his method, far from scientific, was hermeneutic. Indeed, in a most interesting passage, we have another anticipation of Collingwood's notion of human thought as the essential medium of historical knowledge, but he substitutes economic activity (or perhaps one should say 'thought about economic activity') as the factor that is sufficiently constant in human affairs to permit understanding across the centuries. He started by attributing the relative neglect of economic history in England to the fact that economic change was often slow and unobserved by contemporaries and, thus, little recorded, and absent from traditional sources; also to its lack of appeal for those inculcated with the individualist approach. He explained the second point, closely linking it to the first, thus:

> economic changes were movements that were brought about unconsciously, and cannot be ascribed to the deliberate policy of any known individual, and they are therefore unassociated with any great name; the personal element was for the most part lacking, and the annalist who recorded the doings of men, was apt to treat economic affairs as the mere setting of a drama that derived its interest from the play of passion and the triumph of the strong man or the wise ruler.

An additional factor was that the classical economists regarded modern society as the age of economic science, made possible by the free market economy, and everything that predated this age of enlightenment was hopelessly unscientific, irrelevant and impenetrable. Cunningham could accept neither the traditional individualism of the historians nor the anti-historicist attitudes of the political economists. Though economic history had to be a separate branch of history, dealing with man's material needs, needs he shared with other species, 'the chief attraction of historical study is due to the elements that are distinctly human; it lies in the growth of politics, in the institutions for administering justice and for organising mutual defence, in personal aims and national aspirations and the effort to realise them'. There was a close relation between 'material progress' and institutional or religious development — but, more than this, the 'Body Politic, with the institutions by which free men govern themselves, is a more admirable creation of Reason than the Economic Organism in which men cater for each other's needs. The development of the State is the final object of research'. So economic history was not an end in itself; its purpose was to give a 'clearer view of the actual development of the State'. Not only did he elevate the Body Politic above the Economic Organism, but as he rejected economic determinism (possibly an oblique reference to Marxism), he did not even claim fundamental significance for his own branch of history — it was a part of the whole, but not a determining part. Thus he established an organic, as opposed to a mechanistic, model of state and society. The great value of economic history was that it forced the historian to look beneath the surface; from this he developed some very interesting points. It was easiest, he said, to get into the minds of men in past ages through economic history; one often felt bewildered, even shocked, by the religious ideas or the ethics of past ages; but the practical, and material, problems of economic life — food, shelter, clothing — 'involve the use of the same products and a similar struggle with nature . . . With a little effort we can place ourselves in thought on the industrial level of primitive man'. Once credit and money were established they acquired a universal characteristic and, therefore, have always had 'analogous effects'. The forms of economic organisation were what human societies had most in common because they dealt with material problems: 'in their ideals and aspirations men differ fundamentally; but the touch of practical necessity makes the whole world kin'. This held true despite recent technological advances. Thus: 'the economic interpretation of history not only helps to call attention to underlying tendencies, but brings the men of the distant past on to a plane where we can, if we try, enter most closely into their interests and find their action thoroughly comprehensible'. The necessary continuity of economic activity was the basis for the continuity of human history 'and the organic connexion of the past and present'.[25] Cunningham was propounding a hermeneutic method, partly empathetic; it was Idealist, both in its anti-individualism and organicism, and in the Collingwood sense of rethinking the thoughts of the past, but the thoughts that would be most accessible were thoughts about the ever present material conditions of life — which were not, however, determining (though we may possibly detect some, perhaps second-hand, Marxist influence here). As befitted the convert to Tory imperialism and protectionism, he believed that the state or Body Politic was the supreme arbiter of human life and that its ideals differed from place to place and from time to time, but that understanding through reasoning by analogy was possible because the material factor was constant.

The other key figure in the early development of economic history was W.J. Ashley. By the time he went up to Balliol in 1878 he had already read and been influenced by Carlyle and Ruskin, had been coached by Tout, and had felt the lasting imprint of an evangelical upbringing. At Balliol he came under the influence of Stubbs, A.L. Smith (of whom more later), and Jowett. As a private tutor in Oxford, after he graduated, he was influenced by Toynbee and the German school of historical economists. He always maintained a holistic view of society and a teleological view of history, and advocated a hermeneutic method. For him, we may recall, constitutional history was an aspect of the life of society; it made one think about 'the *meaning* of institutions, their growth and decay, their relation to one another. And thus one gets into the way of regarding the whole of human history as having a meaning, as not being purposeless, as moving to some goal'. He said he was a 'fatalist' about the inevitability of socialism, one of the reasons for this being the development of corporate capitalism in place of the old individual entrepreneur. The old individualism and its accompanying ideology, classical economic theory, were dead; but society also evolved, without discontinuities, and the state would have a full role to play, as a watchdog against monopoly capitalism, in the evolution of socialism. His statism was based on a holistic presumption that was in turn founded on a strong moral, evangelical sense that history had to have meaning and purpose, on a belief in progress and evolution (which interested him greatly) and on historicism. His first inaugural lecture, at Toronto in 1888, clearly shows the influence of Toynbee's lectures. Like Toynbee, he condemned traditional political economy and its pretension to deal with universal truths. He condemned its tendency to consign the working man to exploitation. He saw economic history taking up the cudgels against political economy in a more effective way than had the 'muddle-headed philanthropists and unscientific men of letters' like Ruskin and Carlyle. Yet, as with others, the relativism of this type of organicist holism led him to advocate an 'inductive' or 'empirical' historical method, whilst warning against even that becoming a new orthodoxy, and advocating a pragmatic or 'practical' approach. The ideological basis of Ashley's work is less clear and explicitly stated than that of Cunningham's, but the result was very similar, Ashley becoming a pillar of Tory protectionism and statism at Joseph Chamberlain's Birmingham University. He was particularly strong against Whiggism and individualism.[26]

At first sight, the other major economic historian before the First World War, George Unwin, appears to be an exception to the rule — a confirmed liberal who was hostile to statism. Though a brief period of study in Germany had brought him into contact with Schmoller's statism, he had reacted against it. As secretary to the Liberal politician, Leonard Courtney, he had become deeply antipathetic to imperialism and to protectionism. He regarded the history of states as the history of futility and crime. Unwin was particularly concerned with the role he felt Seeley had played in directing English historiography towards the state, both in his evident admiration for the monarchical and bureaucratic Prussian state and in his exaltation of foreign and imperial affairs, indeed, of war itself, as the ultimate test of a state and as a potentially creative force.

Unwin, however, was not solely an individualist opponent of statism; on the contrary, his main thrust was in the direction of pluralism, as an analysis of one of his early works shows. The theme of *The Gilds and Companies of London* (1908) was dear to his heart: a story of economic progress at the hands of merchants' companies rather than the state. But this was no mere individualism. He was writing, he said, 'an outline of the continuous organic development' of the gilds and companies, and he recommended going to Germany, in particular to Gierke (especially), Gothein and even Schmoller for 'the largest body of suggestive theory' that would help to explain organic development. Though he equated western progress (which he contrasted with eastern stagnation) with the pursuit of liberty, this liberty 'is no mere casting of fetters. It is the slow putting on of new habits and capacities, new sympathies, and new insight. It is a growth, the most gradual and most permanent of all growths, a psychological growth'. Positive liberty, organic growth, and the organic relationship of mind and matter — these were all Idealist presumptions. The modern state, he admitted, allowed to a greater extent than its predecessors for the 'positive liberty of equality of opportunity'. This was possible because of the many 'intermediate powers and agencies, offensive and defensive, which not only prevent the state from oppressing the individual, but actually enable individual initiative to gather power about itself and to bring pressure to bear on the state'. So Unwin rejected the sort of individualism that would place nothing between the individual and the utilitarian state, as strongly as he rejected statism itself. True progress and liberty lay with the organic growth of intermediary bodies. He itemised: the judicial and administrative bodies of the state itself, which could acquire their own *esprit de corps* and independent concept of duty; local government, which in England was safeguarded from undue centralism and was even the very basis of the parliamentary state; and voluntary associations, amongst which he numbered the two main political parties. These had grown slowly; they could not be created artificially or written into a constitution; true safeguards of liberty had to be integral and traditional — as the constitution makers of Russia had been discovering from the recent history of the first Duma. He was particularly impressed with the growth of these social and political organs in western Europe between the twelfth and seventeenth centuries, and in particular with the growth of the town, essential to the growth of the nation, and itself the product of the gild. In a highly teleological passage he described how, though they did not exist as we know them, in the middle ages, the state, the municipality and the individual 'were each in a condition of becoming. They were helping each other to grow into their present definite shapes by constant interaction on each other. Each needed the counteracting influence of the other as a condition of healthy growth'. In the early nineteenth century in England the individual had been overmighty, but had been curtailed by the factory and the school inspector, the officers of a newly-created form of self-government. Generally, however, English constitutional development had avoided unhealthy extremes, and had thus maintained a uniquely continuous and healthy life. The parallel with Stubbs's version of the conflicting dangers of feudal anarchy and royal despotism and the eventual happy outcome are close. Noticeable, too, is the similarity between the Idealists' view of the importance of organisations or organisms within the state and Unwin's view of the role of gilds and municipalities and other organic growths, despite the latter's refusal to top the whole thing off with an omnicompetent state. The gilds, to which he attributed so much in western civilisation, such as its freedoms and its progressive spirit, were the products of dynamic forces of 'germination' from below. They needed to be balanced by forces from above, whose purpose and nature were to formulate and control; but Unwin had a clear temperamental preference for the dynamic forces from below. However, though opposed to statism, he was prepared to go a very long way along the holistic path when he talked about a social mind and even about the state as the embodiment of a social will:

> The progress of society, like the progress of the individual, is a moral fact which cannot be derived from any cause outside of itself; but it rests on psychological conditions. The individual or the society must first acquire good habits of mind and will, and then learn to use these habits as an instrument for the achievement of higher ends, which gradually emerge when the individual mind or the social mind has become master of itself. The fundamental habits of the social will are embodied in the state. Society at first creates the state as an instrument of self-preservation and of inward order.

We see here not only the classic Idealist assumption of an organic society with its innate characteristics, but also the assumption that 'higher ends' will be served when the mind, social or individual, masters itself — in other words when right reason prevails over instinct and appetite. As we shall see, the other side to Unwin's pluralism, his anti-statism, was to receive a powerful boost amongst the intelligentsia at large during the First World War, forcing Idealists like Bosanquet onto the defensive.

Amongst the political historians, however, one man at least, Unwin's *bête noir*, Sir John Seeley, had been a convinced exponent of statism. As we have seen, he was not the committed Positivist that he has sometimes been painted; indeed, though difficult to classify, he felt the Idealist influence strongest; the result was definitely holistic. His background and the early influences upon him are instantly recognisable: a strongly evangelical family background was rejected in favour of Broad Church attitudes; he acknowledged the influence of F.D. Maurice and Thomas Arnold, and approved of A.P. Stanley. Though influenced by Positivism in the 1860s, he also appreciated the German-Coleridgian tradition and the Christian Socialist. As his biographer has noted, he shared the Liberal Anglicans' cyclical view of national history. Cambridge-based for most of his career, and educated in the 1850s, he was largely untouched by the Idealism of Green and his Oxford colleagues, but there was some direct German influence — albeit more Rankean than Hegelian. Pauli, a pupil of Ranke, had direct influence on Seeley's *The Life and Times of Stein* (1878); and Ranke himself is credited with influencing Seeley's organicist view of the state. Wormell suggested that, though Seeley had an imperfect understanding of Hegel, he did comprehend notions of positive liberty in terms of self-realisation within an organic society — an understanding derived from Maurice, from Fichte and from German historians.[29] Thus, though he rejected Carlyle (along with Macaulay) as a 'literary' historian, the German Idealist influence was considerable.

What did all this mean in terms of Seeley's attitudes to historical writing and teaching? He believed that God's purpose was revealed to and through nations and their leaders, not as individuals but as groups. He believed that history was a suitable education for such leadership groups; he believed in a 'clerisy'. He wanted 'to idealise the nation and familiarise it in its unity to the minds of its members'. Both church and nation were ideas of God; modern nationalism was the most developed expression of God's will and thus national churches were integral parts of this purpose. As Wormell has put it, this relationship between church and state 'was neither a legal contract nor a prudential political arrangement, but the necessary expression of the unity of national organic life'. For Seeley, they were the soul and the body of the corporate being. The religious basis of Seeley's statism, probably derived from Broad Church ideas, was not unlike Ranke's attitude to the state, and explains why Seeley could seriously suggest that his *The Life and Times of Stein* was the sequel to *Ecce Homo*, his study of the life and moral teachings of Christ. His best known historical works, his *Stein*, and *The Expansion of England* (1883) which was adopted by the Imperial Federation movement, well illustrate his attitudes. Stein's Prussia was a moral conception and an organic state; states like the Napoleonic Empire were immoral because non-organic or artificial, in that they attempted to be supra-national. Wars in pursuit of a national aim, as in the German War of Liberation (1813), the Austro-Prussia War (1866), and the Franco-Prussian War (1870-1871), had 'reconciled the modern World to war, for they have exhibited it as a civilising agent and a kind of teacher of morals'. He admired and publicly defended Bismarck's record. Like the Liberal Anglicans before him, he believed in a cyclical theory of national history. As a Broad Churchman, he wanted people to see that 'the true Bible of every nation is its national history' for it was through the modern nation state that man could relate to God. He saw the Empire as a Greater Britain — in other words as an organic state — though he found insuperable difficulties with India as a consequence of his hostility to artificial empires of conquest.[30]

The enormous influence of Seeley's view of the Empire, as expressed in *The Expansion of England*,[31] need not be laboured here. Less influential, however, was his attempt to redirect academic history away from constitutional history, with its emphasis on parliament and individual liberty, and towards a new emphasis on the corporate destiny of the nation and the state and a recognition of the primacy of foreign policy.[32] Stubbsian constitutional history remained central to academic history for some time; it was deeply rooted in, and helped to sustain, Victorian attitudes.

When new corporatist attitudes became more widely influential, they were less statist, more pluralist, in character, though not always as liberal or laissez faire as Unwin's. Many of their exponents were Cambridge men, but it would probably be misleading to talk of a Cambridge connection. Seeley himself had not been a natural leader nor an inspiration; he established no 'school'; even friends, like George Prothero, were critical; and the disputes over the reform of the History Tripos in the mid-1880s, in which Seeley found himself aligned with the eccentric Oscar Browning against the rest of the Cambridge historians, limited his influence. Creighton was the stronger influence — and he was a product of Oxford and its Idealism. J.N. Figgis, one of the new pluralists, greatly admired Creighton, 'incomparably the greatest man' of the three Cambridge historians he eulogised — the other two being Maitland and Acton, with Seeley noticeably absent.[33] Figgis, it seems, needed a leader, and Creighton fulfilled that role.[34] Apart from Prothero and Figgis, the key figures were Cunningham, who we have already considered, and Maitland.

Homage to Maitland seems to have become almost obligatory, so if conventional pieties are avoided here, this had best be attributed to a non-medievalist's ignorance. But Maitland does not seem to have been an original thinker. As in so many other instances, the chief influence seems to have been from Germany; in this case it was Gierke's ideas on corporate personality. Maitland's own grounding in law helped him towards the crucial idea of a corporate legal personality; and both evolutionary holism and British Idealism seem to have made their mark. In his introduction to his own translation of Gierke's *Political Theories of the Middle Ages* he committed himself to the idea of corporate personality. Using biological terminology, he talked of 'a genus of which State and Corporation are species', and claimed that Darwin's principles were applicable when studying the relationship between the State and other forms of social wholes — in other words there was an evolutionary relationship between them. This sort of evolutionary pluralism was quite popular around the turn of the century. Maitland believed that England had suffered from being 'a singularly unicellular state', and had been unable to cope with the needs of the Irish or the American colonists as a result. But the so-called 'Empire' of recent times was a true 'multicellular' state of self-governing colonies and communities, developing earlier tendencies to self-government discernible in the corporate bodies or commonwealths of the East India Company and 'the puritan commonwealth of Massachussets Bay'. Any serious study of English history had to take account of these communities. It was at this point that he took on board the lawyers' notion of state and man as legal personalities, quoting Pollock: 'the greatest of artificial persons, politically speaking, is the State'. Over and above that, however, was a sociology of social organs and organisms that could not be sharply distinguished from the biological organisms and organs of which they were, ultimately, composed. It is often recognised that there was a powerful alliance of Comtist or Spencerian thinking with evolutionism in this period; what is less often recognised is the link between Idealism and evolutionary ideas. Maitland, however, could see the connection, referring to the growing influence of Idealism in England and to its holism. Above and beyond even these scientific concepts, he said, was the view of the state, or even the community, as having 'not only a real will, but even "the" real will'. And he suggested that other organs, such as the Catholic Church, should be included in this ascription. Corporate groups, he said, had been increasing at a greater rate even than natural persons, and just as law had to take account of this, so had philosophy. He thought that contrary individualist tendencies, which, for example, dissolved a company into its component shareholders, would be disastrous, for the general result would be, not true individual freedom, but first a monolithic state, and then an erosion of that isolated singular power into an anarchy. Only through plural corporate wills could the state secure its own true position as the possessor of 'real will'. Maitland clearly wished to turn political and legal theory away from what he called 'mechanical construction', 'dynamics', and contractual obligation (which he associated with Roman Law and with Austin), towards concepts like 'organisation', 'corporateness' (which he associated with German influences and with Gierke, especially) and towards biological concepts.[35] Amongst the Idealist philosophers, Bosanquet was impressed with Maitland's 'delightful' introduction to Gierke, paying tribute, in the second edition of *The Philosophical Theory of the State* (1910), to the elucidation of a position 'according to which the real or general will is present in all human groups' in a way comparable to the philosophical theory of the state.[36]

The influence of Maitland and, through him, of Gierke, and of their anti-Austinian stance, was acknowledged by Figgis in his *Churches in the Modern State* (which consisted in the main, of four lectures, first delivered in 1911). Of the practical concerns, such as the government of the Empire, and the growth of state powers and collectivism, that were fuelling these speculations, it was the role of churches that excited the interest of Figgis, who (like Cunningham) was an Anglican priest. Like Maitland, he argued that no statist ideal was acceptable unless 'the reality of small societies' was recognised.[37] In 'A Free Church in a Free State' (a title that echoed Cavour's dictum), he showed himself to be deeply concerned about the future of the churches in an increasingly omnicompetent parliamentary state, taking on board Dicey's ideas on parliament and the rule of law. Soon, he said, neither churches nor secular societies, nor even the family, will appear to have rights under the state, and already for many people 'any notion of a rule of morality, as distinct from a rule of law, seems almost blasphemy'. He was also worried that in international law amoral and Machiavellian justifications of state action were now acceptable. This growing fear of international *raison d'état* is something we must return to later, particularly with regard to the impact of the World War. The main concern, however, was with the domestic consequences of Austinian theory. Austin's *The Province of Jurisprudence Determined* (1832) had sought to separate law from morality, regarding a law as simply a sovereign command. Generally thought to have had great influence in the mid-nineteenth century, Austin's ideas were bound to cause an Idealist reaction, just as surely as Positivism and Utilitarianism had excited Idealist wrath. Not only did Figgis fear Austinian theory but also state practice. In England and Scotland he saw a great threat to the churches from recent legislation. In France, the secularising policies of Combes, culminating in 1905, also caused concern. He attributed the omnicompetence of the French state, and its denial of the rights of religious bodies as 'corporate personalities', to the individualism of the French Revolution, the influence of Roman Law, and the baleful influence of French Positivists who wished to establish a Positivist state church maintained by persecution. In Germany, in contrast, Bismarck had lost the *kulturkampf*, an outcome which Figgis hailed as a triumph for the principle of the liberty of conscience — a somewhat odd interpretation of the Catholic Church's position. The question of church establishment was not crucial in Figgis's thinking: what mattered was that the church, established or not, had a 'living power of self-development' that made it more than the mere creation of the state bound by its trust deeds and 'thereby enslaved to the dead'. Figgis asked rhetorically:

Does the Church exist by some inward living force, with powers of self-development like a person; or is she a mere aggregate, a fortuitous concourse of ecclesiastical atoms, treated it may be as one for purposes of convenience, but with no real claim to a mind or will of her own, except so far as the civil power sees good to invest her for the nonce with a fiction of unity?

He tried to widen the argument to include non-religious bodies, and cited Gierke as an authority in this matter. All corporate bodies had 'real personalities' with 'a life greater than the mere sum of the individuals composing the body'; they were 'not merely a matter of contract', for their actions showed 'mind and will', and therefore 'personality'. They were regulated by the state but not its creatures. The family, the club, the trade union, the guild, the religious order, even the universities and their colleges, none of these had owed its life to the state. Waxing lyrical, he felt that we would be 'scandalised' if told that our school, college, parish, county, union, regiment, or family was merely 'a contractual union of a number of individuals, whose individuality was in no way changed by these social bonds, and were each of them purely independent and atomic — so that social life is like a heap of sand, rather than a living being'. He also acknowledged Maitland, alongside Gierke, as a source of these ideas.

The churches, he suggested, might find supporters against an overmighty state where they least expected them; presumably he meant from other, perhaps more radical, corporate bodies. 'Liberty in England', he concluded, 'is a far more popular cry than equality, and it is with liberty that we are concerned.' The individual needed corporate support against the state; 'efficiency', for some time a watchword of statist reformers, was not everything, nor was the material prosperity to which the security and 'vast wealth' of England had accustomed 'the more comfortable classes'.[38] The state, or 'The Great Leviathan' as he called it in another lecture, was a particular threat because: 'too often on the part of those who believe in human personality, the necessities of controversy against doctrines which virtually deny it has led to an insistence on the individual to the neglect of the social side'.[39] Thus nothing stood between the individual and the state. This seems to be a perceptive summary of the impact of the Positivist controversy of the late 1850s and 1860s upon the historians of the Liberal Anglican tradition. They had inherited a partially holistic view of the nation state which had retained a strongly individualist free-will element. In opposing Positivism they had over-emphasised that element of free-will whilst retaining the Idealist and Christian bases of their thought. The balance was now being shifted again. In a third lecture he took, interestingly enough, an English public school as an example of a social organism in which authority arises naturally rather than categorically or legislatively.[40] The public school must have been an inestimable influence running counter to the individualist trends in Victorian society.

Apart from acknowledging Creighton's influence, Figgis was also aware that at Oxford similar issues were being considered, mentioning in particular A.L. Smith of Balliol as somebody who was concerned with the legal theory behind corporate life.[41] The role of Balliol in propagating both Idealist philosophy and an accompanying sense of public duty has already been noted. A.L. Smith's role was in some ways a typically Oxford one, in that, though he published virtually nothing, as senior history tutor and later as Master he was credited with enormous influence. His pupils included Tait (later of Manchester); Lodge (later Professor at both Glasgow and Edinburgh); H.W.C. Davis; Powicke and Galbraith (three successive regius professors at Oxford); G.N. Clark (one of Cambridge's regius professors of modern history); and Namier, arguably the most influential, if controversial of them all.[42] Smith's position, despite his expressed admiration for Maitland, was unlike that of the Cambridge pluralists; he was an out-and-out statist, authoritarian and interventionist, and hostile to church influence. Notes for a lecture probably delivered at Girton in 1913 or in 1914,[43] show him complaining about the English tendency to regard the state as 'something profane' or as a mere policeman after the utilitarian model. He welcomed the recent rehabilitation of the modern state which was counteracting the powerful commercial and industrial influences in political life by evoking a sense of social duty and making 'citizenship not the enemy of Christianity, but its fulfilment'. Alongside the anti-social tendencies of industrial and commercial activities, landowners evaded the new taxes, nobody responded favourably to a recent call for military service, and Oxford and Cambridge were short of benefactors. His scale of virtue is most illuminating. Meanwhile the gulf between Christianity and the state widened under the influence of secular tendencies within the socialist and labour movements. He wanted 'to reconstitute the state' with more than mere coercive functions. The long English struggle against monarchical control, the extremes of laissez-faire economics, and the impact of the French Revolution, which had inaugurated a century of 'acute individualism' and 'manifest Manchesterdom', had overemphasised liberty and rights at the expense of the community and duties. Between Mammon and 'extreme socialism' a balance had to be struck. If this looks like a rather crusty reaction to Victorian industrial society as well as being in the tradition of Green and Toynbee, it was also imbued with the new spirit of national efficiency and even with the ideas of the eugenics movement. Not only would a new approach to education be needed, but it was necessary 'to face the facts of heredity, the transmission of lunacy, criminality and dipsomania'; and scientific research had to be organised on an unprecedented scale. There had to be 'new ways of handling crime and pauperism'. As for the once revered constitution, the much-loved object of the studies of Stubbs and Freeman, that fount of English liberties, and as for the new-found democracy, it would be necessary to reconsider the machinery of government, devise 'new kinds of legislation' and 'new formulas of representation'. The powers of the state had been 'ordained of God' and had an ethical and religious authority that the church had tried to usurp. The practical way of restoring this sense of authority was to encourage the altruism and the *esprit de corps* of the school, the college, or local pride. Academically, topics for research should be chosen in order to emphasise the communal as opposed to the individual point of view 'or rather the communal as the fuller realisation of the individual's place as a member of a great organism'. He claimed Maitland's later work as the model for such an approach. He was, however, enough a product of his time to claim that his statism was not inimical to the rights of smaller corporate bodies, and he was prepared to enrol the Webbs, alongside Maitland, as supporters of, in this instance, local government bodies; and he claimed that even the Trust, properly conceived, was not the enemy of the state, 'but its best ally, a schoolmaster to bring man to the higher sense of political and social duty'. He still looked to Germany for guidance; but he believed that through history a sense of community could be regenerated. This would be history written as the 'history of ideas' in the sense that ideas clothed themselves with institutions, such as laws, which were theories 'made to walk the earth'. So he adopted an explicitly Idealist approach to historical knowledge, that also anticipated Collingwood, and used it to justify holistic presumptions in the sense that laws and institutions represented the ideas of the community. He concluded: 'the State itself acquires fresh majesty when we come to think of it as a mighty personality, with a will of its own and a conscience of its own'. ('Yes, a conscience', he had emphasised in a handwritten addition to his typescript.) Man was not in opposition to such a state. The state was a personality, the body politic an organism, and sovereignty was the general will. In assessing the English attitude to holism, he regretted that insular security had robbed the English of 'the bracing effect of military duty' and had encouraged them to think of the minimal state as a necessary evil, but did credit them with 'clubbosity' and a sense of fair play, which tells us something about Smith's perception of the world. Public schools and Oxford colleges would, moreover, play a role in recapturing a sense of patriotism, social duty and religious devotion to a state 'ordained of God'.[44]

Unlike others who were sickened by the Great War, Smith was to stress its educative value and the lessons to be learnt from Germany.[45] A slight unease about the outcome of an excessive sense of national duty did surface,[46] but he was one of those least affected by the wartime hostility to things German, the impact of which we will be considering later.

Despite his references to the benign influence of Maitland, Smith was not, himself, a trained lawyer; but the influence of legal theory in the all-important area of constitutional history is well illustrated by the work of the Scot, W.S. McKechnie. McKechnie was a lecturer in Constitutional Law and History at Glasgow University when the discipline of history was first introduced to Glasgow (and the other Scottish Universities) in the 1890s as a form of English cultural imperialism. His post in law had preceded the rise of history at Glasgow and he was to find promotion later as a professor of conveyancing in the law faculty. However, working closely with Lodge, a product of Oxford, who was to move to Edinburgh (where he replaced Prothero), McKechnie helped to establish a school of history that was firmly based on the study of the English constitution. His own speciality was English medieval constitutional history.[47] Two years after Lodge's arrival at Glasgow, McKechnie published *The State and the Individual*; intended as an introduction to political science, it was more schematic than most of the publications we have considered. There were, he said, five ways of treating the parts of society, that is, the individuals of which it is composed. With the monadistic approach, the part was a monad or atom unrelated to the whole — indeed, strictly speaking, there was no wider whole. With the monistic approach, in contrast, only the whole was real; and it was indivisible. There was the mechanical approach, with the state as a machine. And there was the chemical or synthetic method, in which atoms could be seen to join to form molecules; this method, which he associated with Huxley, assumed that the part was changed within the whole. The favoured method was the organic, however: according to the organic theory of society 'the life of the whole pulses through all the parts, which in turn contribute something needful to the welfare of the whole'. Though these were analogies only, the organic analogy was particularly apt.[48]

In practical terms there were five options for governments. They could continue to pursue an opportunist path, unsystematically piecemeal in their 'commonsense' policies. They could become socialist and, if following the extreme form of the doctrine, try to regulate everything. They could go to the other extreme form and be individualist. Or they could listen to the compromisers, amongst whom he numbered Mill and, rather more surprisingly, Spencer, who thought that between state and individual 'a hard and fast boundary line exists somewhere, and the problem is to discover it'. But such a line would be 'artificial and arbitrary', and the preferred solution was, of course, an organic one, which by avoiding the false distinction between state and individual avoided the need for *a priori* rules and dividing lines. With an organic approach, changing circumstances could be accommodated and mechanistic formulae abandoned. As the sub-title of the book suggests, McKechnie was entering the lists against both socialism and individualism, currently perceived to be fighting it out for the nation's future, and making a plea for a third way, informed by an explicitly organic conception of the state, which would regenerate society after the disruptive effects of rampant individualism.[49]

With the possible exception of McKechnie, the man most aware of these contemporary debates was Ernest Barker, whose perceptive *Political Thought in England* was published in 1915 in the Home University Library series. Barker's long career cannot be categorised in the modern manner of subject disciplines; he moved easily between political thought and history, first at Oxford then at Cambridge. He remained influential up to the 1950s when he helped to edit *The European Inheritance* (1954). Though a wide-ranging textbook, *Political Thought in England* leaves the reader in no doubt as to the author's sympathies. The old individualism of Adam Smith and Bentham, he said, was dead; even as modified by Mill, it remained the creed of 'an empty liberty and an abstract individual'. Green's Idealism had put political thought on the right lines, restoring Plato's *Republic* to its deserved authority, taking the social system, rather than the individual, as its starting point. Here the state was 'the product and organ of man's moral will'. Barker's great strength was that he saw the wider intellectual context within which political ideas had developed. He saw that the very English subject of classical political economy, individualist to the core, had been counterbalanced by the German tradition, whether of List or of Marx, of holistic thinking. He saw that biology, which he also thought of as very English, also had its individualist and its interventionist tendencies — the internal and the external Social Darwinists, amongst which latter he mentioned eugenicists in particular. Jurisprudence, though dominated for so long by social contract theory, had now begun to support pluralist corporatism — he mentioned Maitland and Gierke in particular. In psychology he was interested in recent work in the fields of the group mind, mentioning Graham Wallas and MacDougall.[50]

It is difficult to estimate the influence of the new psychology. Bosanquet had seen *The Philosophical Theory of the State* as, in part, a response to new psychological theories, claiming to incorporate them into his Idealist version of the State — indeed, no doubt seeing this as one claim to originality.[51] But McDougall, who dedicated *The Group Mind* to L.T. Hobhouse, an ardent opponent of the Idealist theory of the State, and of Bosanquet in particular,[52] was not in sympathy with 'German' Idealists, preferring French and English authors, including Buckle.[53] It is true that *The Group Mind* was not published until 1920, when a strongly anti-German atmosphere existed after the War, but it was, in the main, written before 1914, and was seen by its author as the sequel to his *Introduction to Social Psychology* (1908); it remains the classic expression of the new social psychology. It clearly represents an alternative basis for a holistic social philosophy. Like the Idealists, McDougall saw himself as providing an alternative to the extremes of right wing individualism and left wing collectivism, 'of aristocracy and democracy, of self-realisation and of service to the community'. Criticising Spencer, he attacked the idea that 'the structure and properties of a society are determined by the properties of the units, the individual human beings, of which it is composed', for 'the aggregate which is a society has a certain individuality, it is a true whole . . . an organic whole'. This led him to the 'collective mental life' of society, and, in turn, to the 'collective mind', though he did not go so far as a 'collective consciousness'. A well-established, organised society became 'an organised system of forces which has a life of its own, tendencies of its own, a power of moulding all its component individuals', which perpetuated itself true to its own identity and subject to only slow and organic change. But McDougall's was not an Idealist conception; there was nothing metaphysical (nor mystical) about it, he insisted. A collective mind, like any other mind, could be defined as 'an organised system of mental or purposive forces' which, in the case of the collective mind, was constituted by trans-personal relationships.[54] There is something reminiscent of Dilthey's 'mind-created structure' here. Dilthey had argued that, beyond the enriching effect of individuals' relations to 'their environment, to other people and to things', each individual was also 'a point where systems intersect; systems which go through individuals, exist within them, but reach beyond their life and possess an independent existence and development of their own through the content, the value, the purpose, which is realised in them'. Now, Dilthey did not see psychology as a means of understanding human activity; it was through the study of the organisations (economic, religious, political, scientific and informal) which came into existence to serve these 'systems', that the historian could reach such an understanding. It is also true that Dilthey remained at bottom an individualist who, even more than McDougall, had a deep suspicion of the idea of 'a real super-individual unit, whether this unit is determined transcendentally or in terms of racial psychology'. For Dilthey, divine activity was no more manifest in collective action than in individual action.[55] However, though there are some striking differences between McDougall's and Dilthey's approaches to the role of the individual in society (noticeably in how we can know it, i.e., by Dilthey's hermeneutic method or McDougall's social psychology), there is a similarity in their views of the individual as part of a mind-created structure or 'organised system of mental or purposive forces', and in their denials of supernatural forces.

The truth is that thinking men in all disciplines — sociology, history, psychology and philosophy — were turning their minds, in these years, to this crucial issue of the individual and society, and were coming up with differing but, in nearly all cases, structural or organic solutions. McDougall did not even criticise all Idealist political philosophy: he praised T.H. Green and Ernest Barker, the latter having drawn attention to McDougall's own work; McDougall seemed to regard them as less statist and Germanic, more liberal and British, than other Idealists. He too acknowledged the 'lawyers' like Maitland.[56] McDougall was in no sense a great thinker; in fact, his passages on 'The Part of Leaders in National Life', which in effect tried to rehabilitate the Great Man approach to history, must rank as some of the most banal in any book claiming some sort of scientific character.[57] But he did influence Barker, who was still referring, with approval, to his views several years later.[58]

Barker also acknowledged the importance of Maine's work on ancient law (despite Maine's own individualism) and of anthropology, both of which demonstrated 'the continuity of human life' by tracing 'the roots of the present in the past' and discovering 'in tribal societies the germs of the moral person which we call the state'. But his main interest was in the Idealist philosophy of Green, Bradley and Bosanquet, and their crusade against Utilitarian and Spencerian individualism. He saw 1880 as the turning point in terms of political influence: educational and social reform, socialism, nationalism, imperialism and protectionism were all manifestations of the new spirit. Even anarchists, he claimed, had by 1914 ceased to campaign for the freedom of the individual but spoke for the freedom of organised groups *vis à vis* the state. Thus Barker recognised statism and anti-statism as the opposing tendencies of the new holism.[59]

Whilst recognising the Hegelian influence on Green, he identified two issues of dispute between Hegel and the English philosopher: one was the question of international morality and of war (an issue to which we must return when we look at the impact of the Great War); the other was the worth of absolute monarchy and of England's representative institutions. Green's task, he perceived, had been to adjust continental Idealism to the English representative constitutional tradition. Barker himself, when acknowledging Bosanquet's efforts to incorporate the new psychology into his philosophy of the state, chose to illustrate the idea of the group mind, with reference to parliament which, he said, was 'a connecting idea', not just six hundred men sitting in a room, but 'an idea backed by a purpose we may call an ethical idea'. Parliament had a 'common mind' — though such a mind only existed in each individual mind.[60]

This is not to argue that the acceptance of Idealist and holistic notions was universal amongst British historians; and the holistic tendency, in any case, was divided into statists and pluralists. But it is true to say that a large number of leading figures at both Oxford and Cambridge (and at other universities too) were influenced by Idealist philosophy. The strength of the Liberal Anglican tradition and the maintenance of the social attitudes and conditions that produced that tradition will all have contributed to that influence, as did the lawyer's concept of a legal personality. A similar point about Idealist influence has been made by Collini in relation to the development of sociology in this period.[61] (It is ironic that there seems to be a greater awareness of the history of sociology than of the history of history). He questions the standard assumption that social thought in Britain was stifled by a predominant positivism or empiricism in the period 1881-1920. He also challenges the notion that British theorists were somehow backward or out of step with the more cosmopolitan Europeans. Yet he, too, suggests that, though there were historians 'with promising intellectual connections', they were few and rather unproductive. It is true that Toynbee died young and that Maitland was cautious; and Collini claims that Barker was ambivalent in his attitude to Idealism. But it would be wrong to minimise the influence of Idealism upon historians.

However, there were already signs that the new holism, in its various forms, and historians' conscious acceptance of this theoretical basis for their work, might meet damaging resistance. First, there was a certain stubborn resistance to foreign influence, and a resistance to theory — which in an age still largely dominated by German ideas, could combine powerfully into a sort of patriotic empiricism. Secondly, the political and epistemological realism, which in some respects was part of the anti-liberal, anti-individualist tendency of the time, could work against other individualist tendencies. As suggested earlier, the epistemological and methodological individualism of Tout, Maitland and Pollard, though destructive of the old Whig interpretation with its strong ethical individualism and attachment to the idea of liberty, produced an historiography that had less sense of purpose or direction than mid-Victorian historiography had had. Those that did not share this political realism, however, developed traditional liberal scepticism about metaphysics and holism into a number of ethical reservations about Idealist philosophy. They were not all convinced that the individual could fulfil his potential for positive liberty within the state or even within society; in other words, they were not convinced that, in practice, the rights of the individual would not conflict with a powerful state or a repressive society if the distinction between the part and the whole was not maintained. Additionally, they were wary of denying all international moral authority, of seeing the state as the sole source of morality and, therefore, as unrestrained in pursuit of its legitimate goals. The First World War was to crystallise these doubts into a powerful hostility to German Idealism; thus a third source of opposition was brewing. Fourthly, there was, by the turn of the century, the growing assumption that history was a science. This assumption, with its apparently positivistic overtones, worked against the Idealist influence in ways which will be examined in the next chapter. The claim that history was a science, no less and no more, continued to be a source of endless confusion.

Finally, though Idealists predominated at Oxford, a sort of neo-Utilitarianism, based on an intuitive theory of morals, maintained the older tradition at Cambridge, in particular through Henry Sidgwick. We have already seen its influence upon Lecky. The standard work was Sidgwick's *The Methods of Ethics*. First published in 1874, it was in its seventh edition by 1907 and had been continually revised by Sidgwick, especially in what it had to say about free-will, clearly a subject of continuing controversy — though Sidgwick himself professed to find it relatively unimportant in matters of ethics. Sidgwick claimed to have started out as a disciple of Mill and Whewell, but had turned to Kant and Butler (the latter, it will be recalled, had also influenced Lecky), before formulating his ideas on institutional ethics. Though the tendency of this form of intuitionism was to reinforce traditional commonsense ideas of morality and social duty, in a way not dissimilar from the teaching of the Idealists, intuitionism was nearly as individualistic in its presumptions as the original utilitarianism had been. It also reinforced the attitude that not everything was subject to rational analysis, to progress, or to systematising. For Sidgwick at least, this was so, not because the 'mysterious citadel of Will' stood alone against the otherwise prevalent scientific belief 'that events are determinately related to the state of things immediately preceding them', but because the best way to achieve an understanding of ethics was by a comparative Aristotelian survey of prevailing commonsense ideas about morality, in order to arrive at a set of presumed fundamental moral intuitions, rather than by formulating from basic principles and rational inquiry.[62] Thus he too justified an empirical method.

However, of all these countervailing tendencies the most potent in the last two decades of the century, and the first decade of the new century, seems to have been the assumption that history, despite its concern with the individual event, was somehow a science, and it is to the confusions surrounding this notion that we now turn.

NOTES

1.   F.H. Bradley, 'My Station and its Duties', *Ethical Studies*, second edition (Oxford, 1927), p.174.

2.   M. Richter, *The Politics of Conscience: T.H. Green and His Age* (London, 1964), pp. 47-48.

3.   T.H. Green, *Lectures on the Principles of Political Obligation* (Oxford, 1941), pp. 122, 124, 139.

4.   C.J.W. Parker, 'Academic History: Paradigms and Dialectic', *Literature and History*, 5 (1979), pp. 168-171.

5.   T.H. Green, *Op.cit.*, p. 121.

6.   F.H. Bradley, *Ethical Studies*, second edition (Oxford, 1927), pp. viii-ix, 9-15, 17, 20, 40-41.

7.   *Ibid.*, pp. 162-165, 174, 176-178.

8.   B. Bosanquet, *The Philosophical Theory of the State*, fourth edition reprinted (London, 1965), pp. viii-ix, 17, 29.

9.   For an elaboration of this theme see C.J.W. Parker, 'Bernard Bosanquet, Historical Knowledge, and the History of Ideas', *Philosophy of the Social Services*, 18 (1988).

10.   Bosanquet, *Op.cit.*, pp. 33-39, 139-141, 144, 277, 286, 298-299.

11.   *Ibid.*, pp. 299-300, 302-305.

12.   L. Creighton, *Life and Letters of Mandell Creighton* (London, 1904), pp. i. 26-27, 29, 49, 128, 185-186, 368-375, 376.

13.   M. Creighton, 'The Picturesque in History', *Historical Lectures and Addresses* (London, 1903), p. 284.

14.   O. Chadwick, *Creighton on Luther: An Inaugural Lecture* (Cambridge, 1959), pp. 23-24.

15.   A. Toynbee, 'Ricardo and the Old Political Economy', *Toynbee's Industrial Revolution* (Newton Abbott, 1969), pp. 22-25; see also p. 199.

16.   Toynbee, 'The Industrial Revolution', *Ibid.*, p. 86.

17.   Toynbee, 'Ricardo and the Old Political Economy', *Ibid.*, p. 20.

18.   Toynbee, 'Popular Addresses', *Ibid.*, p. 200.

19.   Richter, *Op. cit.*, pp. 36, 47-48.

20.   Toynbee, *Op cit.*, p. 59.

21. See, for example, Goldwin Smith's inaugural lecture: Goldwin Smith, *Lectures on Modern History, delivered in Oxford, 1859-1861* (Oxford, 1861), pp. 11-19.

22. A. Cunningham, *William Cunningham, Teacher and Priest* (London, 1950), pp. ix-x, 14, 17, 19, 20-22, 37, 39, 50, 52-53.

23. W. Cunningham, 'The Relativity of Economic Doctrine', *The Economic Journal*, ii (1892), 12; see also; W. Cunningham, 'The Perversion of Economic History', *The Economic Journal*, ii (1892), pp. 491-506; and A. Marshall, 'A Reply', *The Economic Journal*, ii (1892), pp. 507-519.

24. A.W. Coates, 'The Historist Reaction in English Political Economy 1870-1890', *Economica*, 21 (1954), 145.

25. W. Cunningham, 'The Teaching of Economic History', in F.W. Maitland *et al.*, *Essays on the Teaching of History* (Cambrisge, 1901), pp. 40-46.

26. Ashley, *William James Ashley, A Life* (London, 1932), pp. 9, 15-16, 18-19, 22-23, 32-40, 49-52. See also: Muirhead's chapter in A. Ashley, *Op. cit.*, on Ashley at Birmingham; and W.J. Ashley, 'On the Study of Economic History' (Harvard, 1893) in N.B. Harte, *The Study of Economic History* (London, 1971), pp. 3-17, and *Harte, Op. cit.*, pp.xxii-xxiii.

27. C. Parker, 'History as Present Politics', *Contexts and Connections: Winchester Research Papers in the Humanities* (Winchester, 1980), pp. 19-23. See also: G. Unwin, *Studies in Economic History: The Collected Papers of George Unwin* (London, 1927); and N.B. Harte, *The Study of Economic History*, pp. xxvi-xxvii, pp. 39-54.

28. G. Unwin, *The Gilds and Companies of London* (London, 1908), pp.v-vi, 4-13.

29. D. Wormell, *Sir John Seeley and the Uses of History*, pp. 5, 14, 18-19, 28, 37, 78, 80-81, 83-84, 96, 110, 125-126, 145-146.

30. *Ibid.*, pp. 28, 35-39,, 77, 84-85, 129-131, 141-142, 155-161, 178.

31. *Ibid.*, pp. 154-155.

32. *Ibid.*, pp. 93, 131.

33. J.N. Figgis, *Churches in the Modern State*, second edition, (London, 1914), p. 229.

34. G.R. Elton, 'Introduction to the Torchbook Edition', J.N. Figgis, *The Divine Right of Kings* (Torchbook edition, New York, 1965), pp. vii-xxxviii.

35. F.W. Maitland, 'Translator's Introduction', O. Gierke, *Political Theories of the Middle Age* (Cambridge, 1900), pp. ix-xii, xxxvii, xli-xliii.

36. Bosanquet, *The Philosophical Theory of the State*, p. xxix.

37. Figgis, *Churches in the Modern State*, p. ix-x.

38. *Ibid.*, pp. 12-31, 39-42, 47-52.

39. *Ibid.*, p. 71.

40. *Ibid,,* pp. 158-159.

41. *Ibid.*, pp. 224-225.

42. H.W.C. Davis, *A History of Balliol College* (Oxford, 1963), pp. 242-243.

43. Balliol College Library, A.L. Smith Papers, 'History and Citizenship — A Forecast'. The Smith Papers are uncatalogued; these lecture notes are in a small box labelled 'Korpora', and an appended note suggests the place and date; reference to the the 1906 trade union act as 'recent' (p. 613), and the absence of references to the World War also help to date this lecture.

44. *Ibid.*, pp. 604-618. On fair play, Smith had written: 'An English sailor classes men as white men, Dagos, niggers; Dagos use a knife, niggers bite in fighting'.

45. A.L. Smith, *The War and our Social Duty* (Christian Social Union Pamphlet, No. 4, Oxford, November 1915), pp. 2-3.

46. Smith Papers, 'The War, Education, and Co-operation', (Address to the Education Meeting of the Co-operative Union Ltd., Manchester, 1916), Box 211 A-i.

47. C.J.W. Parker, 'The Development of History Courses in British Universities' (Exeter University, MA thesis, 1975), pp. 139-140, 144-145.

48. W.S. McKechnie, *The State and the Individual: An Introduction to Political Science, with special reference to Socialistic and Individualistic Theories* (Glasgow, 1896), pp. 8-18.

49. *Ibid.*, pp. 164-260, 264-269, 443.

50. E. Barker, *Political Thought in England* (London, 1915), pp. 9-11, 14-16, 175-182.

51.   Bosanquet, *The Philosophical Theory of the State*, pp. viii-ix.

52.   For Hobhouse's opposition see S. Collini, 'Hobhouse, Bosanquet and the State: Philosophical Idealism and Political Argument in England 1880-1918', *Past and Present*, 72 (1976), 89-90.

53.   W. McDougall, *The Group Mind* (Cambridge, 1920), pp. ix-x.

54.   *Ibid.*, pp. xi, 7, 9-10.

55.   W. Dilthey, *Meaning in History: W. Dilthey's Thoughts on History and Society* ed. H.P. Rickman (London, 1961), pp. 69-70, 77-78, 154. Dilthey's works, which are reprinted in this edited collection, first appeared in print, in German, in 1905 and 1910, or (dating from the same period) were left in manuscript form.

56.   McDougall, *Op.cit.*, pp. 17-19.

57.   *Ibid.*, pp. 135-141.

58.   E. Barker, *National Character and the Factors in its Formation*, fourth edition (London, 1948). The first edition was in 1927, which in turn had been based on his Stevenson Foundation Lectures at Glasgow, 1925-1926.

59.   Barker, *Political Thought in England*, pp. 17, 19-23, 181.

60.   *Ibid.*, pp. 29-30, 45-46, 58, 73-74.

61.   S. Collini, 'Sociology and Idealism in Britain, 1810-1920', *Archives Européenes de Sociologie (European Journal of Sociology)*, XIX (1978), pp. 3-50.

62.   H. Sidgwick, *The Methods of Ethics*, seventh edition, (London, 1907), pp. vii, xii-xx, 62-63, 75-76.

CHAPTER 4

History as a Science — More or Less

Why did historians like J.B. Bury proclaim that history was a science, provoking the excitable, if ill-directed wrath of men like Trevelyan? As we have seen it was certainly not because they were Positivists; this explanation has been based on Collingwood's misunderstanding of Bury, which was as great as Trevelyan's, and has been the cause of much subsequent ill-founded strictures against the English school of history. But perhaps we should not be too critical of Bury's harshest critics, because (even if Bury knew what he was about to a far greater extent than his detractors allow) there was much confusion at the time in the minds of many of those who proclaimed the scientific character of history. Worse, this confusion adversely affected the way history developed, and in particular helped to determine the negative way historians responded to the intellectual influences that played upon them.

Perhaps a growing isolation was evident even by the 1870s, when Bradley's essay on 'The Presuppositions of Critical History' appeared (1874). Bradley provided a typically Idealist critique of historical knowledge as a distinct form of knowledge, an approach that should have been calculated to appeal to the developing historical profession, particularly as many of its members were to be influenced by the social holism of Bradley and his fellows. We now recognise that Bradley's ideas were taken up by Oakeshott and that there is a definite line of development from Bradley to Collingwood;[1] but at the time and sometimes subsequently Bradley's essay was seen as an immature work of little significance. Not only was Bradley's work unjustly ignored at the time, but the common assumption that British Idealist philosophers were not, in general, interested in historical knowledge is quite wrong. Part of this misconception may be due to the lack of interest amongst historians in the epistemological issues raised by the philosophers — a state of affairs surely unthinkable in the first three quarters of the century. Bosanquet, usually credited with dismissing history as a hybrid form of experience, was actually very interested in the history of ideas and their relationship to society.[2] Furthermore, a *Festschrift* for T.H. Green, published in 1883, *Essays in Philosophical Criticism*, contained two essays of an Idealist persuasion on the nature of historical knowledge, one of which, by D.G. Ritchie (Fellow and Tutor of Jesus College; Lecturer of Balliol), is quite substantial.[3] Of Bradley's essay itself, Collingwood was to say that it was a Copernican revolution in the philosophy of history,[4] and so it is to this that we now turn.

All history, said Bradley, is critical history, because all history has to be selective, and 'if we exclude or alter or rationalize to the very smallest extent, then we have criticism at once'. This might have offended any naive realists amongst historians, those who believed they were recreating the past; but Bradley could reassure them that history (as the objective past) did exist, and would exist without the historian, so that the historian had no licence for complete subjectivity and was not the sole creator of history. However, with 'the growth of experience' each generation would rewrite history, with or without new historical evidence. This apparent relativism was linked to a classically Idealist presumption that history was mind or spirit realising itself — 'the rise of the spirit to a fuller life'. Thus Bradley anticipated Croce in asserting that all history was contemporary history, but avoided total relativism by means of his Hegelian progressivism. But he insisted that only the critical mind could cope with this: the uncritical mind would resort to 'the barren scepticism which sees in history but a weary labyrinth of truth and tangled falsehood, whose clue is buried and lost in the centuries that lie behind', because such a mind could only recall and not construct.[5] So, at the height of Whig history's success, Bradley anticipated and criticised the pained scepticism of historians like H.A.L. Fisher when events seemed to have demolished the old constructions.

For Bradley, each historical event or fact, even the most apparently simple, was actually so complicated and part of such an interdependent complex of phenomena, that it defied *analysis*, but could be *understood* by a whole complex of historical judgments. 'The historical fact then (for us) is a conclusion . . .' though not a random invention. Judgment was constantly necessary; every apparently isolated recorded event rested upon a theory, and every narrative of events upon a wider theory. Historical truth was arrived at by inference, and that inference was dependent upon the character of our general consciousness, and so the past varies with the present and can never do otherwise. Reversing the position of the naive realist and, indeed, of Whig presentism and finalism, Bradley asserted that the past rested on the present and that, therefore, the past presupposed the present, which was the past's 'necessary preconception'. Bradley thought it important to recognize those historians that were self-aware and knew that what they wrote derived 'its individual character from the standpoint of the author' and his own conception of 'truth';[7]

the unaware we would characterise as naive realists. That this aspect of Bradley's historical thought went largely unheeded may be due to a number of factors, such as the developing historical profession's disregard for philosophy or a realist resentment at the degree of relativism involved in Bradley's approach. But the most important reason was the developing obsession with the notion that history was, or could be a science. Embedded in this notion were two necessarily linked concepts, both inimical to Bradley's idea of critical history. One was the presumption that history, like science, had to deal with causation, the belief, as Sidgwick put it, 'that events are determinately related to the state of things immediately preceding them'.[8] The other was the assumption of objectivity, which appeals to the naive realism always inherent in non-philosophical minds, and was bound to appeal to the new sense of professionalism evident from the 1870s amongst those historians who sought to increase their own prestige and that of their subject by researches in the archives.

As a result of this gulf between Bradley and the historians the individualist methodological implications and non-scientific character of his version of historical knowledge were largely lost upon the latter, who might otherwise have agreed with these aspects of his epistemology and resisted the call to be 'scientific'. Bradley identified history as, by definition, individualist in method. True he would have none of the argument that history and science were distinct because the former dealt with human volition as an 'uncaused' factor: 'If the freedom of the will is to mean that the actions of men are subject to no law, and in this sense irrational, then the possibility of history, I think, must be allowed to disappear, and the past to become a matter of almost entire uncertainty', because history, like science, was based on an assumption of causal connection. Bradley could go this far with the scientific parallel. But it was still the human element in history which distinguished it from science because human nature was common to both history and the historian. Because 'nothing human is alien to ourselves', every particular realization of human nature is of interest — and this is what the historian has chosen as his special concern. Whereas, for the scientist, the particular is a mere example, 'the object of historical record is the world of human individuality, and the course of its development in time'. The historian cares nothing for the universal as such; at most he sees it 'embodied in a single person or the spirit of a nation'. Thus, for Bradley, because no man was an island, his interest in the doings of his fellows was infinite, and the historian had chosen to reveal these intimacies.[9]

However, because he was committed to Idealist progressivism, Bradley could not accept that the mind of the historian could acquire complete identification with the minds of the past. Though there was human nature in common, 'the consciousness of an earlier stage of humanity is never the consciousness of a later development'. Additionally, the historian's interest is naturally directed to the most apparently distinctive elements of a passing stage of human history — 'the striking, the temporal, in a word the individual'. The result is necessarily imperfect knowledge: 'the event perishes as it arrives . . . It cannot repeat itself and we are powerless to repeat it' and 'we cannot prepare for it'. Moreover, it is too complex for the sort of observation possible, for we cannot fix it by isolating it. He suggested that he might be accused of criticising existing historical practice and knowledge without considering the possibility of a more scientific type of history as a future possibility. He accepted that general laws dealing with 'stationary' phenomena or 'permanent relations' were feasible; though he did not use the terms, these could be described as sociological or structural laws or even social statics. But laws of social dynamics or social evolution were not feasible, for each stage of development was a 'qualitative new-birth of an organic, and more than an organic, unity . . . ' Of course, just as we could not enter into the immature minds of the past, because history was mind realising itself, so we could not predict or comprehend future developments which would, in turn, be as a maturity to our childhood. And as we cannot know the end of human development, we cannot know the means.[10] So historical knowledge was imperfect, could never be scientific, could never produce laws, and could never predict; yet had its own individualist purpose and value. Much of this anticipated Oakeshott and Collingwood, although Bradley's emphasis on the imperfection of historical knowledge seems to be at odds with Collingwood. But even here, there were similarities. Whereas Collingwood was to argue that it was possible to rethink the thoughts of the past because thought was common to all men, Bradley argued that the history of science at least, where the conditions of observation could be minutely and objectively created and recreated, and the observer's consciousness was only employed in a specific way, was one area where a complete form of historical knowledge was possible by rethinking the thoughts of past scientists.[11]

The basis for an historist justification of historical knowledge after the manner of Dilthey, or an Idealist philosophy of history similar to Oakeshott's or Collingwood's, was already there. But British historians did not follow up Bradley's ideas; there was no British Dilthey — only a Pollard, a Tout and a J.H. Round. Acton was impressed with

Dilthey and recommended him to Prothero,[12] but Acton himself was notoriously unproductive, and no equivalent theorist emerged in Britain. Ritchie's essay, though quite substantial and raising some interesting points, some of which seem to echo the Liberal Anglicans (his assumption of the rise and fall of peoples, for example), and others of which seem to anticipate Collingwood (the claim that we only know what people are by what they do), was still basically Hegelian. He believed in the *Zeitgeist*, denied the relevance of individual happiness or destiny to the study of history, and believed that history was an *intelligible* whole because it was an *intelligent* process, claimed (like Hegel) that there were 'unhistorical races and unhistorical periods', and that some peoples were 'elect' to be the bearers of civilization. He identified six types of philosophy of history.

First there was the belief that history was ruled by chance; this was not true scepticism (for that would be agnostic), and, though a denial of any plan to history, was 'as much an interpretation of the facts by an intellectual conception as the assertion of a plan'. It was a pity that the coming anti-Whig generation of Round and co. had not taken this point on board. Secondly, there was belief in the rule of Divine Providence, a teleological conception prone to over-generalization and irrational or partial treatment. Then there was the assumption of a pattern of decadence, a decline from early innocence. This denied the rationality of history and lauded anachronism; he reserved especial scorn for this 'philosophizing of romanticism which is really a protest against reason'. Fourthly, there was belief in linear progress — the case for which was unproven. Fifthly, there was the idea of cycles, an idea that was unhistorical and unscientific. Lastly, and his personal preference, there was the idea of progress by antithesis, with the sequence of thesis, antithesis, and synthesis as 'the struggle for freedom (in no merely negative sense), the liberation of man from the domination of nature and fate. Or . . . humanity making itself, or coming to a consciousness of itself . . . '[13] This restatement of Hegelian dialectic, in purest form, did not recommend itself to practising historians and did not really add to the sum of ideas about the nature of history or of historical knowledge. The profession went its own, rather confused, way.

Professionalization is a favoured theme at the moment and many historians have studied the phenomenon in relation to the development of their own subject.[14] Heyck, in particular, has linked professionalisation with the idea of being scientific. Jann refers to the amateur emphasis on empathy and imagination, which contrasts with the professional's desire to analyse and explain.[15] Goldstein deals with the acquisition of professional institutions and apparatus — a journal (*English Historical Review*), societies (the Royal Historical Society and the Historical Association), and research institutions and forums (the Institute of Historical Research and the British Academy). The necessary base for this activity was the establishment of history courses in the universities and the gradual organisation (from often very casual beginnings) of the teaching that was needed as a result.[16] This process was rounded off by the establishment of the PhD in most universities in and after 1917, which placed at least partial control of entry into the profession in the hands of its members, a significant feature of professional activity. The British system has never been as rigid as that of, say Germany, but training in professional activity through research is clearly important. The professional monograph is sometimes blamed (if that is the word) upon the PhD thesis; though to an extent the monograph preceded the thesis. As we have seen, the production of specialised studies of limited topics, some would say of limited appeal, highly professional in terms of their technical competence in handling sources, but part of no general thesis or interpretation of history, was becoming a major activity of the profession by the end of the century, as part of the anti-Whig reaction. This was generally noted at the time. In 1894, H.A.L. Fisher believed that the current need was for 'minute and critical study, at any rate at the Universities. The long majestic histories are already written, the "great outlines" are already known.' What he called 'special histories' for a specialised audience, were needed to deal with economic, diplomatic and legal history and with 'special reigns and periods'. Perhaps new 'majestic' historians, new Gibbons would arise, who could base their work on the specialist studies currently being produced — but that lay in the future. For the moment, Fisher was content to think of this monographic culture as 'scientific history' because it was based on the critical and careful study of sources and because, supposedly, it was not partisan. He was confident that, with accurate research methods, there would be relatively little room for doubt about the findings of such work.[17]

The point here is that Fisher's 'science' was clearly of very limited application; history was not a science in the Positivist sense, in the sense that an inductive method could be used to produce general laws; it was 'scientific' only in the sense that it involved careful and critical analysis of evidence, mainly documentary, and aspired to objectivity. In similar vein, Fisher said of Maitland that he neither claimed nor cared to possess a conscious theory, but that 'he was simply a scientific historian'. Fisher himself felt that 'nothing is so tedious as a history constructed upon severe philosophical principles'.[18] Though this technocratic, pseudo-scientific, supposedly value-free culture was not Positivist, its ready acceptance by an increasingly technological society that was having a love-affair with 'efficiency', brings to mind the supposedly value-free 'culture' of logical Positivism some years later, as explained by Kolakowski. 'That to which we agree to apply the term "knowledge" is logically arbitrary and historically related to the culture within which such decisions are made', wrote Kolakowski. He continued: 'Logical empiricism then is the product of a specific culture, one in which technological efficiency is regarded as the highest value, the culture we usually call "technocratic". It is a technocratic ideology in the guise of an anti-ideological, scientific view of the world, purged of value-judgments'.[19] Perhaps this explains the confusion between 'scientism' of this low order, as expounded by the historians, and the full-blooded scientism of the Comtists. The common factor was not philosophical Positivism but the technocratic ideal of society, which gave birth to both Positivism (Comtist and logical) and to the 'scientific' history of J.H. Round *et al.*, which latter slid over the question of induction and causation. Dilthey, at about this time, was proclaiming his hermeneutic method of understanding (*verstehen*) as opposed to causal explanation,[20] but, despite Acton's interest, other English historians were unaware of Dilthey and seem to have been very vague about the relationship between minute narrative and causal explanation. There was even perverted national pride and wilful ignorance: Fisher himself relished being 'a beastly phlegmatic Englishman with a taste for facts',[21] and such insularity is quite common.

Bury, in his famous inaugural lecture, was to show an awareness, as Fisher had done, of the potential for the limited works of his own day to be utilised in the future; but he went further. First the 'patient drudgery' and the 'microscopic research' was performed for 'remote posterity' to use in a way which his own day could not envisage. 'We are heaping up material and arranging it, according to the best methods we know; if we draw what conclusions we can for the satisfaction of our generation, we never forget that our work is to be used by future ages'. Secondly, however, because his own generation would continue, willy nilly, to write 'constructive works of history' as well as technical monographs, these constructive works, which would not have permanent value in themselves, would 'abide as milestones of human progress', documents of the age, for the disposal of posterity.[22] All this was echoed some years later by F.M. Stenton. Notes for a lecture (dated some time between 1914 and 1919) refer to the 'technical monograph' as the type of current historiography and the great book as a thing of the past. The modern historian needed an arduous technical training and great caution before making judgments. If he looked more like a man of science than of letters, if his work, however modest, was even then destined for obsolescence, such work was the necessary preliminary to any return of great literary works, with grand themes, in the future.[23]

Today, we might well ask: where is this new wave of constructive history, of great works with grand themes? There has developed a growing unease about the long survival of post-Whig microscopic history. Even orthodox, academic professionals worry about the tendency merely to add facts to facts, 'in the grip of the D. Phil business where all the emphasis falls upon making no mistakes', and even the acknowledged masters write without clear message or purpose.[24] The projected golden age of post-scientific history, whether central or peripheral to the hopes and intentions of those who talked of it, has not materialised and eighty-odd years of microscopic histories have failed to satisfy even the professionals. As for the educated general public, they have occasionally latched on to the work of those atypical historians who have provided either grand theses or literary histories, which in the main have been either sterile Whig survivals, totally divorced from their original intellectual environment and carrying no weight in the academic establishment, or mere fanciful, baseless creations. We shall be looking at several aspects of this state of affairs in later chapters, but for the moment the initial confusion over the 'scientific' character of the new specialist histories must be our starting point.

An exchange, in 1898, between the leading Comtist of the day, Frederic Harrison, and the most uncompromising exponent of the new minute scholarship, J.H. Round, is most revealing. Harrison wrote two articles in *The Nineteenth Century*, one on Froude and one on Freeman, two mutual enemies who had died earlier in the decade, Froude briefly succeeding his old enemy as Regius Professor at Oxford (1892-1894). Attacking Froude, the old opponent of Positivism, with particular reference to his lecture on 'The Science of History', Harrison drew a distinction between sociology as a science of society, and history which could never be a science but only provide the facts on which social science could be based. Comte's great conception of human affairs as 'ordered by law' had been fully worked out by Mill, Spencer, Buckle and others, claimed Harrison somewhat optimistically, scathingly dismissing the opposition of 'theologians and metaphysicians'. But the mere historian, perhaps because he had been influenced by such lightweights, was banned from theorising; he merely narrated events and described the actions of those who participated in them. Even this lowly function would be inexpertly carried out, however, unless the historian accepted that a philosophy of history was conceivable and also abandoned his literary pretensions.[25] There is an obvious similarity between the Positivist view of history as a compilation of facts, which should be narrated but not distorted by artistic rearrangements, which could then be used by others for a higher explanatory purpose, and the views of those historians who settled for their objective, 'scientific', but limited monographs and were prepared to leave grand interpretation to future, better-informed generations. The process of arriving at the overview was clearly going to be different in the two cases, with Positivist social scientists employing an inductive method and historians using more intuitive methods, but it may be that the Positivists, though increasingly confined within sectarian boundaries, had had their unacknowledged influence. An additional and critical difference from the historians' point of view, however, was that fact-gathering history was itself denied the status of science by the Positivists. Harrison likened the relationship between history and social science to that between 'natural history' and natural science, whereas the historians saw more objectivity and expertise in use of sources as enough to qualify themselves as scientists, with philosophical histories as a somewhat vague potential in the future. Two notions were held in common, however: science was a matter of status; and narrated facts could be objectively delivered, unsullied by any artistic reconstruction.

Turning his attention to Freeman, or at any rate using a discussion of Freeman's approach to history as a convenient peg on which to hang his own ideas, Harrison was to show, however, that his belief in objectively delivered facts was not as naive as might at first sight appear. He launched a scathing attack on the fetish of documents and the publishing of unedited manuscripts; he complained of 'the modern superstition that the past can be interpreted by laboriously copying out and piecing together such scraps of written paper as time has chanced to spare'. It needed political 'instinct and experience' to understand political acts and politicians; he numbered Freeman, Thomas Arnold, Macaulay and Gibbon among the successful interpreters of political history. He had no time for those who thought that proof lay in documentary evidence alone or in piling up minute facts; facts had to be grouped, condensed and synthesised. He admitted that Freeman, though the champion of the unity of history, got bogged down in pointless detail in his own works; but even if the historians failed to deliver the goods, the concept of the unity of history was the very basis of all social science; properly composed, history was the main 'organon', or instrument, of any social philosophy. Interestingly, he named three Liberal Anglicans

(Arnold, Milman and Thirlwall), alongside Gibbon, Hallam and Grote, as capable of synthetic history, honourable exceptions to the general rule of microscopic research and analytical pedantry. History was about 'organic wholes' (nations, centuries and 'inspiring forces') which could only be understood by an appropriate synthesis of the facts. As for these historical 'facts' themselves, they were at best 'high probabilities'.[26] So Harrison, who had mocked historical research before, was not a naive realist; and the Positivists did not accept the historians' ideas about history as a science. The response to all this by J.H. Round is equally revealing. He was inspired mainly by the chance of delivering yet another drubbing to the memory of his old enemy Freeman, who had suffered as much in his later years from the attentions of Round as Froude (and Kingsley) had once suffered from Freeman. Where Freeman had castigated Froude for inaccuracy and inexpert use of the archives, Round had exposed Freeman as something of a fraud in that he too was inaccurate and, above all, in that he relied on chronicles rather than true archival material. Much of this new article was in like vein. But the ferocity of Round was also directed at Harrison, in explicit defence of historical research. 'The truest history', he averred, 'like the truest art, is that which is least influenced by motives external to itself. Freeman has shown us the danger of writing as a politician; Mr Harrison would have us increase the danger by writing from the necessarily subjective standpoint of a philosopher with a system'. Here we see the crucial disagreement between the true Positivist and the mere empiricist; the former needed a system; the latter believed that systems and theories distorted the facts. Even Round, however, declared, perhaps a trifle inconsistently, that 'we are but paving the way for the "synthetic" historian of his [Harrison's] desire'. At first sight it might seem that Round actually committed himself to a Positivist programme: accumulation of evidence was to be followed by 'sifting and classification', and then there could be established a new theory 'on a sure foundation'. But he was adamantly opposed to any overarching 'philosophy' like current Positivism; and his new 'theory' even if inductively arrived at, was only a low-level, limited interpretation of a given set of facts — not a law applicable in all, or several, instances; for he cited his own work on the introduction of military tenure as an example of a 'novel theory' derived from a new type of archival evidence found in unedited manuscripts. Minute research was the key to scientific handling of history; this need not involve the use of trivia in narrative which was one of Freeman's sins, but it did involve the search for and the accurate use of authentic evidence.[27] In a way it is easy to see why this model of what constituted scientific activity was accepted by historians. In their academic environment they were often comparing their own research activities with research in the natural sciences of a similarly limited kind. At Manchester, Tout (whilst claiming T.H. Green as one of his mentors, and certainly no Positivist) laid great emphasis on the natural science parallel. The status of history, the acquisition of further knowledge, and professional training in the technical aspects of research were his main concerns. He wished to establish an historical 'laboratory' at Manchester, where students could learn to practise the methods of the 'observational' sciences using archival material. There was no high-flown methodology here, rather 'the processes' whereby history was made in contrast to the mere results of other men's scholarship. He used phrases such as 'training in the technique of our craft' and believed that 'the best training in method is an attempt at research'. He thought Bury's dictum on the scientific character of history was 'a self-evident truth', but wished to eschew any philosophical or methodological issues raised thereby, consideration of such being unprofitable.[28] Not surprisingly, one of his disciples testifies, without a hint of criticism, that he had no 'system' of historical education, no special method to impart, and that he had a totally eclectic approach to the use of theory. Echoing Acton's inaugural lecture, where historical method had been defined as 'only the reduplication of common sense . . . best acquired by observing its use by the ablest man in every variety of intellectual employment', [29] Powicke continued: 'He [Tout] was thoroughly English' in this respect, caring little for consistency, and relying on a strong vein of common sense and 'a powerful and well-disciplined imagination', the kind that 'follows the facts' rather than the needs of artistic creation.[30] Tout's 'scientific' method then consisted of an unsystematic, commonsense approach, learnt from experience like a craft, and dependent as much on a disciplined 'imagination' as on induction for any conclusions it might draw from the available facts. Even the amateur historian was caught up in the cult of facts, though in one instance not without eventual disillusionment. Belloc wrote to his friend H.A.L. Fisher in 1904:

> I am deep in my Marie Antoinette . . . I am making it up entirely of facts: there are hundreds and hundreds of references. It is very entertaining like putting a puzzle together. In this way one avoids all dullness. Most people think that writing nothing but facts makes history dull. The truth is that history is only dull if the selection is inartistic . . . the thing lives — without any paragraphs of one's own. It becomes just like life.[31]

Unlike Tout, Belloc believed in selection for artistic reasons, yet he had faith in the selected facts speaking for themselves and being, indeed, 'just like life', a clear form of naive realism. Yet Belloc's enthusiasm waned: 'Marie Antoinette apalls [sic] me!' he wrote less than a year later, 'I have not the slightest idea who all the people are whom I come across as I write about her, and they all bore me to . . . [illegible] . . . , anyhow'.[32] And in the following year: 'I am taking the bull by the horns in the matter of Marie Antoinette, and writing the book with violence. I cannot go on for ever accumulating material . . . you cannot write a book in that way'. He ended by heartily wishing Marie Antoinette had never been born.[33] A cautionary tale indeed! But the professionals had more stamina.

If Belloc had thought that the demands of artistic selection were adequate safeguard against dullness or irrelevance, his naivety was more than matched by S.R. Gardiner, not technically a professional, but certainly professional in his approach. Gardiner's method was ruthlessly taken apart by the American, R.G. Usher, in 1915. It seems that Gardiner was so concerned to adhere to a strict chronology that he tried to ignore any knowledge of succeeding events, refusing to consider evidence subsequent to the time he was studying — it had to wait till he got there. 'He wrote as he worked', even to the extent of sending every few pages to the printers as they were written, only very rarely correcting or amending. He never bothered about style or experimented with different ways of relating a passage. He tried to live the story day by day, and tried to get his readers to do the same. He said he 'watched' Charles I or Cromwell and wrote down what he 'saw'. He refused to sift, prune, correct or alter his 'facts'. This, as Usher averred, was not the scientific history it was reputed to be: 'A few facts roughly grouped together in chronological order do not make a history'. Narrative was not the form of scientific history.[34] Belloc had assumed that artistic selection, perhaps for literary effect, was the key principle of selection — but did not believe that this interfered with the essential reality of the historiographical product *vis à vis* life itself. Gardiner went further: no principle of selection was required; he could observe the past as if it was the present, as if it was life itself.

It is usually presumed that the loudest, if most misguided, voices on the nature of scientific history were Bury and Acton. Though Bury succeeded Acton as Regius Professor at Cambridge, they were as unlike as Freeman and Froude. Yet again and again their words have been quoted in association, as evidence for the dominance of the scientific ideal. The contention that there was a coherent concept of what constituted historical science is dealt a further blow if we examine their two famous statements.

With Bury we can be brief, for we have had occasion to mention his views several times in passing, and Goldstein has delivered what must surely be the authoritative verdict on what he meant. For our purposes, the crucial point is that Bury's idea of a science of history, though not Positivist, was based on causality: history was a study of causes; sometimes different causal sequences met in contingencies, so events were not predictable, but the historian's business was the study of appropriate chains of causation. Such study had to be based on 'systematic' and 'minute' analysis of sources and 'microscopic' criticism of those sources. This was indispensable for the achievement of a more exact standard of truth. History as art could only distort the truth by interfering with the process of selection (*pace* Belloc); the principle of development was the selective and organising principle upon which historical research had to be based. History might, as a side-line, produce materials for social science, but history as development was the most important form of history, for thus was ensured both the accuracy and the importance of historical scholarship.[35] Belloc (at least the early, optimistic Belloc), Gardiner and Bury, perhaps surprisingly, shared the presumption that the selection of history as narrative was the key to correct representation of the past; but Belloc believed in artistic selection, Gardiner in the facts presenting themselves ineluctably in sequence, and Bury in the principle of development.

Acton's position, however, was quite different. The passage usually quoted is from his letter to the contributors to the *Cambridge Modern History* series. Figgis and R.V. Lawrence, the editors of his *Lectures on Modern History* (1906), included it in their volume on the grounds that it was characteristic of Acton's ideals. Ever since, because of Acton's somewhat inflated reputation, of his tenure of the prestigious post of Regius Professor at Cambridge, and of the semi-official status of the *Cambridge Modern History*, it has been seen as characteristic of the age. But Acton was not typical; the Regius Chair, which he occupied only briefly, was prestigious but largely powerless, and he lacked influence; his editorship was, like the rest of his career, somewhat unproductive. Moreover, the basis of his views has often been misunderstood. Basically, what he said was that 'the scientific demand for completeness and certainty' could now be met by scholars using the abundant primary material now available; 'we approach', he said, 'the final stage in the conditions of historical learning'. The consequent composite narrative could be so free of bias that, in the oft-quoted words, 'nothing shall reveal the country, the religion, or the party to which the writers belong'. There should be no disclosure of personal views.[36] The prevalent association of science with original sources and with objectivity does, of course, appear here. But, as we have seen from Acton's earlier statements, 'the inflexible integrity of the moral code' as well as original research, gave history its objective or scientific character. Acton's pious rejection of moral relativism, however typical of his youth, was quite atypical by the end of the century and was a somewhat quirky basis for the establishment of a science. As he testified in his inaugural lecture (1895), he held to his principle though 'the weight of opinion' was against him.[37] His faith in the new objectivity has, perhaps a little unkindly, been dismissed as pathetically naive;[38] but his critic failed to notice that two distinct elements were involved in Acton's objectivity — the acquisition of all available evidence of course, but also the unchanging moral code; the delivery of magisterial judgment, the ultimate purpose of history for Acton, was dependent on both these factors.

The weight of opinion most certainly was against Acton in this, as York Powell believed. 'The majority of scholars' in England accepted that 'the formation and expression of ethical judgments . . . is not a thing within the historians province', he said. 'The historian's business was to investigate the facts', then to present them clearly and 'lastly to consider and attempt to ascertain what scientific use can be made' of them.[39] (We might add that it is not clear what this 'scientific use' might have been). Moreover, Acton's successors in the editorial chair were much less certain that final judgments and neutrality were possible. A.W. Ward, George Prothero and Stanley Leathes advised their contributors in somewhat different vein. True, they started with familiar words: 'Each chapter is intended to be an exact scientific summary of the history included under its title' and should be 'based on original testimony and the latest research'. But it was only a summary, and was intended as a foundation for wider study; and, though 'treatment should be as far as possible objective', they recognised that facts had to be selected and that the point of view indicated by the very title of each chapter would influence such selection; they wanted 'controversies about disputed points' to be identified (though not pursued).[40] The tone is much more tentative than that of their predecessor. Acton is much quoted, but his successors did the bulk of the editorial work and were probably more typical of the age; for them, objectivity was relative, final judgments had not all been made, and the term 'scientific' was once again a very vague concept.

There was no real excuse for the vagueness with which most English historians used the term 'science'. They obviously meant more than simply organised knowledge, but rarely, if they used the term with approval, did they mean a fully-fledged Positivistic, law-inducing science. Bury, and perhaps Acton, had more precise if idiosyncratic ideas about what constituted historical science, but even after Bury's inaugural lecture there was a tendency to be airily dismissive of the issue he had raised. In Germany, however, not only had Dilthey developed a distinctive approach to *Geisteswissenschaften* or human studies, studies of *geistige Welt* or the mind-affected world, as distinct from natural science,[41] but Rickert, in a critique of Positivism, was distinguishing quite clearly between the historical sciences of the individual and the law-making, generalizing sciences.[42] In England, as we have seen, the philosophical basis for the distinctions had already been propounded by the Idealists. In France, where Positivism still had much influence, Langlois and Seignobos, in contrast, attempted to define the historian's task in more Positivistic terms. Recommending the division of labour, they perceived three stages in the production of mature historical scholarship. First, there was the work of the specialists, the critical scholarship that uncovered, restored, authenticated and classified the documents. Then there was the production of 'partial syntheses' or monographs. Lastly, 'workers of experience' (professors, like Langlois and Seignobos, no doubt) 'should be found to renounce personal research' and devote their whole time to the study of these partial syntheses, in order to combine them scientifically in comprehensive works of historical construction. And if the results of these labours were to bring out clear and certain conclusions as to the nature and the causes of social evolution, a truly scientific 'philosophy of history' would have been created, which historians might acknowledge as legitimately crowning historical science. To achieve this it would be necessary to co-ordinate the efforts of the primary researchers and to standardise the methods of the authors of the partial syntheses. Langlois and Seignobos were not naïve realists, nor vulgar Comtists, if one may use such a term; their book is quite conceptually sophisticated, and they did not believe they were on the verge of 'fixed' historical truth; they also believed it necessary to reason by 'analogy' with the present day, using an understanding of human nature as the common factor in past and present. But they did attempt, in a Positivistic way, to explain what they meant by a scientific method in historical scholarship. For them, the scientific part of the whole process was the final synthesis, the grand conclusion.[43] Nothing could be in greater contrast to the English presumption that the scientific element lay in the painstaking work of initial critical scholarship in the archives. The English confused the technical with the scientific. Of course the assumption of a synthesising 'scientific' role for the French professorial class of historian was largely a reaction to the ambitions of French sociologists like Durkheim to play such a role themselves, reducing all historians to the technician's role.[44]

It seems that historians in England were only dimly aware of these issues, and failed to define their position in a clear or helpful way, despite the challenge of sociology. Bury had been aware of such a challenge, wishing history to be more than 'the handmaid of social science', a mere furnisher of 'examples of causes and effects'.[45] Recently, both Collini and Soffer have drawn attention to the challenge of sociology,[46] a challenge that many English historians were intent on avoiding rather than meeting. It may well be that the great rift between history and social science was based on the historian's continuing preference for free-will; or it may be, as recently suggested, that the historians had already acquired 'their professional interest in variety' as opposed to establishing models of social change.[47]

Be all this as it may, the presumption that 'objective' and 'scientific' are synonymous terms, and that no further thought it needed on the nature of *Geisteswissenschaften*, was typical of English historical thought at the turn of the century. We still live with the legacy of that period; indeed, its major interpreter, Blaas, has himself fallen victim to it. He sees the anti-Whig reaction of the era as a fight against anachronism and as resulting in the successful establishment of 'autonomous' history, that is, history freed from presentism. He unequivocally equates past-centred or 'autonomous' history with scientific history; he believes in the ideal of professional objectivity.[48] It is extraordinary that the anti-Whig tendency of the period should be seen solely in these terms, its own terms as value-free, especially when the political implications of anti-Whiggism are recognised, and when 'realism' had strong conservative political overtones at the time. For our present purposes, however, the significance of this shallow love-affair with 'science' it that it detracted from serious consideration of the nature of historical knowledge. It must be regarded as a major factor in the failure to develop any thesis comparable to that of Dilthey or to clarify the role of history within the Positivist scheme. Probably the most serious loss was the failure to build upon Idealist hermeneutics. Additionally, with the emphasis upon analysis, factual evidence, accurate representation through a narrative of events, and the role of the actors in those events, actors who recorded their role in the archives, the naive realism of those who adopted the scientific ideal militated against the otherwise fruitful consideration of social wholes, or of what moved nations, beyond the individual will. There was no attempt to define attitudes towards causation in society. Methodological individualism reinforced the ethical and other forms of individualism that once typified mid-Victorian historiography. Yet the sense of purpose had gone, beyond that of pursuing a spurious, half thought-out, low-level scientific ideal.

Perhaps the saddest aspect of all this was that any true awareness of the contemporary natural sciences would, in any case, have provided an alternative model for any historians who genuinely wanted to emulate the scientists. Their concept of science was anachronistic. Bury had thought, with some effect, about the impact and meaning of Darwinism, but the Darwinian revolution had been the last major scientific innovation to make an impact in wider intellectual circles. It was not until 1925 that a philosopher (not an historian) attempted a major reassessment of the impact of science upon thought in modern times. A.N. Whitehead's *Science and the Modern World* argued that, for three centuries, the modern era had been increasingly dominated by a 'cosmology' derived from science (as opposed to aesthetics, ethics, or religion, for example).[49] According to this cosmology the only valid method of inquiry was 'the study of the empirical facts of antecedents and consequences', which led to a concern for origins and to an inductive method. Alongside this dominant cosmology was a less influential Idealist culture, which had organicist implications, but had never succeeded in breaking into the world of inductive natural science. He wanted to bring the two worlds together. 'Matter' and 'spirit' were both 'abstractions', both intuitively understood, both part of an organic whole. Intuitively because of our own self-knowledge, he felt that we had 'an organic conception of nature' — the nature of 'electrons, protons, molecules and living bodies'. 'Organism', not 'matter', was to be the new basic concept for the natural sciences. This would bring to an end the unhappy dualism in western thought since the scientific revolution of the seventeenth century. 'A scientific realism, based on mechanism is conjoined with an unwavering belief in the world of men and of the higher animals as being composed of self-determining organisms. This radical inconsistency at the basis of modern thought accounts for much that is half-hearted and wavering in our civilization'. The appropriateness of this remark to the half-hearted acceptance of a supposedly scientific method by the historians, who nonetheless rejected a mechanistic view of human affairs, need not be stressed. Whitehead himself illustrated his point, not from history, but from literature, quoting in particular from Tennyson's *In Memoriam*: '"The stars", she whispers, "blindly run."' Here, said Whitehead, was the agony felt when a mechanistic universe was set against mind and volition. But this was a false antithesis if the doctrine of 'organic mechanism' was accepted; faith and reason no longer stood in unhappy opposition.[50]

During the nineteenth century, according to Whitehead, a fourfold transformation of natural science had occurred: physical activity was now seen as pervading all space; all matter was seen as atomic, and all living matter as cellular; the doctrine of energy worked on a presumption of a quantitative permanence underlying all change; and, of course, there was the doctrine of biological evolution. The most important basis of the new science was the concept of 'energy' which had replaced 'mass' or 'matter'. The study of energy was the study of 'a structure of happenings'; it was, in other words, an organic concept. The primary entity of both atomic physics and evolutionary biology had become 'the event', whether within a large biological organism or within a smaller molecular one subsumed within the larger. Though scientists had not yet learned how to study the life history of individual molecules or electrons, they had learned how to study individual living things, their propagation and life history, and, as a necessary concomitant, the environment within which 'the family, the race, or the seed in the fruit' endured and propagated. The moral of all this was clear to Whitehead — and it was the antithesis of the social Darwinism that emphasised the 'struggle for Existence' and 'Natural Selection'. He complained that there was a spurious belief 'that there was a peculiar strong-minded realism in disregarding ethical considerations in the determination of the conduct of commercial and national interests'. The creative and cooperative side of evolution was neglected. He denounced the false realism of 'romantic ruthlessness'. On a broader front he chided materialists for lagging behind the advance of science, which they professed to emulate, and for maintaining a false dichotomy between mind and matter.[51] Unlike the historians of the preceding thirty-five years, Whitehead was acutely aware of the changes that had occurred in the nineteenth-century scientific world view. The supposedly scientific analytical method had been replaced; new concepts like 'process' and 'organism' needed to be taken on board by those who professed to be part of the dominant science-based culture.

The only historian who had shown even an inkling of the issues Whitehead was raising, was Bury. Interested as he was in both methodological issues and in the history of ideas (as in *The Idea of Progress*), it is not suprising that he turned his attention to the significance of scientific advances. In *Darwinism and History* (1909) he had drawn a parallel between the genetic or historical idea in nature and the development concept in history, particularly in terms of systems and organisms:

> The 'historical' conception of nature, which has produced the history of the solar system, the story of the earth, the genealogies of telluric organisms, and has revolutionised natural science, belongs to the same order of thought as the conception of human history as a continuous, genetic, causal process — a conception which has revolutionised historical research and made it scientific.

He recognised the holistic implications of this — 'the notion that all the institutions of a society or a nation are as closely inter-connected as the parts of a living organism'. For Bury, 'the conception of the history of man as a causal development meant the elevation of historical inquiry to the dignity of a science'. Evolutionary theory had emphasised that man was part of the system, not a separate creation, and that history was one of the sciences, not a separate kind of knowledge. Bury did not concern himself greatly with the issue of 'mind' and 'matter', so he did not go as far as Whitehead in suggesting a fundamental rethinking of the dichotomy, but he did recognise the similarity between evolutionary biology and developmental history, neither of which was a law-making, inductive Comtist science. Organic and social events were manifestations of the same processes.[52]

Bury, however, was no more typical of his age than Acton. Though he continued to explore his inaugural lecture's dictum about history being a science, and explored it with some sophistication, anticipating to some extent even Whitehead's far-reaching ideas, others either dismissed his message as a statement of the obvious or reacted against it with misconceived chauvinism, as did Trevelyan. Thus the supposedly 'scientific' methods of minute critical analysis of supposedly discrete phenomena remained the ideal; methodological and epistemological individualism were untouched by the fascination with science, and if, as the previous chapter has indicated, the social, political and ethical individualism of the mid-Victorians had for some time been weakening in the face of Idealist assumptions of holism and organicism, events in the wider world of European politics were about to intervene in such a way as to reinvigorate the old individualist tradition. It was not only reinvigorated but it was charged with a new combative spirit, for added to the old desire to preserve an intellectual and ethical tradition against unsettling influences was a growing conviction that the threat was political as well as intellectual. The history of historiography has to be drawn into the maelstrom of European politics.

NOTES

1. D. Boucher, 'The Creation of the Past: British Idealism and Michael Oakeshott's Philosophy of History', *History and Theory*, XXIII (1984), pp. 193-214.

2. See C.J.W. Parker, 'Bernard Bosanquet, Historical Knowledge, and the History of Ideas', *Philosophy of the Social Sciences*, 18 (1988).

3. A. Seth, R.B. Haldane (eds), *Essays in Philosophical Criticism* (London, 1813): W.R. Sorley, 'The Historical Method', pp. 102-125; D.G. Ritchie, 'The Rationality of History', pp. 126-158.

4. R.G. Collingwood, *The Historical Imagination* (Oxford, 1935), p.12.

5.   F.H. Bradley, 'The Presumptions of Critical History', *Collected Essays* (Oxford, 1935), pp. i. 1, 7-10.

6.   I refer, of course, to the oft-quoted passage from Fisher's preface to his *History of Europe* (1935): 'I can see only one emergency following upon another . . . there can be no generalization . . .' etc. H.A.L. Fisher, *A History of Europe*, revised and enlarged two-volume edition (London, 1943), pp. i, vi.

7.   Bradley, 'The Presuppositions of Critical History', pp. 14-20.

8.   H. Sidgwick, *The Methods of Ethics*, p. 62. The first edition of *The Methods of Ethics* (1874) was contemporaneous with Bradley's essay.

9.   Bradley, 'The Presuppositions of Critical History', pp 21-23, 36.

10.   *Ibid.*, pp. 39-42.

11.   *Ibid.*, pp. 40-41.

12.   Royal Historical Society Library, Prothero Papers, 4, 5, 6, Bundle 3/9 (uncatalogued) Acton to Prothero, 26 October 1987.

13.   D.G. Ritchie, 'The Rationality of History', in Seth, Haldane, *Op.cit.*, pp. 127-130, 133, 136, 143-147, 149-152.

14.   See, for example, D.S. Goldstein, 'The Organisational Development of the British Historical Profession, 1884-1921', *B.I.H.R.*, LV 132 (1982), pp. 180-193; T.W. Heyck, *The Transformation of Intellectual Life in Victorian England* (London, 1982), pp. 120-150; R. Jann, 'From Amateur to Professional: the Case of the Oxbridge Historians', *Journal of British Studies*, 22 (1983), 122-147.

15.   Jann, *Op.cit.*, p. 123.

16.   See C.J.W. Parker, 'The Development of History Courses in British Universities, 1850-1975' (Exeter University MA thesis, 1976).

17.   H.A.L. Fisher, 'Modern Historians and their Methods', *Fortnightly Review*, CCCXXXVI N.S.(1 Dec. 1894), pp. 811, 813-814. It is not clear whether Fisher was later to believe his own 'majestic' three-volume *A History of Europe* (1935), which was based on pre-Great War scholarship, was one of the new generation of outlines — if so, his message, as we have seen, was no more than one of despairing liberalism.

18.   H.A.L. Fisher, *Frederick William Maitland, Downing Professor of the Laws of England. A Biographical Sketch* (Cambridge, 1910), pp. 107, 174, 178.

19.   L. Kolakowski, *Positivist Philosphy from Hume to the Vienna Circle* (Harmondsworth, 1972) p. 235.

20.   See, for example, W. Dilthey, *Meaning in History: W. Dilthey's Thoughts on History and Society*, edited and introduced by H.P. Rickman (London, 1961).

21.   Bodleian Library, Fisher MSS.54 (Letters to and from Gilbert Murray 1889-1919), Fisher to Murray, 2 November 1982.

22.   J.B. Bury, *Selected Essay* ed. H. Temperley (Cambridge, 1930), pp. 16-18.

23.   Reading University Library, Papers of F.M. Stenton and D.M. Stenton, MS. 1148/8/– 5 'General 1914-1919', notes for a lecture on 'historians as men of letters'.

24.   R.H.C. Davis, 'The Content of History', *History*, 66 (1981), pp. 363, 366.

25.   F. Harrison, 'The Historical Method of J.A. Froude', *Nineteenth Century*, XLIV (1898), 381.

26.   F. Harrison 'The Historical Method of Professor Freeman', *Nineteenth Century*, XLIV (1898), 796-799, 801-802, 804-805.

27.   J.H. Round, 'Historical Research', *Nineteenth Century*, XLIV (1898), pp. 1004-1008.

28.   T.F. Tout, 'A Historical "Laboratory"' (1910), *The Collected Papers of Thomas Frederick Tout with a memoir and bibliography* (Manchester, 1932), pp. i. 79-80.

29.   J.E.E. Dalberg-Acton, 'The Study of History', *Lectures on Modern History* (London, 1906), p. 20.

30.   F.M. Powicke, *Modern Historians and the Study of History* (London, 1955), pp. 34-35, 42.

31.   Fisher MSS. 53, fols 1-20, H. Belloc to H.A.L. Fisher, 29 September 1904.

32.   *Ibid.*, 14 July 1905.

33.   *Ibid.*, 9 June 1906.

34. R.G. Usher, *A critical study of the Historical Method of Samuel Rawson Gardiner, with an excursus on the historical conception of the Puritan Revolution from Clarendon to Gardiner* (Washington University Studies vol. III, part II, October 1915 No. 1), pp. 20-23, 159.

35. J.B. Bury, *Op.cit.*, 'The Science of History', pp. 4-11; see also 'Cleopatra's Nose', pp. 60-61.

36. Acton, Appendix I, *Op.cit.*, pp. 315-316.

37. *Ibid.*, pp. 24-28.

38. J. Kenyon, *The History Men* (London, 1983), p. 138.

39. F. York Powell's 'Introduction' to C.V. Langlois, C. Seignobos, *Introduction to the Study of History* (London, 1898), pp. V-VI.

40. Eastbourne Central Library, Oscar Browning Papers OB1/949, Letters from S.M. Leathes, 'Scheme and Plan of Work, with suggestions to authors: Cambridge Modern History'.

41. W. Dilthey, *Op.cit.*, pp. 66-67.

42. H. Rickert, *Science and History: A Criticism of Positivist Epistemology* trans. G. Reisman, ed. A. Goddard (Princeton, 1962), p. 55. First published in Germany in 1902.

43. C.V. Langlois, C. Seignobos, *Op.cit.*, pp. 316-319.

44. For the impact of Durkheim on the historical profession, see W.R. Keylor, *Academy and Community: The Foundation of the French Historical Profession*, pp. 111-116, 167-170.

45. Bury, *Op.cit.*, pp. 369-370.

46. S. Collini, *Liberalism and Sociology: L.T. Hobhouse and Political Argument in England 1880-1914* (Cambridge, 1979), p. 204; R.N. Soffer, 'The Revolution in English Social Thought 1880-1914', *A.H.R.*, LXXV (1970), 1963-1964.

47. P. Burke, *Sociology and History* (London, 1980), p. 93.

48. Blaas, *Op.cit.*, pp. 369-370.

49. A.N. Whitehead, *Science and the Modern World* (London, 1948), p. vii.

50. *Ibid.*, pp. 41-42, 46, 62-63, 65, 71-76, 78.

51. *Ibid.*, pp. 90-97, 100-106, 137-38.

52. Bury, *Selected Essays*, pp. 23, 26, 31-39.

CHAPTER 5

The Great War and the Revival of Traditional Liberalism

So vain it is by the best-laid scheme and the wisest design to prescribe wisdom for future ages.[1]

Beneath the intellectual uncertainties and personal doubts of the Victorians lay a massive confidence, based on their island's prosperity, peace and security. That confidence, the perhaps necessary foundation of tolerant liberalism, suffered a series of devastating blows in the first half of the twentieth century. If the post-Whig realism of the 1890s and early 1900s had been the beginnings of doubt, the Great War was the first hammer blow. There was an immediate revulsion against all things German, including the German political system, and Idealist philosophy, especially its organicist and statist tendencies. Paradoxically, there was an anxious reassertion of anything that could lay claim to be part of a native tradition; even more paradoxically, the new chauvinism was associated with renewed enthusiasm for the liberal national tradition which had become unfashionable before the War.

The university historians rushed to condemn Germany and her political and intellectual traditions. At Oxford, for example, Ernest Barker, H.W.C. Davis, C.R.L. Fletcher, A. Hassall, L.G. Wickham Legg and F. Morgan, all members of the modern history faculty, produced *Why we are at War: Great Britain's Case* (1914), which ran to three editions before the year was out, the profits going to the Belgian relief fund. Davis also published *The Political Thought of Heinrich von Treitschke* which claimed to be dispassionate, but was very hostile to Treitschke;[2] chapter six of *Why we are at War* ('The New German Theory of the State') may well have been mainly his. Barker, clearly sympathetic to Idealism before the War, was happy to be associated with this indictment of German ideas. According to the Oxford scholars, the war was between 'two different principles — that of *raison d'état*, and that of the rule of law'. Within England this conflict had been decided in favour of the latter in the seventeenth century; the conflict had now been internationalised. The German doctrine of the state was associated with Treitschke, the ardently nationalistic historian of the 'Prussian school', whose *Politik* was the gospel of German nationalists. Treitschke had exalted the state, with Germany as his ideal; he had disavowed any principles above the state, believing that all power, principles and culture derived from it. To this political, ethical and cultural nationalism he added the economic nationalism of List. The state was about power (*macht*). This had led Germany to renege on her international obligations and to see war as legitimate, even glorious. 'The absolute sovereignty of the state is necessary for its absolute power; and that absolute sovereignty of the state cannot be bound by *any* obligation, even of its own making'. Thus the state could not be judged, and 'the end justifies the means'. General Bernhardi, Treitschke's disciple, was credited with direct influence on the rest of Germany's policy makers. Bernhardi's doctrine was: 'Each nation evolves its own conception of Right' and 'No self-respecting nation would sacrifice its own conception of Right'. The glorification of war, said the Oxford historians, was the striking feature of this doctrine. War was seen as the greatest achievement of the state, the healer of national sickness and the creator of a healthy organism: 'Thus the idealization of the state as power results in the idealization of war'. With offensive war glorified even more than defensive war, German ambitions had turned naturally to new naval and colonial outlets and, therefore, had turned against Britain. This, said Oxford, was nothing but a new barbarism 'with a moral veneer . . . the worship of brute force' disguised as a moral crusade. Rejecting pan-German calls for racial unity, they averred: 'Better be traitors to blood than to plain duty' and denied that the English were of pure blood in any case. The gospel of the state, they said, was the gospel, not of the whole of Germany, but of Prussia. And Prussia would be fought 'in the noblest cause for which we can fight . . . the public law of Europe', the 'comity of nations', and the defence of a small nation (Belgium) which had right if not might. 'Our cause', they concluded, 'as one would expect from a people that has fought out its own internal struggles under the forms of law, is a legal cause. We are a people in whose blood the cause of law is the vital element'. We had fought so before, in 1793 against the French revolutionaries; and Anglo-Saxon America and had also fought on these principles.[3] There was just a hint of Anglo-Saxon racialism (now in some disorder because of its German associations, but stressing still the American connection), but crucially a teleological link was forged between domestic constitutional advance towards the rule of law and the recognition of international law. The liberal national spirit was clearly going to be on one of the ideological bases of the intellectual war effort, albeit intolerant of foreign ideologies. It is striking that Barker and Davis had been students together at Balliol (where they had shared rooms) and A.L. Smith had supposedly been a great influence upon them,[4] yet they rejected German statism. Smith, himself, drew different lessons from the War, arguing that, despite its horrors, it called forth the highest ideal of the community spirit, that the 'ferocious individualism' of the English past had to be replaced by a wartime sense of 'discipline, unity, self-sacrifice', and that, though the Germans were currently abusing the idea, we could still learn from their sense of social duty.[5] Even by 1916 he still railed against Manchester individualism and wanted the English to learn from the German sense of public duty.[6] Smith, however, was atypical in wishing to fight Germany with German weapons.

Historians rushed to put their skills at the service of the war effort. George Prothero (of Cambridge, Edinburgh and the Royal Historical Society, but currently of the historical section of the Foreign Office) wrote a number of patriotic, not to say jingoistic, anti-German pamphlets for the Central Committee for National Patriotic Organizations, railing against Germany's militarism, maltreatment of Belgium and plans for the domination of the British Empire.[7] Meanwhile, in November 1914, Ramsay Muir had published *Britain's Case Against Germany: An Explanation of the Historical Background of the German Action in 1914*; it had been proof-read by Tout. Muir, who had held the Chair of Modern History at Liverpool (1906-1913), was no doubt regarded as an expert, having spent the second half of a sabbatical year in Germany immediately prior to the outbreak of the war and before his own translation to the new Chair of Modern History at Manchester in 1914. His argument was similar to that of the Oxford historians: the war was the result of a slow poison in the European system, the source of which was Prussia, for the German action in 1914 was the result of a theory of international politics which had arisen out of the example of Prussian policy over a 250-year period. This prevailing ideology had triumphed over the more liberal tradition of Goethe because of Bismarck's successful *Realpolitik*. Prussia had then moved inevitably towards the crime of 1914, ignoring the nobler precepts of the concert of Europe, protection of small states, arbitration, and the Hague Peace Conferences — all of which Britain had supported. It was even claimed that the British Empire represented 'the antithesis of the German ideal: in its belief in self-government, in freedom, in variety', in peace, and in justice. Between Germany and Britain there was 'a conflict of national ideals'. German political thought was then, once again, identified as the source of Germany's iniquities. It is interesting to note that this attack on Germany employed (whether consciously or not) the very concepts of national ideals, of nations representing ideas in conflict, that derived from nineteenth-century Idealism. Germany's rulers, asserted Muir, bore prime responsibility for the War and its horrors, but behind them stood the creators of opinion, journalists, politicians and 'perhaps especially the professors'. The tone was violent; the wrath of God was invoked: German policy was 'the policy of Hell. And since a God of justice rules the Universe, it will not go unpunished'. The Oxford historians had invoked God in a rather different, fatalistic way: though Bernhardi and his ilk saw war as the highest objective of the state, fulfilling its vital purposes, 'the living God will see to it that war shall always recur as a terrible medicine for humanity'.[9] Evidently the international crisis had quickly stripped away the historians' rationalist explanations of cause and effect. The *deus ex machina* could still be invoked in a crisis'; once it had been Napoleon, now it was the Kaiser's Germany that would incur the wrath of God. It could be argued that this was hasty wartime propaganda, not considered historical scholarship, but this would be to exaggerate the difference between the two modes of expression; and though invocation of God's Providence in such a directly interventionist form seems to be a reversion to older, unacceptable forms of explanation, it suggests that such assumptions were close to the surface; and indeed we find them surfacing later in the century when crisis threatened.

In a chapter specifically on 'German Political Theories', Muir developed the argument further. Again, Bernhardi and his book *Germany and the Next War* (translated in 1911) were identified as the source and type of German attitudes and as a part of a deliberate preparation of the German people for war. Bernhardi's ideas on war as a 'moral necessity', as biologically justifiable, as evidence of might being right, and his views on the powers of the state are cited and criticised. Behind Bernhardi, however, were discerned the more violent figures of the Navy League, the Army League, the Pan-German League, and so on. Treitschke and the entire 'Prussian school' of historians were condemned. Treitschke was 'the teacher and inspirer of the ruling classes of Germany, in the headquarters of Prussia'. But the 'doctrine of power' would destroy itself; 'brutal, immoral, repulsive', it had to be opposed by a doctrine of non-statist individualism, international justice and the rule of law. Englishmen, however dimly they were aware of these principles for which they fought, would triumph in the end because of them.[10] He also looked forward to a programme of international arbitration, projects of disarmament, the creation of a humane code of war, as well as the traditional ideals of the concert of Europe and the defence of small, powerless states who had right, not might.[11]

In this atmosphere it is not surprising that those associated with the spread of German Idealist views on the state were rounded upon as traitors to their own national tradition; as Collini has pointed out, Hobhouse and many others identified Bosanquet especially, as the pedlar of an alien Prussophil philosophy.[12] Indeed, McDougall, advocate of the new 'group mind' psychology, believed that Hobhouse had destroyed the credibility of Bosanquet and of German Idealism.[13] Bosanquet was only too aware of the delicacy of his position during and immediately after the War. He took the opportunity of a public lecture in 1915 to tell his audience that a great philosophy had been degraded, in Germany, into a justification of violence, hatred and self-interest in 'the hands of ignorant and biased amateurs, soldiers, historians, politicians'. The war was not a product of the Idealist conception of the state; on the contrary, it was the result of a failure to live up to that conception. The well-organized state, in harmony with its ideal, would be peaceful at home; its citizens would therefore have right attitudes to questions of law and justice which they would carry over into their foreign relations.[14] In correspondence, Bosanquet agreed with the stand made by Haldane, who he had once seen as the representative of Idealism in government,[15] when the latter had argued that the General Will had now to be seen as potentially international.[16] Muirhead tried to get Bosanquet to join with Hobhouse and other Idealist philosophers in making a collective statement about the moral and political issues raised by the war 'to clear the atmosphere', but Bosanquet chose to steer clear of such a controversial enterprise, and as a consequence it foundered. By the time he published *Social and International Ideals* in 1917, 'the hue and cry' after the Idealist conception of the state, as Muirhead put it, 'had gathered force. Bertrand Russell was pouring scorn upon it as a collection of elderly gentlemen in control of power, gambling with the lives of their fellows, and as the incarnation of the possessive instincts'. Others argued for decentralisation. Bosanquet alone remained faithful to the old ideal.[17]

Bosanquet tried to steer a course between renunciation of his earlier beliefs and exoneration of Germany, but this was complicated by the need to sustain a warlike spirit in Britain whilst condemning the supposed intellectual foundations of such in Germany. He reverted to the argument that the well-ordered state represented internal peace and justice, and would, from habit, sustain international peace and agreements. This association was to become a popular theme. However, he could not resist the old idea that war was perhaps a legitimate moral test.[18] He was careful, however, to reprint 'The Teaching of Patriotism', a pre-war piece, to demonstrate that he had always distinguished between aggression and enlightened patriotism.

Even after the war, Bosanquet still felt the need to defend himself in the light of wartime experience, especially when he republished *The*

Philosophical Theory of the State. It was, he said, 'not the State, nor Sovereignty, nor merely the Germans nor the Kaiser, who made the war. It is all of us, pursuing our mingled aims, which take no account of others, and which, apart from due subordination of means to ends, must lead us into collision. Under the influence of material aims you can misuse and misinterpret the State, as you can the family or the shop'. In other words, individual selfishness and materialism had been at fault; the ideal had been betrayed.[20] But he also stressed that England had always tried to represent high, humane ideals, the principles of justice and liberty, which would now become embodied in the wide sphere of the British Commonwealth and should be embodied in a yet wider sphere, 'the League of Humanity', which would set limits to the state itself yet not be hostile to it.[21] We shall see that towards the end of the war hatred of Germany and all things German, and the invocation of God's punishment upon her, had generally softened into a more positive desire to establish a higher ideal. As early as 1916, Pollard, whilst warning against infection by German *Realpolitik*, distinguished between the bureaucratic, authoritarian, statist German tradition and the noble traditions of German *Kultur* as a whole.[22] The Germany of Goethe as the alternative to a Germany of Treitschke and Prussianism was a frequent theme. But it was also said that Britain (or more usually, England) had always represented these higher ideals, had kept faith with these ideals through the war, and that now they could be internationalised. Though, as H.A.L. Fisher was to note, there was a feeling during the Peace Conference 'that war was a crime' and that the Germans should be punished for it, which was in itself a nobler feeling than mere vindictiveness,[23] one can see how that feeling could be transformed into a yet nobler sentiment of forgiveness once the war was over and the old 'Prussia' no more. The historians had their full share of this optimistic, forgiving ideology that had turned the Great War into the war to end wars. Thus, having turned their backs on Idealist holism, they found a new sphere for the operation of liberal principles.

Three figures attract our attention here, key figures in the development of international history after the war: two professionals, Charles Webster and Harold Temperley; and a gifted and privileged amateur, G.P. Gooch. As we have seen, the dominance of constitutional history, that traditional vehicle for the Whig interpretation, had been threatened before the war by the rise of administrative history in the new 'realist' mode; but there had also begun to develop an interest in international history and the study of foreign policy. Though Seeley had pointed in this direction, he had few followers prepared to assume the primacy of foreign policy: this concept had been crucial to the mainstream Idealist, German view of the role of the state. But diplomatic history written in England before the war suggested that different criteria were being used. The English approach to the writing of international history was confirmed and strengthened by the experience of war, by wartime diplomacy, and finally by peacemaking after the war, which was often a highly personal experience for historians with expertise to offer their government. Webster, a product of Cambridge, was already a young professor (28 years of age) at Liverpool when the war began. He volunteered for war service in 1915 and was seconded first to military intelligence, then to the historical section of the Foreign Office to write *The Congress of Vienna* (1919) as a guide for the peacemakers, and finally to the military section of the British delegation to the Peace Conference, as assistant secretary. Some years after the war he left Liverpool for the Chair of International Politics at Aberystwyth, and then moved to the Chair of International History at the London School of Economics (1932-1953). His major works were on the Congress of Vienna and the foreign policy of Castlereagh.[24]

The Foreign Office and the various intelligence departments were gathering places for historians during the war. Prothero was Director of the Foreign Office's Historical Section and general editor of the handbook series of which *The Congress of Vienna* was a part. Webster's immediate superior was Harold Temperley, until the latter was transferred to Belgrade, as Assistant Military Attaché, just before the end of the War.[25] Namier, seconded to the Peace Conference in 1919, had spent the war in intelligence, specialising in the Polish Intelligence Department; he contributed to the official history of the Conference, which was edited by Temperley, though Namier, alone of the historians, despised the League of Nations.[26] A younger member of the British delegation in Paris was E.H. Carr.[27] R.W. Seton-Watson worked for intelligence, specialising in Eastern European affairs. H.W.C. Davis's war work was in trade intelligence for the blockade of Germany; he too was a member of the Peace delegation.[28] Temperley's editorial, 'Suggestions to Contributors' to the official history of the Conference, is instructive. After acknowledging, unlike Acton, the impossibility of freedom from national bias under existing circumstances, he nonetheless instructed Webster and co. to 'aim at the international point of view, to adopt a Geneva perspective'. Their guiding principle was to be that the Peace was 'a great constructive experiment', not just a balancing of national interests but 'a definite attempt to establish the reign of law above that of force'. It involved, therefore, the concept of 'punishment of the guilty', establishing machinery for penalising future guilt and guarantees for protecting the innocent. Summaries of facts were to be eschewed in favour of indicating 'how far each measure or set of events assisted or retarded the establishment of this great guiding principle'. In the post-war world the wicked ways of the past were no longer relevant: 'Guilty nations have been punished and war, which was previously regarded as justifiable, is henceforward looked on as a crime'.[29] Gone were the national sentiments of Seeley or Treitschke; gone was the fatalistic acceptance of war as a necessary trial of strength. The early belligerent denunciation of German aggression, typified by Prothero's pamphlets, had been officially transformed into a new internationalism. Diplomatic history, the cinderella branch of British political historiography, came into its own, with official histories and enormous contemporary interest in international affairs because of recent events and future hopes, at a time when the emphasis was clearly on peace not war, on international law as opposed to national interest. Through official channels, the spirit of the League of Nations and the Paris Peace Conference descended upon the diplomatic historians, transforming their subject in importance and turning it into another vehicle for liberal ideals. Once again, the historians merely mirrored their age.

Writing from the British delegation's headquarters in Paris, in January 1919, Webster found time to consider his plans for the post-war teaching of history at Liverpool after his demobilisation. He wanted to modernise the curriculum, weighting it towards recent history and away from the medieval: the war, he felt, had convincingly demonstrated the need to relate historical study to the present; his words carry a sense of urgency and mission.[30] This sense of purpose arising out of the need to understand the modern world and to inculcate the right principles, so evident in the plans of both Temperley and Webster, also affected the men who funded the new chairs of International Affairs. Two of these were held by Webster. The first (the first of its kind in Britain), the Wilson Chair (after Woodrow Wilson) of International Politics at Aberystwyth was founded by private gift in 1918. Its trust deeds were completed by 1922 and Webster became its first occupant. The subject of the Chair was defined as 'Political Science in its application to international relations with special reference to the best means of promoting peace between nations'. It was founded in memory of the students of the college who had died in the Great War, and its teaching duties were limited to one term a year explicitly to allow the occupant to travel and research in pursuit of the founder's ideals.[31] Webster, given his background and his membership of the League of Nations Peace Union, was a natural for the job. When he later applied to be Toynbee's successor as the Stevenson Professor of International History at the London School of Economics in 1932, he found similar expectations: the holder had to be 'in sympathy with the

desire of the founder of the Chair to promote a spirit of international
co-operation, peace and goodwill through the teaching of history on an
international basis'. His work should be 'free so far as possible from
national prejudice, bias or prepossession'.[32] Sir David Stevenson had
worried about the jingoistic effect of nationalist history in schools and
elsewhere; and believed that history, property taught, could be a force
for international goodwill.[33]

The mood of relevance was very strong generally. Another wartime
intelligence veteran, R.W. Seton-Watson, had written a plea for the
study of contemporary history, specifically arguing that 'a close study
of recent history is an essential corollary of the new international peace
movement which centres round the League of Nations, and on which
the avoidance of fresh upheavals must so largely depend'. A proper
study of recent times would help to create a new world and mentality'.[34] Charles Manning, Professor of International Relations at the
LSE, wrote to Webster as the recent appointee to the International
History Chair, to ask if he would ensure the relevance of his lectures
to current international problems; Webster, of course, accepted this
principle.[35] At about the same time, Eileen Power, another recent LSE
professorial appointment, who was on a committee to revise school textbooks 'from the point of view of international friendship', bewailed the
'remoteness' of Oxford scholarship: Oxford historians, she told Webster,
'were just like flies in amber'. She recalled the story of how Emperor
Frederick Hohenstaufen had shut up twelve infants with dumb nurses
for ten years to see what language they would speak: she was sure
'that when he came back again they were all talking with Oxford
accents'. (She had similar worries about the teaching of economics
— 'all curves and disdainfully remote from any application
to real life', even at the LSE.)[36] Later on, Webster claimed to have
been influenced by Croce in his belief 'that history must be continually
reviewed and rewritten in the light of subsequent events'.[37] References
to Croce's dictum that all history was contemporary history proliferated
in the interwar period; though this probably does not reflect any deep
understanding of Croce's metaphysics, it does illustrate the extent to
which recent events had converted many historians to the principle of
relevance.

Of course, not all had been converted. Powicke, even in 1921, when the
tide ran strongly for both internationalism and relevance, had doubted
the wisdom of revising textbooks along League of Nations principles.
Scholarly expertise and scientific standards were enough to ensure
impartiality; the occasional rogue would be all too evident; nationalism

had not been the major inspiration behind historical works.[38] Professional-ism ensured impartiality. The scientific ideal, with the emphasis upon professionalism, was still alive. In general, however, the war and the peace had stimulated a lively concern to be relevant and to be on the side of the angels. It can be argued that each new branch of the discipline of history had been introduced into the curriculum, and its works into the canon, in order to fulfil a political and moral purpose;[39] and international history seems to have been no exception, its mission being to international-ise morality.

That Webster should have followed up *The Congress of Vienna*, which had been explicitly and officially relevant, with his major study of the foreign policy of Castlereagh (published in 1931), the British statesman whose diplomacy most strikingly represented an attachment to the con-cert of Europe, was wholly appropriate to the post-war years. His old Foreign Office colleague, Harold Temperley, who was finally posted to Belgrade, was, it is true, an ardent supporter of nationalism in Europe, as befitted an expert on the nationalities of Eastern Europe. But his nationalism was very much the liberal nationalism of self-determination; he was well suited to assist into practice the Wilsonian ideals of the Peace Conference. Just as Castlereagh was an ideal subject for Webster, so Can-ning's foreign policy, with its support for liberal nationalism, was an ideal topic for Temperley. A recent comment upon Temperley has described his works as 'tombstones on the grave of the romantic liberal of 1905 who, like so many other Liberals of his generation, was left high-and-dry by the death of the Liberal party in the 1920's;' Temperley's 'natural home' was 'the Liberal party and the Liberal university'.[40] This seems somewhat glib; though it is true that foreign affairs, from the 1848 revolutions to the Vietnam War, have proved highly seductive to liberals unsure of their role at home.

Included in the list of Temperley's 'tombstones' was the multi-volume collection of *British Documents on the Origin of the War* which he and Gooch edited. G.P. Gooch never held a university post; he came from a prosperous upper middle-class background and did not need a career. A product of Trinity College, Cambridge, in the 1890s, he later claimed that Acton had been the key figure in his early intellectual development. He visited the University of Berlin and heard Treitschke lecture, admiring his skill but deprecating his chauvinism and worship of force. In France he admired French democracy and individualism but, as a devout Angli-can, objected to French scepticism. Significantly, his first work was *The History of English Democratic Ideas in the Seventeenth Century* (1898), a defence of Protestant individualism as the basis of modern egalitarian ideas. He acquired a growing sense of the social responsibilities inherent within society. Hostile to the Boer War, he was politicised, becoming acquainted with both Liberals like Leonard Courtney, who was the key influence on Unwin, and socialists of varying persuasions, such as the Hammonds and Ramsay MacDonald. He opposed the *Realpolitik* notions of imperial expansion then common, regretted the influence of Bismarckian methods of diplomacy, and opposed the influence of Social Darwinism in foreign affairs and the ideas of Karl Pearson. He believed that states were bound by the same moral standards as individuals.[41] In short, he had the classic liberal attitudes of the Edwardian period, including a strong dose of individualism mitigated by a sense of social duty, and a commitment to internationalism. There was a Christian basis to his individualism: nothing stood between the soul and God. His liberalism found practical expression as a Liberal MP and as PPS to Bryce between 1906 and 1910. His approach to history has been summed up as follows:

> It was fundamental to Gooch's conception of history that he rejected any determinist view of the past. There are no foregone conclusions, there is no inevitability in history. He was entirely out of sympathy with attempts by different philosophies of history to detect a pattern in development, such as were later made by Toynbee. Personality plays a part, not only in the shape of the occasional 'great man', but also through the many human beings in humbler roles who collectively make their contribution to the course of events. There is room for individuals to make their decisions, which in their sum total can change events. Gooch could not envisage the past without at least a limited freedom of will. He also allowed for the effect of passion and accident in history.[42]

Unwittingly perhaps, we have here an almost perfect summary of the liberal tradition in history.

With a German wife, and four years of experience as co-editor of *The Contemporary Review* which, under his leadership, was known for publishing articles with a liberal approach to international affairs, Gooch resisted the rush to denounce the entire German cultural heritage in 1914 and 1915, pointing to the alternatives to Treitschke and the worship of the state. He allowed Morel and the Union of Democratic Control access to *The Contemporary Review*. Though he wrote for the historical section of the Foreign Office, he also wrote for the League of Nations Society. He denounced the doctrine of the state as unfettered by no higher moral code, identifying Machiavelli, Hobbes, Hegel and Treitschke as its authors. He also contributed to *A Century of British Foreign Policy* (1917), prepared by the Council for the Study of International Relations; he dealt with the fourteen years prior to the outbreak of the war. The evidence of this is that he had already established his ideas on the origin of the war, the ideas that guided his selection and co-editing of *British Documents on the Origins of the War*; and that these attitudes were underpinned by his liberal ideas.[43]

He and Temperley, the latter specifically requested by Gooch, were perfectly placed for resisting the considerable pressure brought to bear upon them in the late 1920s by the Conservative Government to adapt their works to the diplomatic needs of the day: Temperley had Foreign Office experience himself and was by then an experienced diplomatic historian; Gooch had an independent position to go with his liberal views — he even refused payment for his work. Their heroic struggles to maintain their independence, including their final threat to resign, thus leaving any subsequent publications with a real credibility problem, are well charted in Eyck's biography of Gooch, and would make salutary reading for any official or 'public' historians.

Gooch rejected the notions that the national interest was the sole legitimate determinant of state policy, that war was an extension of foreign policy and that power was the state's most desirable and inherent quality. One of the qualities that made democracy preferable to monarchy was the former's relative reluctance to go to war, for war was always 'a bad business . . . whatever the result' for 'Victory can never decide the question of right'. He looked forward to a Europe consisting of 'a loose federation of unarmed and self-governing communities, settling their disputes by arbitration'.[45] This was a world away from *Realpolitik*, the *Machstaat*, and war as a test of national principle.

Though he had deliberately avoided the anti-German hysteria of 1914, which had focused on Treitschke in particular, Gooch did in due course deliver a considered but very powerful statement on the importance of the countervailing liberal tradition in international relations. The occasion was a lecture on *The Prince*; the message was one of hope for liberal principles in the future. He saw a link between Machiavelli and Hegel in that Hegel had moralized Machiavelli's *raison d'état*, denying the binding validity of international law, legitimizing war as a natural product of state action, seeing the state as 'the realized ethical idea'. Treitschke had followed Hegel, praising Machiavelli for recognising the state as power; but criticising him for not seeing that power was *moral*. Treitschke's message was:

> . . . the moral and spiritual grandeur of large and powerful states. Little states are out of date for they cannot defend themselves. The state stands high above the individuals who compose it, and it exists in order to realize ideals far above individual happiness. It can only fulfil its function if it is strong. It need not inquire if its actions are approved or disapproved by its subjects, for it is the guardian of the national tradition and a trustee of unborn generations.

Nor did it owe allegiance to any external authority. War could be 'whole-some and elevating . . . an instrument of statesmanship and a school of patriotism' and 'the only medicine for a sick people. It is idealism that demands war and materialism that rejects it. Dreams of perpetual peace are the mark of a stagnant and decadent generation, for conflict is the law of life'. Then he quoted Treitschke directly: 'The hope of banishing war is not only meaningless but immoral, for its disappearance would turn the earth into a temple of selfishness'. And he quoted Moltke in similar vein. Gooch concluded: 'With such a philosophy we shall never succeed in organizing the world; for the cult of power leads to the twin evils of the idolatory of the state and the glorification of war'. Gooch was committed to a liberal progressive view of international relations; he saw peace and the rule of law between nations as the logical extension of the rule of law in domestic affairs. He regarded the view that the state was the sole source of morality as primitive and outmoded. He had an optimistic view of human nature, and believed in the moral superiority of democratic principles. Democracies did not have a will to power, and the will to power was not 'the sole key to human nature'. Democracy and pacifism were both expressions of faith in the ultimate sanity of the common man. Though he was speaking in 1935, he insisted that the contemporary dictatorships would prove but a temporary setback. The 'supermen' would pass away; western civilization would find its characteristic way once again, foster-ing individuality, humanizing social life and 'moralizing' policies. The cataclysm of the Great War should have taught men wisdom. The nation was not an end in itself, merely an (indispensable) bridge between the individual and the wider human family. Nations were a necessary, indeed organic, stage in the evolution of mankind; but were only the first part of the story. The 'new trinity' (almost blasphemous for a man of Gooch's religious views, were it not for his obvious seriousness of moral, indeed religious, purpose) was the individual, the nation and the whole human family. It was a passionate appeal for the principles of the League of Nations, with Kant ranged against Machiavelli, Gladstone against Bis-marck, and the Wilsonian Peace against the war itself.[46] These were noble sentiments, nobly put, and surely sincerely felt. But more than that, they were an expression of faith in a system of ethics that did not depend on the state but looked to a higher loyalty and a universal code.

By the time Gooch was writing, so eloquently, the liberal individualism resurrected by the Great War had become firmly re-established; but, for many, the ideal of extending liberal principles to the international arena had become soured by events. In the next chapter we turn to consider the extent to which revived liberalism succeeded in providing itself with an effective philosophy and a convincing social and political purpose besides that of internationalism.

NOTES

1. A.F. Pollard, 'The Growth of an Imperial Parliament', *History*, i (1916), 138.
2. H.W.C. Davis, *The Political Thought of Heinrich von Treitschke* (London, 1914).
3. E. Barker *et al*, *Why we are at War: Great Britain's Case*, third edition (Oxford, 1914), pp. 6, 108-117.
4. J.R.H. Weaver, A. Lane Poole, *Henry William Carless Davis 1874-1928. A Memoir and a Selection of His Historical Papers* (London, 1933), p. 12.
5. Smith Papers, Box 211A-1, *The War and Our Social Duty* (Christian Social Union Pamphlet, 47, Mowbray, Oxford, 1915).
6. Smith Papers, Box 211A-1, 'The War, Education, and Co-operation' (Address to the Educational meeting of the Co-operative Union Ltd., Manchester, 1916), pp. 3,6.
7. Prothero Papers, *Our Duty and Our Interest in the War* (London, 1914); *How Goes the War?* (London, n.d.). The latter was written ten months into the war.
8. R. Muir, *Britain's Case Against Germany: An Examination of the Historical Background of the German Action in 1914* (Manchester, 1914), pp. vii-ix, 2-3, 45.
9. E. Barker *et al*, *Why we are at War*, p. 112.
10. R. Muir, *Op.cit.*, pp. 51-55, 63-67, 77.
11. *Ibid.*, pp. 166-190.
12. S. Collini, 'Hobhouse, Bosanquet and the State: Philosophical Idealism and Political Argument in England 1880-1918', *Past and Present* 72 (1976), 89.
13. W. McDougall, *Op.cit.*, p. ix.
14. J.H. Muirhead, *Bernard Bosanquet and his friends: Letters illustrating the sources and the development of his philosophical opinions* (London, 1935), pp. 161-162.
15. Bosanquet to Haldane, 11 June 1912, *Ibid.*, p. 54.
16. Bosanquet to Hoernle, 24 January 1915. *Ibid.*, pp. 163-167.
17. *Ibid.*, pp. 167, 190-191.
18. *Ibid.*, pp. v-vii.
19. *Ibid.*, pp. 1-19.
20. Bosanquet, *The Philosophical Theory of the State*, pp. ix-xii, xlv, xlvii.
21. *Ibid.*, pp. lx-lxi.
22. A.F. Pollard, 'History and Science: A Rejoinder', *History*, i (1916), pp. 27, 39.
23. Fisher Papers, 55, Letters to and from Gilbert Murray 1920-1940, Fisher to Murray, 7 January 1920.
24. These brief notes on his career have been culled from: British Library of Economic and Political Science, London School of Economics, Report on the correspondence and papers of Sir Charles Kingsley Webster (1886-1961), Historian, 1906-1962 (Royal Commission on Historical Manuscripts, Quality House, for the B.L.E.P.S., 1977, LSE) pp. iv-ix.
25. B.L.E.P.S., Webster Papers, 23/6 Draft for a chapter of C.K.W.'s autobiography: on the Congress of Vienna.
26. J. Namier, *Lewis Namier, A Biography* (London, 1917), pp. 122, 152.
27. E.H. Carr, *What is History?* (London, 1961), p. 61.
28. J.R.H. Weaver, A. Lane Poole, *Henry William Carless Davis*, pp. 33, 39.
29. Webster Papers, 1/3 (30), 'Suggestions to Contributors' from the editor, 'The Paris Peace Conference', c/o Sir Ernest Hodder Williams, Hodder Stoughton and Co.

30.   Webster Papers, 3/9 (125), Webster to Veitch, 8 January 1919.

31.   Webster Papers, 5/2 (1), Memo on the Department of International Politics, U.C. of Wales, Aberystwyth.

32.   Webster Papers, 6/1 (3), Information on 'Stevenson Chair of International History tenable at London School of Economics'.

33.   Webster Papers, 6/1 (106), 'Stevenson Joint Committee (LSE and Royal Institute of International Affairs): Agenda for first meeting at Royal Institute of International Affairs, Chatham House'. The R.I.I.A. was itself founded by men who had been delegates to the Paris Peace Conference.

34.   R.W. Seton-Watson, 'A Plea for the Study of Contemporary History', *History*, 14 (1929), 17.

35.   Webster Papers, 6/1 (69), Charles Manning to Webster, 29 March 1932.

36.   *Ibid.*, 6/1 (72), E[ileen Power] to Webster, 5 April n.d.

37.   *Ibid.*, 6/6 (2) 'The position of history in the Examination for the degree of B.Sc. (Econ.)', 20 June 1946.

38.   F.M. Powicke, 'History Lessons and the League', *Modern Historians and the Study of History* (London 1955), pp. 159-163. This piece originally appeared in *The Manchester Guardian*, 12 March 1921.

39.   C.J.W. Parker, 'History as Present Politics', *Contexts and Connections: Winchester Research Papers in the Humanities* (Winchester, 1980).

40.   M. Cowling, *Religion and Public Doctrine in Modern England* (Cambridge, 1980), i, 212-219.

41.   F. Eyck, *G.P. Gooch, A Study in History and Politics* (London, 1982), pp. 29, 31-33, 38-45, 57-58, 62, 73. See also pp. 74-80.

42.   *Ibid.*, pp. 98, 227.

43.   *Ibid.*, pp. 247-253, 272-273, 275, 284.

44.   *Ibid.*, pp. 331-381.

45.   G.P. Gooch, 'The French Revolution as a World Force' (1920), *Studies in Diplomacy and Statecraft* (London, 1942), p. 310.

46.   G.P. Gooch, 'Politics and Morals', *Ibid.*, pp. 317-328.

CHAPTER 6

Liberalism Besieged

The Great War had changed much more than people's attitudes to peace and war; it had changed the map of Europe and changed the colour of many of its regimes. New threats and new instabilities appeared to threaten not only the international peace but the internal security of states, perhaps even of England itself, the home of liberalism, constitutionalism and the rule of law, the national embodiment of those principles that our diplomatic historians were even now seeking to extend to the international stage. Liberals saw militant left and militant right as twin enemies, just as Marxists saw liberal democrats and fascists as merely the less militant and the more militant wings of embattled capitalism (Stalin even seeing social democrats as the social wing of fascism), as Nazis denounced Weimar and Soviet Republic alike, and as *Action Française* saw the Third Republic as a permanent treason that would lead to an equally repugnant socialist republic. Polarity is relative. The assumption that right and left were, not only equally repellent, but repellent for the same reason, goes back much further than the Cold War when 'totalitarianism' in both its fascist and Stalinist forms was the designated enemy. It probably goes back well beyond the Great War and the October Revolution. It certainly was expressed within a few months of the ending of the war.

On 10 May 1919, R.G. Collingwood addressed a conference of Belgian students on 'The Spiritual Basis of Reconstruction'. Attacking 'Prussianism' in a way with which we are now familiar, he denounced it as a theory of the state that denied the individual any power for good or evil, and that insisted the state was the only creative, original power, almost a God — 'a being answerable to no-one but itself, and possessing absolute right and absolute power over its own members, while owning no duties, no obligations, no responsibilities towards any other state'. This theory he ascribed to Hegel. He further characterised it as follows: 'towards other states the state is merely force, and the more perfectly it is a state the more perfectly it shows itself as force. There is nothing one state can do to another except conquer it. The will of the state can only be defined as a will to power'. He identified Nietzsche as the exponent of this logical conclusion of the Hegelian tendency — a highly questionable, but at the time not unusual

119

assertion. Germany had suffered from a 'spiritual disease' that 'caused the war'. As we have seen, this is so far standard stuff. But Collingwood went further. According to him, the Hegelian absolutist tradition had split into monarchist and socialist forms; Marx and Lenin were in the same tradition as Hegel, advocating 'a socialism which is Prussianist in its glorification of aggression, of war, and of tyranny'. Much of what else he had to say was typical of the period: there should be no power above the law, for true power depended on the law, and this principle should be extended to international affairs. Like other historians of the time, he thought that the imperialism of the British Empire was morally superior to recent German expansionism. His explanation was that the rule of the more civilised over the less civilised was a progressive, beneficent force, whereas German imperialism had been attempted in the totally 'improper sphere' of Europe. Though clearly a case of special pleading, this argument fitted with standard assumptions about the benefits of rule under English law, and would have appealed to a recently liberated Belgium. But, again, he took the argument further: 'if Germany had conquered Europe our own civilisations, our own liberties would have been destroyed but the ideal of class-war may yet conquer Europe, and the result will be the same': irrespective of outcome, it would mean 'disaster and death, the destruction of civilisation'.

Collingwood, the major figure in the philosophy of history during the inter-war period, was totally committed to an engaged role in defence of liberalism against fascism and Marxism. Many critics, acquainted only with the closing passages of *An Autobiography* (1939) have found this view of Collingwood unconvincing, seeing only an attempt to catch the transient mood of the aftermath of Munich. But a wider knowledge of his papers and writings of the inter-war period, both on political themes and on the philosophy behind the politics, exonerates him from any charge of opportunism: he knew what he was against and why he was against it.

The oft-criticised passage from his autobiography was an explicit state-ment of his commitment to democracy and the liberal principles of active citizenship and representative government based on a wide franchise, a free press, and freedom of speech, which would prevent oppression and bring grievances to light. Democracy, a national school of political experience as well as a political system, created an informed public opinion and was thus stronger than the strongest authoritarianism; it was worth defending, at all costs. Though Marx regarded democracy as a capitalist fraud for exploiting workers (and there were examples of oppression and exploitation), the point was to change things through the system rather than to abolish it. The system was 'self-correcting'. It was threatened, however by the cheap and nasty popular press such as *The Daily Mail*, and by populist politicians as typified by Lloyd George. So weakened, could it withstand the twin challenges of Marxism and fascism? Collingwood believed that progress could be achieved without class war and that fascism was but 'an incoherent caricature of socialism's worst features'. But he was also highly critical of the National Government, particularly of non-intervention in the Spanish Civil War, appeasement and its rearmament policies. Rather hysterically, perhaps, he ended by suggesting that the government had not only failed to defend democracy abroad but might threaten democracy within; he feared that the half century of misinformation and decline of the public spirit, which he perceived, and blamed on governments and press, would prove fatal to British democracy. Rather portentously, he renounced the role of 'detached professional thinker', and committed himself with these final words:

> I know now that the minute philosophers of my youth, for all their profession of a purely scientific detachment from practical affairs, were the propagandists of a coming Fascism. I know that Fascism means the end of clear thinking and the triumph of irrationalism. I know that all my life I have been engaged unawares in a political struggle, fighting against these things in the dark. Henceforth I shall fight in the daylight.[2]

Self-important as this sounds, it was the logical conclusion of his autobiography, even if he did play down the extent to which he had fought 'in the daylight' before 1938. The 'minute philosophers' of his youth were the 'realists', like Prichard, who had divorced philosophy from the real world of political life, and had destroyed moral philosophy, arguing that knowing does not affect the known and, therefore that human action could not be affected by knowing about it. (The parallel with the 'realist' school of historians is clear.) The realist philosophers had replaced the high seriousness of purpose of Idealists, like T.H. Green, who had believed in their pedagogical function, with an amoral intellectual game, argued Collingwood. They denied their educative responsibility to a generation of future rulers. Consequently, they had trained up a generation well suited to be the 'potential dupes of every adventurer in morals or politics, commerce or religion'.[3]

If we turn from his autobiography to other sources, the picture is consistent. Letters to the Italian Idealist philosopher, de Ruggiero, in the twenties, illustrate this. In English philosophy, he wrote in 1927, the realism of Moore dominated, and its political impact was mainly negative, leading to 'academic paralysis of practical energy, except where, by its materialistic pluralism it fosters socialistic inclinations'. He regretted that de Ruggiero's 'idealistic liberalism' was unlikely to win English adherents, reminiscent as it was of the currently unfashionable Green — and 'today the fashionable colour is red'.[4] It is interesting to note that, whereas adventurers and fascists were likely beneficiaries of amoral realism in 1938, in 1927 it was materialistic socialism that was the threat. Collingwood certainly had a low opinion of socialism in these years, referring for example to Joad as 'not a philosopher but a socialist', who made Collingwood feel ashamed of his own country.[5] Whereas, by 1938, even Marx, the founder of 'Prussian' socialism, received grudging praise: though Marx's ideas were unconvincing, he was at least 'a fighting philosopher' who sought to improve the world, and preferable, therefore, to the realists or even to J.S. Mill, whose liberalism was founded on scepticism as to the value of thought itself.[6]

This changing identification of the main enemy was legitimate, given the changing political circumstances, but his identification of hostile intellectual trends, be they Positivism in historiography before 1920, realism in philosophy after 1919, socialism in the politics of the twenties, or fascism in the thirties, does suggest that he liked to feel isolated, an 'outlaw' as he put it in one of his letters to de Ruggiero.[7] This would square with his heroic stand, in 1938, against the iniquities of his age. His position was sincere, however, and quite legitimate in terms of his Idealist metaphysic. Man, he argued, lived 'not in a world of "hard facts" to which "thoughts" make no difference, but in a world of "thoughts" . . . If you change the moral, political and economic "theories" generally accepted' by society 'you change the character of his world'. Moreover, if you change the theories, you change the way you behave.[8]

A sense of despair and isolation was, however, very strong in 1936. Cataclysm was imminent; society was sick unto death; nobody had confidence in the future; man had gone mad. Characteristics of the madness were the vast extension of warfare and the domination of the state by its armaments programme. He scorned both the deterrent theory and the idea that war was 'the ultimate end of the modern state'. Modern warfare could destroy civilisation. Meanwhile, liberalism had collapsed. He defined liberalism as 'the idea of a community as governing itself by fostering the free expression of all political opinions that take shape within it, and finding some means of reducing this multiplicity of opinions to a unity'. Dependent, therefore, on free discussion, on a 'dialectical solution of all political problems', on common ground, and political activity open to all, it needed a politically mature people and peace. The right attacked liberalism, wanting more efficiency, despatch, expertise, authority and unity; for a generation, liberal principles had been sacrificed to 'efficiency' and bureaucratic authority; parliament was held in contempt, even in Britain, 'the home of the parliamentary system'. Authoritarianism threatened. 'This jettison of the liberal principles which our civilisation so long and painfully acquired — a jettison conscious and violent in Germany and Italy, careless and almost absent-minded in our country — is political madness'. He exaggerated the domestic threat posed by the lethargy of the public spirit in the mid-thirties; but he felt genuinely and legitimately depressed by the European situation in general — not least because of his wide circle of acquaintances on the Continent. In 1936 he still reserved harsh words for the left as well as the right, accusing the left of misreading the liberal position and of pretending to some of liberalism's principles whilst planning to use anti-liberal methods. Marxist socialism, in particular, he still associated with Hegelianism; and insisted that liberalism, though it had failed to implement its principles in foreign relations, was the more advanced form of political thought, unencumbered with the obsolete ideas of left and right. Failure on the international front was explained as follows:

> The liberal state of the nineteenth century conceived itself as an individual among individuals, in that false sense of individuality which makes it synonymous with mutual exclusiveness, and denies that between one individual and another there may be organic relations such that the welfare of each is necessary to that of the other. The liberal government which 'trusted the people' hated and feared peoples other than its own.

In other words, he said, internal liberalism had combined with external illiberalism to create international anarchy, which had driven states to their current militarism. Collingwood touches here upon two of our main themes — the need to extend liberal principles to international affairs, and the rejection of the notion of the state as an historical 'individual' without international responsibilities other than maintenance of its own power. The *Machstaat* principle was rejected on the grounds that just as individuals had responsibility to the state, so the state was organically related to a wider sphere of responsibility and had international duties.

In domestic affairs, the liberal principle had also been taken too far in terms of economic liberalism; echoing Toynbee's Oxford lectures on the industrial revolution, he argued that excessive economic liberalism had fostered socialism. Collingwood clearly takes his place amongst the classic exponents of the New Liberalism and the League of Nations enthusiasts who sought to extend these principles onto the international stage. By the mid-thirties, however, he had also become something of a Cassandra:

the following teleological passage shows the strength of the Whig-Liberal tradition of thought, but grown pessimistic with the years:

> For three hundred years, civilised man has been working out a liberal system of political method, applying it, bit by bit, to the various parts of his corporate life. Now, because the application has not proved exhaustive, because there are still some regions unreclaimed by this method, it seems that man had decided no longer to use it, but to throw it away and live a life solitary, poor, nasty, brutish, and short.[9]

Thus Collingwood, deliberately echoing Hobbes, feared for the collapse of the liberal spirit that had held sway between Hobbes and modern authoritarianism. These passages, from a 1936 manuscript, 'Man Goes Mad', anticipate much that Collingwood later published in *An Autobiography*, in an article entitled 'Fascism and Nazism' (*Philosophy*, 1940), and in *The New Leviathan* (1942). It also closely paralleled Croce's contemporary work in Italy.[10] Idealism in its individualist form had clearly become the dominant form of liberalism since the war, yet it still felt threatened by new forms of authoritarianism. In 'Fascism and Nazism', Collingwood argued that the basis of individualist liberalism in the West had been religious — a belief in the 'love of God who set an absolute value on every individual human being' and whose son died to save every individual soul. Whilst the religious spirit died, liberal Christian morality lived on, secularised but without inspiration, unable therefore to withstand the onslaught of fanatical, authoritarian-minded minorities in Italy, Germany and Spain. It was the duty of philosophers, he argued, to help towards an understanding of these illiberal tendencies that had inspired the foe: 'what our soldiers and sailors and airmen have to fight, our philosophers have to understand'.[11] The need to understand Treitschke and Bernhardi in 1914 had become the need to understand Nazism and Fascism in 1940.

The New Leviathan was a surely misconceived attempt at political thought on a grand scale, an unsuccessful attempt to replace Hobbes, and a strange mixture of political philosophy, comment on contemporary affairs, and purely idiosyncratic speculation about concepts like 'civilisation' and 'barbarism'. Rather like Whitehead's *Adventures of Ideas* (1933), it was a decidedly capricious piece, more like an eighteenth century 'philosophical history' than anything else. Perhaps its weaknesses owe something to Collingwood's fatal illness. But it was, in other ways, a fitting climax to the work of the politically-engaged Collingwood evident since 1936 at least, if not earlier. He reiterated his criticism of both the Hegelian statist tradition and Marxism, which he still saw as linked.[12] Also, he developed his 'dialectical' theory of liberalism. Starting with individual free will, he argued that 'freedom of the will is, positively, *freedom to choose*; freedom to exercise a will, and, negatively, freedom *from desire*; not the condition of having no desires, but the condition of not being at their mercy'. It was not possible to become free by choosing — that would anticipate freedom; the individual had to become free by an involuntary act, which would bring a 'consciousness of being free' and, as a consequence, 'self-respect'.[13] He then distinguished between social and non-social communities: the former were genuine self-forming and self-ruling societies; the latter, not freely formed, had a distinction between rulers and ruled. The modern body politic, like the family, was a mixed community constantly evolving towards the really social community by a dialectical process: the rulers were constantly being permeated by the ruled (or the adults by the growing children); the rulers were real 'persons', possessed of free will. The dialectical element was in the adaptation of the ruled to being ruled by their particular rulers, and the adaptation of the rulers to ruling their particular subjects: politically, this meant that both conservative and liberal forces were at work in the dialectical process. This system had operated in nineteenth century England, said Collingwood, with great effect; only in the twentieth century had the dialectical process been neglected, and liberalism had disappeared.[14] This seems to be a modern version of Whiggism: gradual emancipation of those who had become free to choose; measured, liberal, open-ended progress. The only problem was, at the time of writing, something had gone wrong with the process.

Each state had within it elements of 'civilisation' and of 'barbarism'. 'Civilisation' involved behaving 'civilly', abstaining from shocking, annoying, frightening or emotionally disturbing a fellow citizen, for this might weaken his self-respect and, thereby, threaten his consciousness of freedom by making it seem as if his freedom of choice was threatened by his passion or desire. Similarly, civil relations had to avoid force. Free will was, therefore, equated with civilisation, just as democratisation was seen as the archetypal progress from a non-social (or partially social) society to a fully civilised and social community. But the process of civilisation could be reversed. Barbarism was also a process which accentuated the barbaric elements in a community — the non-social, non-voluntary elements. The Turks and the Germans had produced the two modern versions of barbarism. This was a negative, destructive process, in contrast to the 'civil' process of living dialectically, respecting the freedom of others, living peacefully, under the rule of law, and with the greater potential for economic and social progress.[15]

The New Leviathan was a brave, if flawed, effort to breathe new life into traditional liberalism, to provide it with a text as influential as the original *Leviathan* had supposedly been. It chimed perfectly with his historical method, which involved the individualistic assumption that history was about the actions of human individuals — actions which could only be understood by a critical rethinking of the thoughts behind the actions; it fitted with his insistence that only such rethinking could be an effective guide to what man could do and what man could be. It was an Idealist approach to analysing social and political trends in terms of 'civilisation' and 'barbarism' — and crucial to his definition of the former was his own version of what constituted free will and the dignity of the individual. Though posthumous publication raised Collingwood's reputation and influence after the Second World War in terms of his philosophy of historical knowledge, *The New Leviathan* and his social and political ideas sank almost without trace. Outside of the sphere of international affairs, the liberal idea looked decidedly insecure in the inter-war years and after.

The sense that liberalism was under threat in the inter-war years, both politically and intellectually, was very strong amongst historians, including those who were much less philosophically inclined than Collingwood who was, after all, from a professional point of view, a philosopher first and an historian second, but not (as we shall see) atypical in other respects. Of two of these historians, Butterfield and Brogan, it has been said that the central political experiences of their lives were the collapse of the Liberal Party in the 1920s and the fall of France in 1940 — both liberal catastrophes, from which they never really recovered.[16] Another in many ways representative of the type, H.A.L. Fisher, was himself involved in Liberal Party politics, having been recruited during the Great War, and active until 1926. In 1920 he was still confident that, thought the party was split, liberalism would remain a force in British politics.[17] When he abandoned political life in 1926, his friend, Gilbert Murray, regretted his loss to the party, but felt that 'if Liberalism is to be re-built it must be re-built slowly and thoughtfully, outside parliament. Jowett and Green and Arthur Sidgwick did probably as much for the liberalism of our time as most of the practical politicians'. Fisher, he felt could do the same in Oxford, as Warden of New College; Fisher's practical experience would be of enormous influence, he felt, even with those who were, strictly speaking, partisan opponents, such as Lindsay (Master of Balliol since 1924, and well known as a Labour Party sympathiser) and G.D.H. Cole. Fisher, he hoped, might save Oxford, 'this appalling place', from itself.[18]

In fact, Fisher's impact at Oxford was slight, despite his excellent connections. His father had been private secretary to the Prince of Wales, and the Prince became Fisher's godfather. 'Eminence', wrote his biographer, 'came to Fisher as a duty and a birth right'. Winchester was followed by 'Greats' and then a New College fellowship. After a spell as Vice-Chancellor of Sheffield University, he became Lloyd George's President of the Board of Trade in 1916, with responsibility for the Education Act of 1918 and a considerable role in drafting and piloting the Government of Ireland Bill (1920); he was also a delegate to the League of Nations in Geneva. Yet, despite all this, his return to Oxford did nothing to regenerate the intellectual bases of liberalism. He remained involved with the League — a touchstone of 'liberal' attitudes, and he got involved with the famous Peace Ballot of 1935, of which episode his biographer wrote: 'he was an idealist member of an idealist political party, and in common with many contemporaries he was induced to give public support to a movement which assumed that these ideals, so much valued by ourselves, can be shipped across the Channel'. (Writing in the immediate post-Second World War years, Ogg assumed that German attitudes were inherently different from British ones.)[19] This could be taken as a partial explanation for Fisher's failure: liberal internationalism seemed to be increasingly ineffective in the 1930s. His now famous pessimism about the lack of pattern in history and the play of the contingent and unforeseen may also account for a lack of dynamism, typical perhaps of liberalism between the wars. His age must also be taken into account — he was sixty when he returned to Oxford; also he had never been a specialist historian and, as Master of a college, had no incentive to become one after a long absence from academic life. Politically, the tide refused to turn for his old party in 1929, and after that it was a broken force. His major literary production, his *History of Europe* (1935), was not a specialist work, nor was it based on up-to-date scholarship and, though vastly influential in schools and amongst the general public, for which it was much reprinted, the day when such a survey, however elegantly written and superficially wise, could have academic influence, was gone.

His Ralegh Lecture of 1928, on 'The Whig Historians', is quite revealing. Fisher's archetypal Whigs were Macaulay and G.O. Trevelyan. Such Whig historians were, he said, well-connected and shared in (or had access to) 'the society of governing people'. They were not academic teachers, but men of affairs and of leisure; so they understood the reality of political life. Of course, he could have been talking about himself. 'They believed that public affairs were best regulated when they were in the hands of the middle-class, supported by the most enlightened members of the aristocracy and the most prudent section of the artisan population'. They had, however, been wrong to fear universal suffrage and colonial parliaments; Fisher blamed these mistakes on their atypical, un-Whiggish acceptance of the Austinian doctrine of indivisible sovereignty. Austin (1790-1859) had been the advocate of law as the command of the sovereign. On this matter alone the Whig historians had accepted (spurious) *a priori* reasoning. Thus Fisher out-Whigged the Whigs! In general, he felt that the Whig approach to history was the historical method *par excellence*, precisely because it took the middle ground. Whig history would survive the challenge of 'Tory' history because it applied principles that met with the widest sympathy. The Whigs' only other failing had been their inability to understand the new industrial world after 1832. One would have thought that such a failure spelt immediate political disaster and ultimate disaster for the efficacy of their historical works, but, despite his reservations, Fisher's sympathies for Whiggism are clear, and his liberalism appears as no more than a democratised version of Whiggism, and as such lacked dynamic appeal.

Within two years Butterfield had harsher things to say about the Whig interpretation; but before turning to his attack, with its rather inflated reputation, we need to consider other responses to Fisher's Whiggism and look further at its weaknesses. His 1923 lecture on 'The Commonwealth' suggests that one of the few additions to his traditional Whig-liberalism was unfortunate, and that he was not immune from some of the more illiberal tendencies of the age. Alongside classic liberal ideas (that the individual had public duties, which appealed to both the Whig aristocrat and the post-Green liberal, that wealth honestly acquired and correctly employed was socially acceptable, that material success and high ideals could be combined, and that European civilisation rested on private property), came the disturbing notion that poverty had a eugenic value, and that, therefore, education (and, by implication, any major social welfare programme) could be disadvantageous.[21] And this from the author of the 1918 Education Act! Such a caveat sits uneasily amongst the liberal protestations of moderation, consensus, tolerance, good sense and humanity; but it may have been a factor in the decision by Eyre and Spottiswood's Douglas Jerrold, renegade liberal and fascist sympathiser, to sign up Fisher for his *History of Europe*, in 1931, as a response to H.G. Wells' *The Outline of World History* (1920), which seemed to worry everybody.[22] Both literary and 'minute' historians worried about anybody who did seem to have a message for the general reader. Populism and, perhaps, even democracy and equality were problems for the Whig survivors, doomed, as Ogg said of Fisher, to 'an accelerating process of disillusionment' in the twentieth century.[23]

Christopher Hill, the Marxist historian, identified the weakness of Fisher's position in a devastating demolition of *The History of Europe* when the 1938 revised edition appeared. It was 'in the worst sense of the word Whig'; because it perceived no pattern in history, it aspired to no explanation of history. In practice, however, through slipshod thinking, an Idealist explanation was offered as a substitute for serious explanatory intent — for example, when 'Europe' was idealised in an anthropomorphic way as a participant, willing events.[24] It is doubtful if Fisher's idealist mode of explanation was as unconscious as Hill suggested; Fisher certainly disapproved of materialist explanations and believed, for example, that Europe's problems were 'not economic, but moral and political'.[25] And we should not be surprised at an Idealist leaning in a liberal of his generation. Hill half-recognised this: 'a consequence of this idealist misinterpretation is to give disproportionate weight to individuals acting in movements of the human spirit, as when Fisher wrote "in the initial stages of that great movement of the human spirit . . . Louis Bonaparte played a decisive role"'. Hill accused Fisher of being out of date in his use of secondary sources, of being similarly old-fashioned in ignoring economic interpretations, of being narrowly partisan, and of representing the interests and outlook of the English ruling classes. In a particularly devastating passage, Hill wrote:

> This manner of writing history is bankrupt, and an absconding bankrupt at that. Its denial of the possibility of interpretation conceals its own bland assumption of the absoluteness of the narrow standards of the English ruling class, its impartiality turns out to be a synonym for Liberal politics. Its concentration on the thinking of the past abstracted from its economic background alone makes possible the postulate of 'wayward events', influenced for good or ill by statesmen, inventors of genius, and members of the royal families. Anything can happen, because everything is in the last resort a flight of fancy. History is not influenced by ponderable, analysable, material factors.[26]

Such an onslaught could have been launched on many historians from Carlyle to Fisher; once the secularisation of ideas had relieved man of the notion that men and 'movements' were agents of God's purpose, the vacuousness of many forms of historical explanation was cruelly exposed. Though we might not all accept Hill's materialist assumptions in the narrow form favoured by *The Modern Quarterly*, his attack on Fisher encapsulated the dilemma of most historians in the inter-war period. The majority were either committed to a realist approach that denied not only pattern and purpose in history, but also, therefore, any explanatory model — for all but the minutest human experience; or they floundered between outmoded Whig-liberal principles and the methodological empiricism of the realists. There was a materialist critique of this approach but, whatever intellectual hold it had in parts of Cambridge or in certain rarefied intellectual and political circles, mainly youthful, it was a critique generally ignored by historians, who regarded it as a product of the rigid dogma of a politically dangerous and mistaken sect.

The Cambridge historian, R.E. Balfour, reckoned that not only were the public issues of the day essentially economic and the focus of historical interest on social and economic matters, but the economic *interpretation* of history dominated in place of what he called the 'individualist' and the 'idealist' interpretations of history. One might question his broad assumption here, but in any case it is important to note that his conclusion about the impact of this was not that it was possible to determine the course of history, that history was explicable, but on the contrary:

> Our grandfathers were impressed by man's increasing mastery over circumstances, we rather by the sense of his impotence in the face of blind forces and of human stupidity. It was as natural that they should think of ideas as being the free offspring of the human soul as that we should regard them as merely the rationalisation of their environment, the product not the cause of historical changes.[16]

In other words, materialism had produced liberal pessimism about the weakness of the individual in the face of 'blind forces', not optimism about man's ability to understand and control the course of history. This pessimism was further evidenced by the relativism of the view that, though materialism appeared to be the dominant and unchallengeable mode of explanation, if it too (like all ideas) was but the product of a particular economic base, then, if the base changed, materialism itself would be superseded. In fact, as this caveat indicates, Balfour, like most of those who had supposedly accepted a materialist or economic interpretation of history, was a most reluctant materialist and not at all consistent. He regarded the question of determinism, for example, as a metaphysical issue that need not concern historians, yet asserted that 'historical changes are not the result of impersonal and inevitable tendencies but of particular events. Whether those events were ultimately inevitable or determined, they have the appearance in the actual course of history of being willed or accidental; and it is with that appearance that the historian is concerned'. Whereas Goldwin Smith had once argued that the appearance of free will caused men to act as if they possessed it, and that this was the strongest evidence for its real existence, Balfour merely argued that the historian limit himself to *appearance* — an appearance of will and accident; there was a higher plane of explanation, no doubt, but it was not for the historian. This low aspiration was further compounded: 'the facts of history always escape from our grasp when we attempt to reduce them to an orderly scheme, because that scheme is merely our rationalisation of something, which we know in part and comprehend imperfectly'. He concluded: 'the greatest art of all in the writing of history is to convey all the complexity,the indeterminateness and the cross-currents of the past in a narrative that shall itself be lucid and clear-cut.[27] And that, of course, is precisely the effect that Fisher, and those who wrote like him, did produce. Hill claimed that Fisher's Whiggism, though influential in non-academic circles, was scorned or ignored by academics; but that may apply only to the grand scale of his effort rather than to his mode of explanation. Hill himself believed that this approach to history lay at the root of modern liberal fatalism and supine acceptance of the rise of fascism: there was no point in trying to understand the phenomenon of fascism; it had to be seen as simply a way-ward misfortune — like everything else in history. As Hill put it: 'if nothing is analysable, nothing is predictable. Events in the future will be as wayward as in the past . . . Nothing we can do will influence history (unless we have had an education which fits us for seats in the cabinet)'. Unfortunately, 'the *thoughts* (!) of men may flow into the channels which lead to disaster and barbarism'; (the words were Fisher's, the italics and the exclamation mark were Hill's). Dismayed by both modern barbarism and modern communism, the Whig shrugged his shoulders and hoped they would go away.[28] Despite Hill's criticism, Fisher's work continued to be reprinted or re-edited every year, bar 1939, until 1943, and again in 1949, 1952 and 1957 — and its popularity was only in part due to the fact that, like Wells, Fisher filled a gap; its style and its content found much favour. As for Hill's Marxism, though Hill was later to stress the flexibility of a materialist approach, and indeed his own work was to testify to this, in the thirties it seemed to be too rigid and unimaginative a framework to win wide acceptance.

Another reason, no doubt, why Fisher or anybody else failed to galva-nise Oxford's decadent liberal tradition was that Oxford was difficult to move. It had, after all, appalled Gilbert Murray and Eileen Power, and its realist philosophy had upset Collingwood. At Cambridge, a similar story could be told, of the history school at least. As a student in the 1920s, W.H.B. Court found history at Cambridge to be unenlightening for a young man interested in the social, political and economic problems of his day. As a consequence, he said, Tawney's 'idealistic socialism' was of great influence, filling what would otherwise have been a desperate void. Moving to Harvard for a time, he came across ideas about economics and the social sciences for the first time. 'General ideas on man and society adequate to explain historical change had come to seem to some of us after three years of study for the Historical Tripos the chief want of the Cambridge Historical School in our day. Impressively good scholarship was, it appeared, not quite enough'. But he and his young colleagues 'did not know the intellectual map well enough' to discover what exactly it was that was missing. He said he fell back on Goethe — Goethe's love of the concrete, particular and individual, his insistence that it was only through individuals that he could think his way towards the universal all . . . reinforced all my natural tendencies and prejudices. He was a great help towards continuing to regard historical studies as serious and worthwhile even in an age of universalising science, for which one had a healthy respect'. Clearly, Court could find no guide or solace amongst the historians, no *raison d'être* for the impressive scholarship of the history school beyond that provided well over a century before by one of Carlyle's heroes. In contemporary Europe he saw only 'Russian Marxists', 'Hegelians in the service of Italian Fascism', and 'the Rankeans, conscious and unconscious, who were ensconced in the Government offices and universities of Europe'. Presumably his 'Rankeans' were followers of the Ranke of Actonian myth — critical, colourless, objective and realist. But the point is that he found two competing ideologies, which by and large he rejected (though confessing to being influenced by Marx), and a professional tradition that no longer satisfied and no longer justified the study of the concrete, particular and individual.[29]

By the mid-thirties, Postan, also of Cambridge, discoursing on history and the social sciences, even claimed that the historian's 'critical attitude to minutiae', ensured that only those of 'a cautious and painstaking disposition, not necessarily endowed with any aptitude for theoretical synthesis' were attracted to the subject. He felt there was a crisis in 'the intellectual state of modern historiography' and urged historians to reacquire some concern with 'social generalisations'.[30] At Cambridge in the thirties, Court said plaintively, the economists had Keynes, but the historians had no-one;[31] his biographical essay is entitled 'Growing Up in an Age of Anxiety'.

Few historians espoused fascism — a hint of admiration for Hitler, by Oman, is a rare exception.[32] And the Marxists remained an isolated, mainly partisan group. It has since been suggested that 'the curious failure of Marxism to develop a conventional constellation of theory in England' can partly be explained in terms of the lack of a tradition of systematic philosophic thought in English culture and, especially, by the accentuation of the native empirical tradition after 1900, but that there was nonetheless 'a remarkable corpus' of Marxist historiography. This corpus was not part of a general Marxist culture, however, because Britain lacked both 'a numerous and radical intelligentsia' and a mass, proletarian-based Communist Party.[33] Britain certainly lacked the latter; and arguably, lacked the former. Yet, as it is also claimed that Marxist thought in general was characterised by a divorce of theory from practice in the half century from 1918 to 1968, one wonders whether the British experience was that unusual and whether the two factors were jointly necessary. Whatever the explanation however, the Marxist historiography that did exist was isolated both within the historical profession and intellectually — in the sense that there was no flourishing Marxist culture of political or economic thought. Developments within Marxist thought occurred on the continent. Few would admit at the time, or (like Court) in retrospect, that Marxism had had even a slight influence upon them. It is true that many historians felt that history had an individualist methodology and epistemology, which were at odds with systematising or philosophising; but the thoughtful or the young needed some justification of this. They did not get it from the tired Whiggism of Fisher and his contemporaries.

It is also possible that historians found difficulty relating to the dominant school of philosophy of the day. The logical positivists (or logical empiricists), it has been said, seemed to believe that they had made history irrelevant by freeing all epistemological enquiry from genetic considerations (that is, considerations of the genesis of that of which we seek knowledge), seeking 'to formulate rules governing the use of words regardless of the conditions under which they came into being'. This, if accepted, would be a fatal blow to the sort of developmental history practised by the Victorians and espoused by Bury. Ironically, as we have suggested, logical positivists shared some of the characteristics of the 'realist' school of historians — a belief in 'an anti-ideological, scientific view of the world, purged of value judgments' and a preference for 'historical scepticism' (which the historians, minimising the potential of their subject, had shared, if less radically, with the philosophers).[34] The end result of either realist history or logical positivist philosophy was quietism — technical competence in small things and neglect of the great issues. As products of the same culture they were fated, by their very similarity, to ignore each other.

As Court has suggested, the one man who could be said to have provided an inspiring sense of moral and political purpose, and could reach a wider audience than either narrowly research-oriented professional historians or sectarian Marxists could hope to do, who could offer something more progressive than old Whiggism and more accessible than Collingwood's Idealism, was R.H. Tawney. A product of Rugby and Balliol, once classic homes of socially-conscious youth, Tawney is the one historian of the inter-war period to qualify as an important political thinker.[35] He was a major influence on the Labour Party and, in the days of William Temple, upon the Church. His influential family circle included William Beveridge. His early admiration for Unwin, one of his pre-war mentors, is obvious; and Unwin's influence is acknowledged;[36] there are also signs of forward links with some modern post-war socialist historians. A convincing case can be made out for a constant interplay between his historical work and his views, writings and actions in the field of contemporary politics: he was an 'engaged' historian.

Tawney's importance, irrespective of whether his interpretations of particular events have stood the test of time, was twofold. Firstly, his *Religion and the Rise of Capitalism* (1926), in the words of Court, 'helped powerfully to destroy the hold which an interpretation of the seventeenth century, cast mainly in terms of Parliamentary politics and constitutional law and devised in the first instance by the great aristocratic houses in order to explain to themselves and the country their actions at a time when they played a leading role in the politics of the nation, still had upon the public mind down to about sixty or seventy years ago'.[37] In other words he struck at the heart of the Whig interpretation of English history, at the Whigs themselves and at their role in the formative years of the early modern period — not by a frontal assault but by a flanking movement; as an economic historian, he changed the terms of the debate by studying, in his own words, 'the economic foundations, the political superstructure and the dynamic ideas', not merely the political and constitutional story. If the first parts of his phrase suggest the influence of Marxism, the last part, at least in the pinched climate of Marxist opinion in the thirties, shows that he had broader opinions of what made history move. As for traditional political history: 'it says so much and explains so little'. He advocated 'l'histoire intégrale'.[38]

This brings us to the second point of his importance. Not only did he reinterpret the moving forces of early modern national history, but he held an anti-individualist attitude appropriate to his anti-Whiggism. He was not a thorough-going collectivist or holist — certainly not a statist. His Christian Socialist doctrine was based on the concept of

duty, as expounded in particular in *The Acquisitive Society* (1920) (published by the Fabians as *The Sickness of an Acquisitive Society*) which,
together with *Equality* (1931), represented his social philosophy in this
period. He argued that the industrial revolution had destroyed the old
corporate society, replacing old values with individualism and its sordid
companion, acquisitiveness. Old duties had been forgotten; property had
once implied duties and, if it was to be enjoyed in the future, then it
should once again assume duties. Rights were to be acquired, not from
possession of property, but as a reward for functions — functions
being activities with a social purpose. So, the purpose of industry was to
supply man with its products, not to make profits for its shareholders.
Industry had to adopt professional codes of practice like the traditional liberal professions. Tawney's targets were the rentiers, speculators,
mine-owners and owners of large urban freeholds — those who
possessed wealth without social function. No thorough-going socialist in
the sense of opposition to all forms of private property, he accepted that
the owner-manager fulfilled a social purpose, and he accepted the liberal
notion that small-scale private property helped to maintain an independence and freedom for some that was of benefit to all.[39] The emphasis on
duty and function owed as much to old ideas of service accompanying
privilege, and to the Idealist function of Green and Toynbee, as to
modern ideas of socialism. However, unlike so many earlier holistic or
organic conceptions of society, Tawney's avoided stratification; equality,
as his book of that name made clear, was the necessary condition of a just
society. But society was integrated, not atomic; and history, therefore,
was not 'a series of past events' but 'the life of society'. And each human
society revealed its own characteristics successively, not simultaneously
— in other words through its history, just as an individual has to
be understood through his or her life history. The imagery was organic
and the implications were somewhat teleological. The historian's role was
to observe 'social behaviour in different conditions and varying environ-
ments', and to discover the essential characteristics of different types of
society and 'the forces in which change has found its dynamic'; also to
criticise conventional contemporary wisdom. For some it had become
almost a conventional genuflection to the Crocean idea to say that all history was present history, but, for Tawney, history with a contemporary
social purpose was vital — for what else could give the historian
himself a 'function'! And this history, because it accepted something
other than individual will or peradventure as a possible motor force,
could seek to explain the changes that shaped society. Research could
not be an end in itself; it needed a purpose. Narrative alone could not

explain.[40] This was the Tawney that Court felt offered some inspiration to a younger generation; but the main body of the profession was largely unmoved.

If the mainstream was moved by anything other than mere professionalism for its own (as opposed to society's) sake, it was still the old individualist ideal that had influence. In particular, the idea that the history of the Empire somehow represented individualism at its best and purest, already seen in Ramsay Muir, found frequent expression in these years. The argument seems to have started in the wartime editions of *History* after it had been adopted by the Historical Association and placed under the editorship of Pollard, who straightaway committed the journal to a policy of relevance to issues raised by the war and likely to be of lasting significance, explicitly wanting to link past and present and bring historical experience to bear upon modern political experiment.[41] As we have seen, this was typical of the time. But Pollard felt that imperial affairs were of most importance here. The first contributor to this theme was C.P. Lucas, not a professional historian at all, but a key figure at the Colonial Office until his retirement in 1911, and a prolific writer of imperial history both before and after his retirement. For Lucas, imperial history, unlike other aspects of the national history, was still 'human' history with the personal element given its due. His model was J.R. Green's *Short History of the English People*, which showed that 'history is the record of peoples; that peoples consist of men and women; and that, as in life, so in history, men and women are really men and women — human beings of like passions with ourselves'. He maintained: 'the full play of human motives can be seen in, say, the formation of the East India Company, or in the Puritan Emigration', because these were the actions of a few, 'not lost in the crowd' — 'the obvious outcome of men and women, who were really men and women, not contingent remainders in a complicated legal-constitutional-social-industrial system'. He obviously saw imperial history as both a frontiersman history of individual initiative and enterprise, and as a refuge from the more institutional or deterministic constitutional, legal and economic histories:

> On the overseas side of English history private individuals, and combinations of private individuals, have done more, and Governments, Parliaments, laws, constitutions have done less than on the home side. It is to the story of our Overseas Empire that we point to illustrate the private initiative on which Englishmen pride themselves. And, obviously, the more elementary the conditions of land and living are, the more depends upon the human factor as opposed to laws and systems.

Thus imperial history was 'English History humanised by bringing in the overseas leaven'. The imperial experience was made by the private initiatives of individuals co-operating as they did in chartered companies or by self-government. He concluded with a plea for the Historical Association to take a lead in the provision of appropriate textbooks on imperial history.[42] All this was argued in the context of the pre-war debates about imperial preference and an imperial parliament, and during a war when the Empire had rallied to Britain, and German inhumanity and authoritarian, statist discipline had become bugbears.

In fact the question of an imperial parliament and the role of the Empire dominated these early issues of *History*. Pollard argued against an imperial parliament on the grounds that it was vain even 'by the best laid scheme and the wisest design to prescribe wisdom for future ages', seeing an imperial parliament as an artificial construct rather than a natural growth, and warning that 'men have lived and suffered and died in this war to little purpose if we have not learnt from our foes to shun the idolatry of the state'.[43] Ten years later, H.W.C. Davis took a line very similar to that of Lucas: in his Ralegh Lecture at the British Academy, 'The Great Game in Asia (1800-1844)', he sang a paean to the 'individualists' (now, he feared, 'suspect or worse'), of whom a great Empire always had need, 'especially on its frontiers or in its outposts'. They had sometimes been unwise or unsuccessful, and they had often faced criticism and gone unrewarded, but these adventurers were the stuff of Empire. They had 'obtained leave to work for the hive outside the hive'. The British Empire had 'used such men more freely than most other Empires'.[44] *The Times* obituary for Davis (1928), by a fellow historian, made special mention of his Raleigh lecture on the doings 'of minorities and individualists' of his 'almost wayward impatience of the verdict of the crowd' and his 'mature sympathy for men destined to bear the responsibility of life and death decision'.[45] Davis, a quiet personality, who had been a day boy at a small, but academic, minor public school, had gone on to become a Balliol tutor, in which capacity he had the task of keeping the Etonian rowdies in check.[46] From Freeman, at times antisocial and eccentric in his Oxford relationships and privately educated by tutors in his boyhood (not uncommon in the early nineteenth century before the reform of the public schools); and from poor, bullied Froude, to Davis, and Trevelyan, who as a Liberal outsider had hated Harrow for its philistinism and Toryism; and Gooch, who had been similarly displeased with Eton; we find again and again that our historians, not presumably atypical of the most scholarly earnest young men, often from a clerical, evangelical or liberal family background, who were destined to be academics, were either privately tutored or were the products of small academic institutions before going to Oxford or Cambridge, or they were outsiders in the big public schools. How much of the strength of English intellectual individualism might derive from the intellectual's rejection of the more ebullient features of the corporate life of the English public school and the Oxbridge college? Just as Arnold's and Stanley's Rugby and Jowett's and Caird's Balliol are held to have fostered both a sense of communal responsibility and Idealist neo-liberalism, and also (more controversially) Positivist and clerisy ideas, [47] could one say that, more typically falling short of the ideal, the majority of these institutions tended to produce an individualist reaction amongst more sensitive intellectuals?

By 1940, of course, we do not need to speculate on the well-springs of individualism; if 1914 had been seen as a crisis year for the individualistic English state, then 1940 was an even more serious challenge — from rampant fascism in unholy alliance with totalitarian Russia. Gooch's British Academy lecture on 'Hobbes and the Absolute State' captures the tone. Hobbes was original but un-English; his pessimism and his opposition to tradition marked him as 'the father of totalitarianism', neither Whig nor Tory, liberal nor conservative, neither optimistic for the future nor careful of tradition. No better sense of the importance of continuity and compromise in the liberal tradition can be got than from Gooch's lecture. Austin too was castigated — an *a priori* thinker, authoritarian and 'pure Hobbes'. He also resented the philsophical radicals, such as James Mill, systematisers who had rescued Hobbes from deserved obloquy — further evidence, if any were needed, that the origins of individualist thought are by no means always or necessarily traced back to the Utilitarians. In the twentieth century, said Gooch, the rise of totalitarian dictatorships had kept Hobbes in fashion, and one of the ironies of history was that he who had failed to find many disciples at home had found them abroad. Mussolini's article in the *Enciclopedia Italiana* was pure Hobbes (though others have seen it as Hegelian). 'Hobbes', he said, 'was the foe of the idealism, the individualism, and the method of compromise which have given Western civilisation its colour and shape' — a civilisation once thought solidly safe but now threatened: Europe in 1940 was as much a 'battleground of ideas as the England of 1640'. He felt that 'the old conflict between the flowering of personality and the iron road of the state has flamed up afresh', fanned by the new realists. [48] Thus Gooch tried to isolate the alien elements in our intellectual tradition, ranging the typical ingredients of traditional liberal individualism (consensus politics, freedom for the personality to bloom and a European civilisation that transcended the state) against the inimical idea of the totalitarian state.

It was easy to revitalise this liberal tradition in 1940 because it had never really died out amongst the historians. They had continued to talk about 'the part played by individual idiosyncrasy in shaping the historical process', of how the wills of individuals did not necessarily express anything like a collective will, and of how history was, by definition, about individuals.[49] They preferred the individual's will, mind and emotions to either 'rarefied abstractions' or analytical 'scientific' methods.[50] It is true that these attitudes were particularly prominent in the pages of *History*, and these theoretical articles were not particularly impressive, but *History* was the one journal of the time that assumed it had a role as a forum on these wider issues, and the contributors probably represent the more articulate members of the profession as far as methodology and epistemology are concerned.

Not that all historians who, like Gooch, took the history of political thought as part of their brief, were prepared to see the totalitarian and liberal traditions as so sharply delimited and mutually antagonistic as Gooch proclaimed them in 1940. Some recognised that the growth of the modern nation state had posed a real problem for traditional liberalism. Alfred Cobban, whose *Rousseau and the Modern State* was first published in 1934, later claimed that 'the main problem of twentieth century political life' was already implicit in Rousseau's political thought: namely, 'given the reality of nationalism, state sovereignty, the demand for the enforcement of economic equality by the state, and the emotional basis of popular polities, how to reconcile these with political principles founded on the idea of the rational, self-determining individual, the free citizen, and derived ultimately from Greek ideas of justice and liberty?' Rousseau, he felt, had tried to hold the balance between the individuals and the community.[51] It is worth remembering that Bosanquet had also identified Rouseeau as an original mind who had yet found it difficult to recognise that the state was the true source of individual freedom.[52] And for most historians the Idealist holism of Hegel, Bosanquet *et al.* remained unreal: individual and state were in conflict. An historian like Galbraith, who acknowledged Bosanquet as a master and who accepted that 'the individual exists fully only in the totality of society' and that we are the state,[53] was a rarity; he may have derived this influence via his Balliol mentor, A.L. Smith. Thirty years after his book first appeared, Cobban concluded:

The collapse of divine right and the bankruptcy of hereditary aristocracy may seem to have launched the world on a sea of change in which nothing is permanent. Yet there still remain, unchanged in a changing world, on the one hand, the community and its will to live, and on the other hand the divine spark of individuality in Western civilisation, the eternal capacity of the individual for taking the initiative, and the perennial life of the principles of political freedom first enunciated in ancient Greece. Delivered over apparently to the mercy of great communal movements of opinion, unforeseeable and uncontrollable, the individual may have seemed helpless and the ideals that Rousseau upheld mere dreams. Yet whereas the tide, when this book was first written, was running strongly against them, in some respects at least it has turned . . .[54]

This could almost be taken as the appropriate epilogue for this chapter: individuality set against the community, largely ignoring the earlier Idealist concept of the positive relationship between state and individual; liberal ideals, challenged in 1914, buffeted in the storms of the twenties and thirties, delivered from their most militant enemies during the Second World War, and finally coming to safe harbour in the fifties and early sixties. But it points us to one last theme that needs to be explored: namely, the creation of a new conservative tradition of historiography which partly involves the transfer of individualism from the liberals to the conservatives; this has happened politically; and it happened intellectually. In general, a new style of conservatism was being created.

Some have been tempted to talk of Whig history being superseded by Tory history, and there is some truth in the idea when applied to Blaas's realists in the 1890 to 1930 period, though the terms simplify the situation. But the inter-war period saw further developments, some of which can be traced back to pre-war intellectual influences different from those typified by Pollard, Tout and Round.

The most famous of the new conservatives was Namier — though his fame derives more from the post-Second World War era, a fact that can be explained by relating the characteristics of his approach to the mentality of British intellectual life in the fifties as well as to the course of his own career; but that is to look ahead. One could argue as to whether Namier, with his Jewish-Polish background, could be included in the national historiographical tradition; but of course he can, on many counts. His influence in Britain, at least in the fifties, was to be considerable. He himself was subject to many English influences after his arrival at the age of nineteen. His peculiar identification with the English ruling classes, coupled with a paradoxical but constant sense of alienation, adds a definite piquancy to his role. And finally, the intellectual life of Britain in the twentieth century has been enriched (though some would deny the verb) by European emigrés, who have made their own distinctive contribution to the tradition of English individualism, which they tend to see as the most distinguishing and healthy characteristic of their adopted society when compared with their original homes. They also see British stability and continuity as distinctive.

Namier's own arrival had nothing to do with the turmoils of the inter-war years; he arrived in 1907, but maintained a somewhat international lifestyle for a while thereafter, visiting America, and living in Vienna and Prague in the twenties. A volunteer in 1914, he was seconded to the Polish intelligence department during the war, becoming intimately involved with the complex issues and rivalries of nationalism and socialism in Austria-Hungary and the Polish lands of the three eastern Empires. He was acutely aware of the disturbed and disturbing nature of international affairs and of the instability and growing authoritarianism of European politics between the Wars which directly affected his own family relation-ships. His Zionism also brought strains and stresses.[55]

Namier had been one of A.L. Smith's protégés at Balliol, and from him he seems to have acquired a certain organicism. Namier's second wife has claimed that the only contemporary philosophical work that Namier appreciated was by his friend, the Manchester medievalist and later Balliol philosopher, C.G. Stone — a book called *The Social Contract of the Universe*.[56] How reliable a guide to his philosphical posi-tion this is, it is difficult to say. It is an uninspiring book, awkward and confused in style and, no doubt, justly forgotten. But it was in the holistic mode of Idealist thought, proclaiming (rather frequently) that 'reality is one action', but denying that determinism had any place in his holistic world. There were limited possibilities within the whole: 'the power of free action is always limited'. Decisions are never freely rational in the sense of being the product of a free intelligence; they are bound by circum-stance and by the limited intentions of their authors. Reality is neither wholly coherent nor wholly incoherent. In Stone's world, therefore, there was neither a totally free, individual, rational will nor an holistic sense of overall purpose. It is true that his ideal was a community of 'organised individuals, all perfectly coherent and rational in their freedom', but real communities were organisations of individuals who pursued their individual aims, bound by circumstance, with limited intentions and knowledge, and without a guaranteed outcome.[57] Namier was certainly imbued with an ironic sense of the unpredictability and irrationality of man's fate as much as with a sense of the interrelatedness of human soci-ety, as many of his shorter essays show. He had none of A.L. Smith's ebullient interventionism and sense of purpose: in the context of the wartime arguments about an imperial parliament, for example, Smith had been confident that 'the theory of deliberate adaptation of means to ends' was correct, and he was against 'the theory of drift' which was 'so fatally attractive to the English character'; he believed in seizing 'the great occasion'.[58] But Namier thought rational purposeful man was a Whig myth. Macaulay's dictum that 'when we see the actions of man, we know with certainty what he thinks his interest to be' was naive in the light of modern psychology. Thus, political ideas were never 'the offspring of pure reason; one had to discover 'the underlying emotions' which produced the ideas which were left behind as doctrine, or, 'at best', clichés. It is worth noting that, for Namier, even a cliché was better than a doctrine. He admitted that he had been accused of 'taking the mind out of history'. He distrusted reason: 'strictly logical conclusions based on insufficient data are a deadly danger, especially when pride is taken in the performance'. Doctrine and dogma were the enemies; and, in contrast, 'the irrational is not necessarily unreasonable: it may only be that we cannot explain it, or that we misinterpret it, in terms of our conscious thought'. The 'economic motive' or the 'will to power', or a host of other irrational factors had to be accounted for. Political ideologies, as the twentieth century had demonstrated, were apt to be 'shams and disasters'. The so-called dictatorship of the proletariat enslaved the masses, whilst the worst scum that had ever wielded power had ruled Nazi Germany in the name of élite rule. 'But even far less cruel or fierce political ideologies have played havoc with human welfare'. Ideologies, he said, get outdated, 'which is the reason why radicals who rely on systems so often produce mere junk . . . they do not repack their ideological baggage. Moreover, almost all ideologies vastly overrate man's capacity to foresee the consequences and repercussions of ideals forced on reality'.[59] Of course, this distaste for ideology, this association of Marxism (never specified but looming large) and Nazism, and the Popperian distrust of prediction, were all typical of the fifties, when this piece was written, but, as we have seen, these had been common themes amongst historians for decades.

Not all had drawn Namier's conclusions from this twentieth century awareness of the irrational, it is true. F.M. Powicke, who claimed to follow Collingwood in terms of knowing the past through the thoughts of other men's minds, reckoned that, nonetheless, there was much that we simply could not bring ourselves to know and understand 'about human wickedness and folly'. Rather than revel in the irrational, he counselled historians to concentrate on 'politics and common sense', on the rational and sensible efforts of man to order his world. Eschew 'the nightmares', he said, because 'life must go on, work must be done. It is for us to make the best of a bad business, and to see the good in it'.[60] Written in 1938, this seems rather desperate, albeit deeply felt; it was more positive than Fisher's helpless pessimism, but it was reminiscent of Balfour in its self-denying ordinance of historical limitations. Powicke had always wanted 'a constructive outlook over the past' and saw such an outlook as a safeguard against both 'mysticism' and 'cynicism'. He recognised that the great deterministic philosophies of history, Christian, Hegelian and Marxist, whilst appealing to man's sense of destiny, were in opposition to 'history as history', in other words to an empirical approach to the study of the past.[61] Yet he retained an optimism about the constructive possibilities of studying the rational past of man and making some sense of it.

In the long run, however, it was Namier's more conservative empiricism that became the historian's dominant ideology — though of course its proponents have never recognised it as such, being supposedly opposed to all 'ideology'. By the fifties, Namier at least was aware that his time had come:

> Some political philosophers complain of 'a tired lull' and the absence at present of argument on general politics in this country: practical solutions are sought for concrete problems, while programmes and ideals are forgotten by both parties. But to me this attitude seems to betoken a greater national maturity, and I can only wish that it may long continue undisturbed by the workings of political philosophy.

Grand solutions were out; reasoning from first principles was suspect. History, therefore, was in; pragmatic solutions to concrete problems were matched by an empirical method and a concern for concrete situations. History, for Namier, had always been about 'man in action', 'concrete events fixed in time and space'. Its approach was 'intellectually humble', for the crowning achievement of historical study was simply 'a historical sense — an intuitive understanding of how things do not happen'.[63] How things do *not* happen! How they *did* happen, he said, was a matter of specific knowledge, by which he meant that each event was unique and so had to be understood in itself and for itself, a classic historicist position. But the historian did also acquire a sort of negative wisdom by learning not to make mistakes and generalisations (synonymous, presumably), and not to argue from first principles.

We are in danger here of trespassing on the subject of our next chapter, namely the tendency to divorce history from its loose association with science (if divorce can be obtained from a loose association), and to see it, once again, as a unique discipline; but we cannot separate our

two themes: ideology is not as easily disposed of or isolated as Namier
had imagined. Namier's own approach was imbued with a world-weary,
pessimistic conservatism, based on the presumption that man could
know little and, therefore, could do little. No doubt, he said, there
were regularities, there might even be cycles, in the course of human
history — though we might also invent them out of psychological
need; but, even if they existed, we could never know them, for they were
beyond 'the range of our experience and knowledge'.[64] This seems to be a
quieter echo of Kingsley's rumbustious protestations of human ignorance
and divine power.

Namier's ideal method of historical research was to treat aggregates
'as entities in which each person retains his individuality', denying that
society could be compared to a living organism.[65] Yet he also used rich
organic imagery about the history of parliament — 'anatomy',
'physiology' and 'living substance', all of which gave a sharper anatomi-
cal meaning to another phrase, 'cross-section of the political nation'.[66]
His two formative historical works were *The Structure of Politics at the
Accession of George III* (1929) and *England in the Age of the American
Revolution* (1930), so we must look to these to see if his early exposure
to organicist tendencies had affected more than his imagery. The cynicism about rational man was already there: he believed that political
and constitutional issues rarely excited profound interest or affected
the lives of people, whose real concerns lay elsewhere. But the true
history of the 'political nation' could be discovered in microcosm, in
the House of Commons, understanding of which could be achieved by
steeping oneself 'in the political life of a period'. So, 'understanding',
rather than induction was the method;[67] rational analysis of rational
statements about rational efforts to control social life was inappropriate.
On examining why men went into Parliament, he found 'an ant-heap,
with the human ants hurrying in long files along their various paths;
their joint achievement does not concern us, nor the changes which
supervene in their community, only the pathetically intent, seemingly
self-conscious running of individuals along beaten tracks'. In dealing with
the electoral structure, he counselled the reader not to mind 'the time
spent over details — we distinguish trees by considering their
general shape and their characteristic details, for instance the leaf or the
bark; while seemingly more prominent features, such as the circumfer-
ence, the number of branches, etc., can be safely disregarded, as can
so many things which lend themselves best to historical narrative'. If
he concerned himself with each individual ant and its only seemingly
self-conscious running, rather than with the ant-heap and its collective

achievement, he retained a holistic view; of the Commons, he said: 'a House, just as a team, has a joint personality superior to that of the individuals who compose it; and while its purpose dominates them, there can be little regarding of men . . . '[68] But society still achieved its purposes without formulae or explicitly stated goals: 'England knows not democracy as a doctrine, but has always practised it as a fine art'. His conservatism was definitely an *English* conservatism, which he saw as being landowning, plutocratic, rooted and free from either threats of war or revolutionary change, and thus less militaristic and ideological than continental conservatism. His own sense of alienation and his outsider's admiration for 'the fine growth of English Conservatism' and 'the English political family', a 'compound of "blood", name, and estate', the landed estate being the most important element, comes through powerfully.[69] His own disinheritance from landed estates, which were still very unusual for European Jews, and his Zionism, made him very conscious of the importance of land and rootedness.[70] He did not believe that institutions could be transplanted or manufactured: 'counterfeits of organic creations do not work', he wrote of the institutions of inter-war Europe where advancing fascism and bolshevism seemed to threaten both personal and property rights and all 'our hard-won, more cultivated modes of living'.[71] He felt a deep need for the stability of the way of life of the English ruling classes, which seemed to contrast with the disruptive tendencies in Europe. After his break with Zionism this need increased; he even joined the Anglican Church. Like all good conservatives he remained pessimistic; not only was man 'a criminally inclined species', but even the British parliament, the national political life it had represented, and the attitudes it had fostered, were by 1957 a thing of the past. Decay had set in on an imperial scale.[72]

The history of parliament, the object of his veneration and subsequent despair, on which he was engaged, has itself had an interesting history, because it was begun under the supervision of J.C. Wedgwood, a Liberal-turned-Labour politician, who had envisaged it as a monument to the mother of parliaments in the Whig and constitutional tradition. After many vicissitudes, typical of corporate historical enterprises (which monsters tend to devour their contributors), it emerged as Namierite prosopography, about parliamentarians rather than parliament, about the ants on their beaten paths rather than the development of the constitution.[73] Although the Namierite method was antithetical to the Whig constitutional approach, it was also conducive to a conservative admiration for the English ruling classes and their method of doing things, and to suspicion of more programmatic or ideologically-based policies or systems. It was a perfect example of the transmogrification of liberal into conservative positions.

Lawrence Stone has divided prosopography into two schools, an 'élitist' school and a 'mass' one, with Namier firmly located in the former, dealing with 'small group dynamics' and, in particular, with 'competition for power and wealth and security' amongst 'small ruling élites'. (Namier, of course, claimed that his élite represented the political nation, but virtual representation does not cut much ice in these more democratic times.) Stone saw the popularity of prosopography arising out of the 'near exhaustion' of the existing system of historiography which had used state archives for studying institutions, administration, constitutional development and diplomacy — an exaggeration perhaps, particularly with regard to the seemingly inexhaustible resources of diplomatic history; but he was nearer the mark when he saw it as a side-effect of a 'contemporary crisis of confidence in democracy'. Elite prosopography, with its cynicism about political theory and programmes, and its distrust of rational behaviour and rational explanation, turned its back on broad-based popular initiatives, ideologies and ideals, to concentrate on 'material interest and kinship ties'. Politics was about tactics and wire-pulling. 'By accident or design', Namier chose a period and a class uniquely suited to this approach.[74] It is difficult to quarrel with the burden of these conclusions, or with the point that mass prosopography, commoner in America and latterly in France, requires more sophisticated statistical techniques and some knowledge of social science theory, whilst Namierite collective biography does not.[75]

If it be thought that Namier's conservative élitism be in some ways unsatisfactory, however, it was preferable to the unthinking way in which a conservative such as Oman reacted. Philosophers were 'the enemies of history, trying to make out of a series of strange and perplexing happenings which we have before us, something logical and tending to an end — evolution, progress, illumination, what you will'. History was but 'a series of happenings' prompted by great men. Unashamedly Carlylean, but without any appreciation of Carlyle's metaphysic, Oman was desperately lacking in originality or depth, and unattractively fond of heroes in an age calculated to bring the concept into disrepute; yet his fears were typical of the conservative tendency.[76]

Beside Oman even Butterfield's *The Whig Interpretation of History* (1931) looks sophisticated, though still undeserving of its fame. Blaas's study of the anti-Whig reaction has put it firmly in its place — at the tail-end of the reaction. Most of its points are immediately recognisable, placing Butterfield (*pace* Cowling) firmly in the conservative, realist school; though it is true that he resigned this position with his wartime *The Englishman and His History* (1944), a thoroughly patriotic piece of Whiggish war work akin, in the nature of its appeal, to Trevelyan's *English Social History* of the same year. However, Butterfield changed his position again after the war, as we shall see. His 1931 essay was definitely in the conservative realist mould. He attacked the study of the past for the sake of the present. Above all, he attacked value judgments in history. He applauded research and monographic scholarship as likely to be value free and free of selective bias — though his own reputation was to be founded by moralising on such themes as history and Christianity. For Butterfield, the dread sin of bias and relevance came in with selection, which was necessary for general outlines, the home of the worst Whiggery and presentism, but unnecessary in original research itself: this is one of the worst cases of naive realism that we have encountered; though, as we shall see, Oakeshott quickly provided a philosophical justification for it. History, so methodologically simple at the level of empirical research, was nonetheless, insisted Butterfield, *about* 'complication and change' when considered as a process. It had to be about the particular and the accidental; and the historian should not disparage this, his material. 'The eliciting of general truths or of propositions claiming universal validity is the one kind of consummation which it is beyond the competence of history to achieve', he said; and continued to asssert that the historian's business was with 'the concrete', with 'facts and people and happenings', with 'accidents and conjunctures and curious juxtapositions of events'. That this could make the reputation of its author says something about the state of theoretical or methodological debate in the interwar period. History, said Butterfield, was 'a form of descriptive writing as books of travel are'; it was not concerned with 'the meaning or purpose or goal of life'. He accepted that historians, therefore, had had little cause to ponder reality or the nature of things, even the nature of their own subject — and, presumably, were none the worse for that. The conservative historian generally has to hold his nose when he ventures into the realms of theory. Like the censor, he warns his colleagues off, lest they be corrupted. Additionally, Butterfield counselled historians to eschew essences and formulae — evidence of an hostility to both Idealism and scientific method that seems to get lost in his general anti-Whiggism.[77] At least, it might be thought, Butterfield gives a clear picture of his ideal historian, but in a later chapter he qualified his remarks to such an extent that he recognised the historian could not be an objective, passive observer and that unbiased history was impossible and would be dull if it were attempted. He was preparing the ground for a retreat from a position that might have suggested an inductive or scientific method. Historians needed, he said, creative acts of historical imagination after the manner of a Scott or a Carlyle; they needed 'historic sense' and sympathy; they would even need to write 'from the point of view of the present'.[78] This is but the knee-jerk reaction of the historian through the ages: it might be valid, but baldly stated it can be but a series of truisms, often no more than a substitute for serious consideration of how the historian achieves historical knowledge, unless it is part of a well-formulated methodology.

If Butterfield was prepared to admit to the impossibility of objective history, why did he make so much fuss about the value judgments and presentism of Whig history? The clue lies towards the end of his book, in his chapter on 'Moral Judgments in History'. Here he took Acton to task, quoting at length from his correspondence with Creighton. Acton, he said, had exalted history until it became almost 'like the mind of God, making ultimate judgments' upon events, with the historian as the voice of God.[79] Butterfield the Christian, so much in evidence (as we shall see) in the post-war world, was there in 1931. We are back with Kingsley and Froude minus their moral judgments; a Kingsley would not trespass upon God's territory by *explaining* history, but he would judge; Butterfield refused even to judge — in that sense, perhaps, he was closer to Rankean historicism than to the English tradition; but his approach was to be typical of the new conservatism, offering little explanation and no judgment. Such an approach, whilst protesting its neutrality, has an inbuilt conservatism by virtue of its very refusal to judge events and its reluctance to explain them. Butterfield's Cambridge colleague, R.E. Balfour, wrote: 'Understanding of history will convince men of their own unimportance, of the incompleteness of their knowledge, and of the transitoriness of the circumstances, intellectual no less than material, of the contemporary world'.[80] A few years later, during the war, E.L. Woodward, proclaiming his dissatisfaction with deterministic philosophies of history, felt that, though there was evidence of design in human affairs, the pattern was beyond comprehension. Between the two extremes of hope and despair, determinism and anarchy, lay 'the wisdom of history', acting as 'a warning and a steadying influence, a mirror of the strength as well as of the frailties and waywardness of human beings'. Unfortunately, there was 'no prescription for acquiring or for applying this wisdom'.[81] Once again, then, history proper is an antidote to dangerous and spurious philosophies of history; there is a pattern but it is unknowable. History is a *via media* between unrealistic optimism and empty pessimism. It is difficult not to see God's Providence at work in this perspective. But the 'wisdom' of history also works in mysterious ways, for it is not an easily acquired or easily applied wisdom: there is nothing technical or scientific about it, nothing demonstrably applicable. Similarly low ground had been taken by Balfour, who concluded his essay:

In an age when old ideals have perished and new ones have been prematurely nipped in the bud, when the humanist conception of civilisation is dying and we are not sure whether we like the scientific one which promises to replace it, when mankind seems to have lost his sense of direction and knows not whither he desires to go nor how he is to get there, when we can seriously question whether more harm is done by well-meaning idealism than by sheer incompetence, when finally there hovers above us the never distant possibility of another catastrophe in which not merely we ourselves must perish but everything that constitutes civilisation as we know it — in such a day man does not require inspiration but reassurance. And history replies by telling him not of the greatness of man in the past and of his achievements but of his littleness and of his mistakes. If man has survived so much already, perhaps he may even yet survive today. Only by a frank recollection of the worst from the past can we find courage with which to face the future; only from a knowledge of despair dare we believe that there is still hope.[82]

Perhaps we should let this be the epitaph of the age.

NOTES

1. Bodleian Library, Collingwood Papers, Address to the Belgian Students Conference, '10 May 1919: 'The Spiritual Basis of Reconstruction'. pp. 6–16.

2. R.G. Collingwood, *An Autobiography* (Oxford, 1919), pp. 153–167.

3. *Ibid.*, pp. 44–52.

4. Collingwood Papers, Folder 27: Collingwood to de Ruggiero, 4 October 1927.

5. Collingwood Papers, Folder 27: Collingwood to de Ruggiero, 2 October 1920.

6. Collingwood, *An Autobiography*, pp. 152–153.

7. Collingwood Papers, Folder 27: Collingwood to de Ruggiero, 4 October 1927.

8. Collingwood, *An Autobiography*, p. 147.

9. Collingwood Papers, Folder 24: 'Man Goes Mad' (Rough MS begun 30 August 1936).

10. B. Croce, *History as the Story of Liberty* (London, 1941), pp. 25–26, 53–54, 167, 288–289, 306–309. Translated by S. Sprigge from *La storia come pensiero e come azione* (1938).

11. R.G. Collingwood, 'Fascism and Nazism', *Philosphy* XV (1940), pp. 170–175.

12. R.G. Collingwood, *The New Leviathan or Man, Society, Civilisation and Barbarism* (Oxford, 1942), pp. 272–279, 375–387.

13. *Ibid.*, pp. 91–92.

14. *Ibid.*, pp. 130–147, 160–184, 189–190, 208–211.

15. *Ibid.*, pp. 291–295, 305–308, 326, 329.

16. M. Cowling, *Religion and Public Doctrine in Modern England*, I, 195.

17. Fisher MSS.55, Letters to and from Gilbert Murray 1920–1940, Fisher to Murray, 7 January 1920.

18. Fisher MSS.55, Murray to Fisher, 14 February 1926.

19.   D. Ogg, *Herbert Fisher 1865–1940, a short biography* (London, 1947), pp. 32, 130, 137.

20.   H.A.L. Fisher, 'The Whig Historians', *Proceedings of the British Academy*, XIV (1928), 325–327.

21.   Ogg, *Op.cit.*, pp. 150–152.

22.   For example: G.M. Trevelyan, 'History and Literature', *History*, 9 (1924), 86; J.N.L. Myers, 'Dr Herman Schneider's Philosophy of History', *History*, 17 (1933), 303; E.F. Jacob, 'Recent World History and its Variety', *History*, 8 (1924), 241–255; A.S. Turbeville, 'History Objective and Subjective', *History*, 17 (1933), 292.

23.   Ogg, *Op.cit.*, pp. 148–149.

24.   C. Hill, 'A Whig Historian', *The Modern Quarterly*, 3:1 (1938), 276.

25.   Ogg, *Op.cit.*, p. 152.

26.   C. Hill, 'A Whig Historian', *Op.cit.*, pp. 276, 283–284.

27.   R.E. Balfour, 'History' in H. Wright ed., *Cambridge University Studies: Cambridge 1933* (London, 1933), pp. 185, 204, 208, 214.

28.   C. Hill, 'A Whig Historian', *Op.cit.*, p.284.

29.   W.H.B. Court, *Scarcity and Choice in History* (London, 1970), pp. 17–24, 26–28, 38–39.

30.   M.M. Postan, *Fact and Relevance: Essays on Historical Method* (Cambridge, 1971), p. 16.

31.   Court, *Op.cit.*, pp. 34–35.

32.   C. Oman, *On the Writing of History* (London, 1939), pp. 133–158. Oman concludes a passage on 'great men' with Frederick the Great and Bismarck, the two creators of modern Germany, adding — 'shall we have to add a third'.

33.   P. Anderson, *Considerations on Western Marxism* (London, 1976), pp. 28–29. See also p. 102.

34.   L. Kolakowski, *Positivist Philosophy from Hume to the Vienna Circle*, p. 235.

35.   R. Barker, *Political Ideas in Modern Britain* (London, 1978), pp. 141–147. This is apart from G.D.H. Cole who was not primarily an historian. Historians in general are quite well represented in Barker's book, e.g., Maitland, Figgis, E.P. Thompson.

36.   R.H. Tawney, 'Introductory Memoir' in G. Unwin, *Studies in Economic History: The Collected Papers of George Unwin*, (London, 1927), pp. xxiv–xxv.

37.   W.H.B. Court, 'Two Economic Historians', *Scarcity and Choice in History*, p. 139.

38.   R.H. Tawney, 'The Study of Economic History' (Inaugural Lecture, 1932, at LSE) in R.H. Tawney, *History and Society: Essays by R.H. Tawney*, ed. J.M. Winter (London, 1978), p. 64.

39.   R.H. Tawney, *The Acquisitive Society* (New York, 1920), pp. 9, 50–53, 64–82, 106–116, 222.

40.   R.H. Tawney, 'The Study of Economic History', *History and Society*, pp. 54–56, 58, 63.

41.   'Editorial', *History*, I (1916), 2–3.

42.   C.P. Lucas, 'On the Teaching of Imperial History', *History*, I (1916), 6–7, 9–11.

43.   A.F. Pollard, 'The Growth of an Imperial Parliament', *History*, I (1916), 138, 145.

44.   J.R.H. Weaver, A.L. Poole, *Op.cit.*, p. 202.

45.   *Ibid.*, p. 55.

46.   *Ibid.*, p. 380.

47.   C. Kent, *Brains and Numbers*.

48.   G.P. Gooch, 'Hobbes and the Absolute State', *Studies in Diplomacy and Statecraft* (London, 1942), pp. 341, 372–373.

49.   N. Sykes, 'The Study of History', *History* 19 (1934), 103–104.

50.   A.S. Turbeville, 'History Objective and Subjective', *History* 17 (1933), 289.

51.   A. Cobban, *Rousseau and the Modern State*, second edition (London, 1964), p. 170.

52.   B. Bosanquet, *The Philosphical Theory of the State*, pp. 79, 227, 229–230.

53.   V.H. Galbraith, *Historical Study and the State. An Inaugural Lecture of Oxford, 3 February 1948* (Oxford, 1948), p. 16.

54.   A. Cobban, *Rousseau and the Modern State*, p. 170.

55. All this, and more, is recounted in a slightly eccentric biography by his second wife: J. Namier, *Lewis Namier, A Biography* (London, 1971). See also: V. Mehta, *Fly and the Fly Bottle: Encounters with British Intellectuals* (Harmondswoth, 1963), pp. 178–221.

56. J. Namier, *Op.cit.*, pp. 115–116.

57. C.G. Stone, *The Social Contract of the Universe* (London, 1930), pp. 2, 9, 41, 49–52, 110, 118.

58. 'Annual Address: Historical Fatalism' from 'Report of the Proceedings of the Eleventh Annual Meeting' (of the Historical Association) January 19 (Leaflet No. 43, Historical Association, February 1919), pp. 2–3.

59. L. Namier, 'Human Nature in Politics', *Personalities and Power*, (London, 1955), pp. 1–7.

60. F.M. Powicke, *History, Freedom and Religion* (London, 1938), pp. 22–23.

61. F.M. Powicke, 'Historical Study in Oxford', (Inaugural Lecture, Oxford, 1929), *Modern Historians and the Study of History* (London, 1955), pp. 174–175.

62. L. Namier, 'Human Nature in Politics', *Personalities and Powers*, p. 7.

63. L. Namier, 'History', *Avenue of History* (London, 1952), pp. 1,4.

64. *Ibid.*, p. 6.

65. *Ibid.*, pp. 1, 10.

66. J. Namier, *Op.cit.*, p. 289.

67. This seems to be endorsed by his wife: 'He always aimed at contemplating the multitude of gathered facts and letting their coherence emerge out of the strivings, writings and sayings' of those involved; and 'the period of gestation needed for such emergence was always long'. *Ibid.*, pp. 328–329.

68. L. Namier, *The Structure of Politics at the Accession of George III*, second edition (London, 1957), pp. ix–xi, 11.

69. L. Namier, *England in the Age of the American Revolution*, second edition (London, 1961), pp. 6, 8, 18–20.

70. *Ibid.*, p. 18.

71. J. Namier, *Op.cit.*, pp. 185–187, 230–231, 236.

72. *Ibid.*, pp. 261–262, 291, 321–322, 328–329.

73. The Stenton Papers contain some interesting papers and minutes of the history of Parliament Trust, which give some insight into these problems: Stenton Papers, MSS.1148/19/1/1, 1148/19/1/8.

74. L. Stone, 'Prosopography', *Daedalus*, 100(1) (1971), 74–84, 52–55, 62–63.

75. *Ibid.*, pp. 70–71.

76. C. Oman, *On the Writing of History* (London, 1939), pp. 84–85, 130.

77. H. Butterfield, *The Whig Interpretation of History* (Harmondsworth, 1973), pp. 16–31, 52–57.

78. *Ibid.*, pp. 68–69.

79. *Ibid.*, pp. 79–95.

80. Balfour, *Op.cit.*, p. 226.

81. E.L. Woodward, *Short Journey* (London, 1942), pp. 141, 144.

82. Balfour, *Op.cit.*, pp. 227–228.

CHAPTER 7

History as a Special Form of Knowledge

Simultaneously with the reversion to traditional individualism, which began as a reaction to German holism and ended by erecting history into a sort of alternative culture to the otherwise dominant ideologically-determined cultures, came a reaction to the idea of history as science. This further reinforced the individualistic strain. It had the virtue of ending a lot of the loose talk about history as a science. Whether it brought more loose talk — this time about history as a distinctive form of knowledge — is another matter. From the complex of ideas involved we can isolate four main features of this development. History was about 'understanding' the human situation as opposed to any scientific concept of knowledge. Secondly, though this met with less general approval, history had to involve value judgments, whereas science was neutral. Thirdly, each age interpreted history in its own way. Lastly, history was idiographic (i.e., an explanation of the unique) as opposed to what we may call nomethetic (i.e., explanation through establishing general laws); this was a logical extension of a nominalist position. Much of this had always been the historian's position, but it could now be clarified in the new anti-scientific atmosphere.

The reaction against scientism, like the revival of individualism, began during the Great War, because Germany was identified as the home, not only of Idealist philosophy and statism, but of modern science; and a culture dominated by science was seen as inhuman. Lucas, in his *History* article on imperial history, had made the point: 'the inhumanity of the Germans in the present war has horrified us all. Is it not connected with the fact that of all peoples at the present day the Germans are the most dominated by science and make the nearest approach to human beings converted into machinery?' He also associated science with the destructive weaponry with which the war was fought.[1]

Pollard, editor of *History*, took up the theme, challenging claims made in a letter to *The Times* which had argued for a more science-based education, especially for those in public service, in supposed emulation of the Germans. The British Empire had not been built upon science, said Pollard; German successes would prove transient and as nothing compared with her failures consequent to her 'neglect of moral forces, contempt of political wisdom and defiance of the humanities', which would ensure her ultimate defeat. Man and matter were distinct, and the Germans neglected the distinction at their peril. Man had mind and soul; he was an ethical being. If 'science' was but a name for accurate reasoning, then history was scientific, though it could never match the precision of the natural sciences for 'mind is more complex than matter and human action cannot be expressed in formulae'. The arts, or humanities, were more creative and intuitive, more dependent on the wisdom gained by experience, and more concerned with ethical issues. History was clearly seen as both a *moral* science and a humane study. The arts were mainly 'synthetic', whereas science was analytic; science depended on 'knowledge', whereas the arts required the more difficult feat of 'understanding'.[2] Ironically, much of this could have come from the German philosopher, Dilthey, before the war — and, to be fair to Pollard, he had confessed that not all German *Kultur* had lacked humanity. He also seemed to anticipate Collingwood: 'history deals with what man has done and how he has done it; and that knowledge is at least some guide to what he can do in the future and how he should seek to do it'. This plea for a humane and less materialistic education was based on a much livelier and more optimistic mentality than that which ensued after the war: Pollard believed that 'the paralysing dogma of the helplessness of mankind' was derived from science, not from history; history was a guide to future action, not in the sense of there being a pattern of development to discover, but in the sense that it led to an understanding of man and his potential.[3] Thus Pollard laid the foundations of the reaction against scientism, concentrating on the first two characteristics that we have identified.

A few years after the war the publication by Harrap of a translation of Croce's *Teoria e storia della storiografia* (*History — Its Theory and Practice*, 1921) added the question of temporal relativism to historians' interests. Croce's impact is rather unusual: rarely have British historians reacted positively and explicitly to works on epistemology by philosophers, especially foreign philosophers. Pollard never mentioned Dilthey; those who expressed a preference for the idiographic as opposed to the nomothetic never did so in those terms or with reference to Windelband. Croce must have had a special appeal, though this does not necessarily mean that his admirers fully took on board the metaphysic behind his famous dictum that all history was contemporary history.

Ernest Barker addressed the Historical Association on the subject in 1922; an article followed. He endorsed Croce's views: all history was contemporary history; history was about the past that was still with us.

He too developed the theme of 'understanding' again, contrasting this with the method of natural science, and comparing the natural world with 'the world of human action'. History was 'the record of human will and action'. The voluntarist principle lay at the heart of these ideas. Furthermore, the basic tool of the historian was his own mind; with this he had to go deep into the minds of other men, for 'history deals with mind and the operation of the mind'.[4] Appropriately this method was as individualist as the subject. Bearing in mind Barker's pre-war interest in the holistic implications of Idealism, it is interesting to note the extent to which Croce's Idealism was providing a more individualistic basis for that form of philosophy; though it must be remembered that Idealism had always leant towards an individualist methodology, even whilst preaching social holism. Croce, however, was to come out strongly against the 'rhetoricians and the sophists' who insisted that particular nations were 'eternal conceptual categories' or that a nation could be a 'physical, intellectual and moral person, with her own private genius and mission in the world'. He reserved especially harsh words for Nazism and state worship; and he attacked the generic concept of the 'epoch', particularly as it assumed some sort of spirit of the age, which effective individuals could not transcend. Similarly, he attacked the generic concept of race, which belied individuality and mutability. The importance of this individualist Idealism in the inter-war period was considerable, avoiding as it did the authoritarian, collectivist and determinist tendencies of pre-war Hegelianism. Croce illustrates the liberal opposition to a predetermined goal in a way reminiscent of Bury's distinction between progress towards a defined goal and an open-ended, liberal concept of progress: 'in contrast with ths idea of a progress towards the terminus of some blessed state of self-satisfaction there has very properly been conceived the idea of the infinite progress of the infinite spirit . . .'[5] Croce naturally thought in terms of a progressive 'spirit', which Bury, of course, had not.

Pollard wrote an article about Bury's *Idea of Progress* and about Croce, but it was not a very powerful piece.[6] If he did not abuse his position as editor of *History*, he seems to have used it unwisely, dashing off essays in response to just about every general issue raised in these years. He also attempted a reply to Barker, which lacked internal consistency and seemed to contradict some of his earlier attitudes, particularly when he appeared to advocate a more scientific and value-free approach. He seems to have assumed that Barker's purpose had been to attack historical research and reacted in a typically 'professional' way. In arguing, however, for a separation of history and philosophy, as if he resented theoretical discussions, he distinguished between the philosophers' concerns with the 'essential unities' of 'mind' and 'spirit', and the historians' interest in the individual and 'heterogenous manifestations' of mind and spirit.[7] His seemingly misguided response to Barker was just as individualist as Barker's own position, in the idiographic sense.

This issue was raised a few years later by H.W.C. Davis in his inaugural lecture (1925) as Regius Professor of Modern History at Oxford. If science was engaged in empirically ascertaining 'the habits of organisms' without explaining their 'inmost nature', then history might have some scientific quality, since history could generalise 'up to a point' about human behaviour — 'the behaviour of that mysterious organism, *homo sapiens*'. But historians did not concern themselves with 'the fundamental axiom of the natural sciences that the same cause will always produce the same effect'. Historians knew that history did not repeat itself, 'that the same cause never occurs twice in their sphere of investigation', and that (of course) human action was purposive and the product of deliberate and real choice. History, by its very nature, was dominated by free human action as opposed to 'the necessity of natural law'. Scientific conceptions of cause and effect were irrelevant when 'dealing with the co-operation of the clash of human wills'. Davis accepted that 'the uniformity of human nature' was the basis of historical understanding because the historian could recognise the activity of human reason, essentially like his own — further evidence that human thought was regarded as the common basis for historical understanding, in this period, by many who did not necessarily derive the idea from Collingwood or back it up with the full weight of his philosophical apparatus. But Davis could not accept the arguments 'of those self-styled "social historians" who think that they find the essence of our common humanity in the life of the common man', the life of the poor and illiterate. These 'historians of the commonplace' forgot that new ideas 'make their first appearance somewhere near the summit of the social fabric and percolate downwards', albeit adulterated and corrupted in the process. 'Our common humanity is best studied in the most eminent examples that it has produced of every type of human excellence. This much there is of truth in Carlyle's hero-worship, though very few of us will accept without challenge his attempts to define the essential nature of the hero'. Despite Davis's proviso, the accents of Carlyle and of Kingsley's denunciation of 'the new science of little men' are unmistakable. For Davis, even the most common element in history, its humanity, its human nature and reason, was a basis for an individualistic approach — and an élitist one at that, which assumed, moreover, that intellectual eminence was found among the socially eminent. His assumptions were Idealist: ideas changed things; the historian had to understand those ideas. But his Idealism was not Hegel's; he did not believe, he said, in the Hegelian notion of 'man's gradual ascent toward omniscience, and therefore towards the perfect social state'. There were too many accidents in history, too many defeats suffered by 'higher reason', too many bad times; despite man's potential for progress, such optimism was unacceptable.[8] This low-key, pessimistic, humanist but élitist Idealism seems to be very typical of the time. The unity and the sense of purpose had gone, perhaps as a result of the secularisation of thought since Carlyle's day — a parallel of the loss of an ultimate standard of good and evil by the secularisation of German historicism, as discerned by Iggers.

The key figure in English idealist thought, especially on the philosophy of history, was of course R.G. Collingwood. He was less pessimistic, more of an enthusiast than many historians. For twenty years, between 1926 and 1946, in a series of lectures, reviews, articles and books (the last published posthumously as *The Idea of History*, being mainly based on his 1936 lectures), he dominated higher level thinking about the methodology and epistemology of history, despite his sense of isolation in the world of philosophy *per se*. Powicke, Norman Sykes, W.K. Hancock and Eric John were amongst those historians who acknowledged his influence, and Collingwood himself was no mean historian and archaeologist. Many others neither acknowledged his influence nor recognised the relevance of any theoretical considerations to their professional work; but, though he liked to see himself as a prophet crying in the philosophical wilderness, he was in many ways simply the most articulate exponent of prevalent attitudes amongst historians. Ironically, because he insisted that the English history tradition was Positivist he presumed that he was isolated here, too.

To see Collingwood's thought in the intellectual context of the time it is worth considering his expositions as they were made, rather than simply looking at *The Idea of History* (1946) which was posthumously compiled from his 1936 lectures and is the best known example of his work. His 1926 lecture notes seem to be atypical, and as they were never prepared for publication perhaps not too much should be made of them. He seemed to set his face firmly against value judgments in history: 'we are not called upon to pass moral judgments at all . . . The real holocaust of history is the historian's holocaust of his emotional and practical reactions towards the facts . . . True history must be absolutely passionless, absolutely devoid of all judgments of value, of whatever kind'. The past was dead and gone — there was nothing to judge![9] It would be tempting to suggest that this was an attitude that he later abandoned, but if such a conveniently linear temporal explanation is adopted (there being some excitement at present about the development of Collingwood's thought), then the change came rapidly. We have already noted his letter to de Ruggiero of 1927 bewailing the academic dominance of realist philosophy and its amoral consequences, so his hostility to non-judgmental academic work, so passionately proclaimed in his autobiography (1939), was formulated early on: it is difficult to see why he would have exempted history from this. Perhaps these lectures were simply not his considered personal opinion. In other respects, however, they have interest because they show the early influence of Bradley, the man whose essay on 'The Presuppositions of Critical History' Collingwood was to call a Copernican revolution in the philosophy of history. Indeed Bradley's assertion that the past did not exist, being but (in Collingwood's words) 'an ideal element in the present', was the source of Collingwood's assertion that the dead should be left to bury their dead and that the historian had nothing to do with judgment. Collingwood's subsequent engaged role marks a break with that particular Idealist mode and contrasts with Oakeshott's approach. Taking up Bradley's idea that the past was only an ideal element in the present, constantly changing, Collingwood moved on to introduce what becomes one of his key ideas — the distinction between what he called first degree and second degree history, the latter being the history of the historiography of an historical problem. Only after second degree history had been studied could 'authorities' become 'sources'. In addition to preparing the ground for more first degree history, knowledge of the history of historical thinking was as important a part of the intellectual life of any civilisation as other forms of knowledge. (The present writer finds nothing to dispute in this justification of his task!) Collingwood then went on to castigate 'the positivistic view of history as a crude lump of magma of existing fact, a real and therefore structureless past, whose elements can be studied by the historian but not without a dangerous concession to subjectivity, arranged in any kind of pattern'. He described this as a 'theory of the real past', in other words as what we have called naïve realism.[10]

In the following year Collingwood published a couple of articles in *Antiquity* on Spengler and historical cycles. Spengler was second to H.G. Wells in exciting historians' wrath; Toynbee's theories of challenge and response and the rise and fall of civilisations later replaced Spengler or were coupled with him. In attacking Spengler, Collingwood showed his commitment to methodological individualism: 'history deals with the individual in all its individuality'; thus, 'comparative anatomy is not history but science; and Spengler's morphology is simply the comparative anatomy of historical periods. The historical morphologist is concerned not to discover what happened, but, assuming that he knows what happened, to generalise about its structure as compared with the structure of other happenings. His business was not to *work at* history, but to *talk about* it', assuming that someone else had already done the work, and arranging ready-made facts, found in books, into patterns.[11] This was a valid point, tellingly put, and one which some modern writers, on state-formation for example, could well bear in mind. It was a natural extension of his hostility to the 'magma' theory of a real past. He had argued that everyone, be he Hegel, Spengler or Collingwood, had the right to arrange his own knowledge of the past, but it had to be *his* acquired knowledge, not somebody else's. One's 'historical sense' was a 'feeling for historical thought as living thought, a thought that goes on within one's own mind . . . ' He is here moving towards his famous idea of critically rethinking the thoughts of the past. Additionally, he argued that, whereas science dealt in 'timeless truths', for 'nature has no history', and science, therefore, was as much about the future as the past, 'for history, time is the great reality', and the future was not foreseeable because, as it had not happened, it could not leave 'its traces in the present' — which was the only way the historian could recognise the past. 'Instinctively', he said, the historian knows he cannot foretell the future — to do so would be science, or clairvoyance, or hoax.[12]

So Collingwood drew a clear distinction between history and science, ignoring the fact that most scientists no longer claimed to deal with time-less truths. It was perhaps ironical that the stimulus for this anti-scientism should have been Spengler.

In the second article, Collingwood stressed the essential humanity of history. Essential change occurred within man himself — 'It is a change in his own habits, his own wants, his own laws, his own beliefs and feelings and valuations; and this change is brought about by the attempt to meet a need itself arising essentially from within'. For, unlike other animals, man does not simply react automatically to external stimuli: 'his humanity consists in his self-consciousness, his power to mould his own nature which comes simultaneously with his awareness of that power'. So we are back to self-conscious will. History consisted of a sequence of changes occasioned by men becoming dissatisfied with themselves, so acting to change themselves, thus creating new selves, new problems and new dissatisfactions . . . and so on 'for ever'. Each situation was unique; and this pattern of change is not actually perceived by the individual historian who understands only small bits of it, and issues only an 'interim report'. There will be apparently inexplicable gaps filled by a seeming muddle and confusion. In any case, the pattern of change was not progresssive in a qualitative sense.[13] So Whig optimism was eschewed, as was Hegelian optimism despite the dialectic between man as he is and man as he wants to be; also out was the assumption that full knowledge could ever be achieved. Each historic event was individual, and its individuality derived from its self-conscious and unrepeatable humanity; it could not, therefore, be a subject for science. We see here the extent to which Collingwood's ideas were simply the most developed and sophisticated expression of those current.

Four years after his demolition of Spengler, Collingwood turned his attention to Bury upon the posthumous publication of Bury's *Selected Essays*, edited by Temperley. He warmed to his theme: the 'essential element' in history was 'the individuality of historical events and agents', an element that, contrary to the Positivist view, made history quite distinct from science. Collingwood believed that Bury had failed to rid himself of his early Positivist assumption that 'only the universal was intelligible', and, instead of delighting in contingency and the individuality of history, had nearly despaired of it.[14] Collingwood did seem to respect Bury — at least he paid tribute to him as both a great historian and as one who realised the integral importance to his work of the theory of history; but he also, both then and later, adopted a more dismissive tone towards him. This is a pity, because Bury's reputation has suffered as a consequence; and these two must be reckoned the most effective theoreticians about historical knowledge amongst practising British historians, by far and away, at least since the Liberal Anglicans. Particular credit is due to Bury, who was, after all, an historian first and only an amateur philosopher; Collingwood's position in both worlds was unique. It is then appropriate that Collingwood developed his own ideas in debate with Bury's — critical rethinking of which he could be proud in terms of the quality of its results, though not in terms of his accuracy in appreciating Bury's original thoughts. Perhaps Collingwood was simply blinded by his hostility to the scientific method and the Positivist philosophy that, he believed, was always at the back of any inappropriate applications of that method. In a letter to de Ruggiero, earlier in 1931, he had bewailed the supposed influence of scientific method upon English philosophy, much as he later explained the ills of historiography; this influence, he felt, had ensured that English philosophers did not take history seriously. He also, however, claimed that the nineteenth century British Idealists were largely lacking in an historical sense — 'just small traces in Bradley, Green and Caird —

none in Bosanquet, and none today'.[15] This has become the received wisdom, but it was simply untrue. Collingwood exaggerated the isolation of his own position. This may have been due, in part, to an awareness of the now stronger current of Idealism running in Italy; apart from Croce, always acknowledged to be a major influence on Collingwood,[16] there was de Ruggiero, whose work on liberalism Collingwood had translated and tried to popularise at Oxford.[17]

The extent to which Collingwood's thinking was becoming dominated by the idea that scientific method, or rather the abortive effort to apply scientific method, was the enemy of true history, is evident in his inaugural lecture as Professor of Metaphysical Philosophy at Oxford (1935). Science, he told his audience, lives in 'a world of abstract universals', but history was about the concrete individual, specifically located in time and space.[18] The nineteenth century Idealists, like Bosanquet, had talked of concrete universals, a somewhat difficult concept. For Bosanquet, the concept of the 'individual' was nothing but 'an empty and exclusive point', that had no purpose because it did not relate to the cosmos; whereas the concrete universal was both 'a positive cosmos' in its own right, and also, as a microcosm, it related to the universal experience — so it was doubly 'universal'.[19] Whether this difficult, not to say tortured, concept has any meaning for the non-Idealist it is difficult to say; for Collingwood, it should have had meaning even if he did not accept it, but he either ignored the point or was not aware of it. He continued to talk in terms of a dichotomy between abstract universals and concrete individuals, the one being the concern of science and the other of history, despite Bosanquet's claim that his concept destroyed the presumption that contingency and the concrete were inseparable;[20] and Collingwood was much concerned with contingency because of his interest in Bury's contingency theory. He felt that Bury's great failing had been his refusal to recognise that contingency was not a fault in the system but the glory of the historical method.

In contrast to the Baconian scientific method of experiment, the historian achieved 'autonomy' by a process of 'historical criticism' of his sources: 'the historian puts his authorities in the witness-box, and by cross-questioning extorts from them information which in their original statements they have withheld'. He can do this because he is his own ultimate authority.[21] Only his own thought is ultimately real to him, and so his own thought is his own criterion when he critically rethinks the thought of others. Bosanquet's 'concrete universal' might have been of some use here in terms of explaining why one 'individual' could relate in this way to another. But Collingwood's method not only took the individual as its subject; its full-blooded epistemological individualism ensured that only the individual mind could be a source of knowledge about the past. The historical imagination, said Collingwood, is 'a self-dependent, self-determining, and self-justifying form of thought'.[22] There is also something reminiscent of other aspects of individualism, as defined by Lukes, in Collingwood's approach — the 'dignity' of the individual, the individual as creative artist and, especially, the 'autonomy' of the individual, autonomy being precisely the term used by Collingwood. It is also interesting to note Collingwood's legal imagery when describing the historian's cross-examination of his witnesses; he was fond of this sort of imagery when dealing with individuality, for there is a strong association of ideas between the legally responsible individual and the individuality of the historical action. In the first of his articles on Spengler, for example, he had written: 'History deals with the individual in all its individuality; the historian is concerned to discover the facts, the whole facts and nothing but the facts'.[23] This was not a sudden outbreak of the despised Positivism, but another example of the legalistic method. Historians are generally very fond of this imagery, especially when claiming that their method, whilst not scientific, can arrive at, if not scientific accuracy and certainty, at least the truth *beyond reasonable doubt*. In a recent debate on the nature of historical knowledge, Fogel has claimed precisely this: the 'legal model', as he calls it, has been used by historians as a substitute for the 'natural science' model.[24]

But how could Collingwood's individual historian understand the historical individual? What was the universal element that linked the two? It was simply human thought. In order to justify this position, Collingwood had to consider the difficult problem of human nature. This he did shortly after his inaugural lecture in the *Proceedings of the British Academy*, with a piece entitled 'Human Nature and Human History', in which he also attended to the challenge that Whitehead's philosophy of scientific knowledge posed to his own ideas. His starting point was: 'Man, who desires to know everything, desires to know himself. Nor is he only one . . . among the things he desires to know. Without some knowledge of himself his knowledge of other things is imperfect: for to know something without knowing that one knows if it is only a half-knowing and to know that one knows is to know oneself'. In much the same way Comte, one of Collingwood's targets, had seen sociology, the science of man, as the queen of the sciences, with the sociology of knowledge as the essential element in all true knowledge. Collingwood, of course, would have no truck with social science. In fact, part of his argument was that the time was long overdue for abandoning the natural science model for the study of human nature. Since the scientific revolution of the seventeenth century, he said, the natural science method had acquired enormous prestige; but ever since then a comparable intellectual revolution, an historical revolution, had been in progress. Not that all reality was historical; that would be to commit the same sort of error as the scientific materialists had done; scientific method was all right in its place. But history comprised the only true knowledge of human nature. It was at this juncture that he considered the implications of the ideas of Bergson, Alexander and Whitehead. He was impressed by Whitehead, but unconvinced, insisting on a difference between natural and historical processes. History was not mere 'timefulness' or change; its crucial characteristic was the human element; and it was the thoughts behind the human documents, artefacts, or whatever, that the historian studied which made the difference between science and history, between the mere 'outside' and the 'inside' of the event.[25] Thus he arrived, by criticism of Whitehead, at the heart of his philosophy of historical knowledge, which he stated in full for the first time:

> In thus penetrating to the inside of events and detecting the thought which they express, the historian is doing something which the scientist need not and cannot do. In this way the task of the historian is more complex than that of the scientist. In another way it is simpler: the historian need not and cannot . . . emulate the scientist in searching for the causes or the laws of events . . . After the historian has ascertained the facts, there is no further process of inquiring into their causes. When he knows what happened, he already knows why it happened . . . The cause of the event, for him, means the thought in the mind of the person by whose agency the event came about: and this is not something other than the event, it is the inside of the event itself . . . The processes of nature can therefore be properly described as sequences of mere events, but those of history cannot'. They are 'processes of actions' which had 'an inner side', or 'processes of thought . . . All history is the history of thought'.[26]

The historian had to rethink the thoughts of the past in a critical way. This was a method for the individual and about the individual; he was sceptical about the notion of corporate minds. The 'mind' of an age or the 'spirit' of a nation could only be known through the thoughts of people. Only by the historical method can we know either ourselves or others, for 'the so-called science of human nature or of the human mind resolves itself into history'. He was adamant that history could not foretell the future, nor establish laws of human behaviour; indeed these were the greatest errors of the social scientists. He would accept only low-level generalisations about human behaviour; as an example, he said that the 'behaviour pattern' of a feudal baron might well exist and be constant whilst there are feudal barons in feudal societies, but in other societies they will not be found, except by loose and fanciful analogies. Constant behaviour patterns would require constant social conditions, and these history cannot provide. A science of mind might well establish uniformities and patterns of human behaviour, but only for given social conditions, just as the 'laws' of classical economics applied to human behaviour only in a particular society at a particular time. He took great offence at what he regarded as Positivistic social science, and psychology especially, for mistaking historical for natural phenomena. Psychology he allowed only a minimal role as a small branch of physiology, dealing with sensations and the like, unless it confined itself solely to the irrational side of mind. Either way it would confine itself to 'the blind forces and activities in us which are parts of human life . . . but are not parts of the historical process: sensation as distinct from thought, feelings as distinct from conceptions, appetites distinct from will'. These might be the necessary basis of our rational life but were not part of it. 'Our reason discovers them, but in studying them it is not studying itself'. Such study might help to keep them healthy and make the operation of reason possible 'while it pursues its own proper task, the self-conscious creation of its own historical life'.[27] He ended with these words, and they are typical of what was at the core of his later writings, so we can be certain of their importance for him. Collingwood, then, was resurrecting not just the individual, but the rational individual, indeed Reason, personified as the true self, not necessarily in opposition to appetites and sensations but requiring them to be healthy for the sake of the Reason, which is the ultimate purpose of life, an end in itself. Collingwood was not concerned about empathy with the emotions but about understanding rational processes of thought: these, not human appetites, sensations or emotions, were the universal element in history. This rigid distinction appears to have emerged as a result of the process of writing for the *Proceedings of the British Academy*, for notes in his papers, dated 1936, which are clearly rough notes for this piece are explicitly hesitant on this distinction.[28]

By 1936 it is clear that the elements of Collingwood's philosophy of historical knowledge had been fully worked out. *An Autobiography* (1939) and the posthumous *The Idea of History* (mainly compiled from his 1936 lectures) did of course carry these ideas to a wider audience; and some occasional notes and pieces add a little to the picture. Notes compiled in 1938-39 show his opposition to the comparative method: 'the apotheosis of anti-historicism in a positivistic interest — you cease to care about what a thing *is*, and amuse yourself by saying what it is *like*'.[29] And an interesting insight into his hostility to scientific method, suggesting an hostility to science itself as an almost sacrilegious attempt to control nature, can be gained from a letter to de Ruggiero in 1938; Marlowe, who he described as the 'only Elizabethan dramatist with any intellectual gift', had created in *Dr Faustus* a masterly critique of 'the phase of history in which European man devoted himself to conquering the "powers of nature"', a phase whose attitudes were only now being recognised as obsolete.[30] He certainly did not underestimate the importance of the intellectual revolution he was attempting. Nor did he confine his attention to traditional fields. Notes he compiled on the then somewhat unusual subject, for an English historian, of folklore and fairy tales show the consistence of his hostility to the scientific method and to psychology in particular: he dismissed any idea of investigating the psychological origin of fairy tales; they had specific historical origins.[31] In other words they were traceable to specific historical events (or actions) and could not be explained in terms of man's psychological needs.

Clearly, the intellectual biography outlined in *An Autobiography* is substantially correct; the ideas generally available in both that volume and in *The Idea of History* are typical of the corpus of his thought as it developed, mainly between 1926 and 1936 in his critical responses to the publications and ideas of that decade. Particularly evident is a growing obsession with the supposed influence of Positivism upon English historiography. But what is also clear is that his philosophy of history was very much a product of typical attitudes amongst historians in this period.

Some historians proceeded to acknowledge Collingwood's influence, using his philosophy to bolster their established attitudes. Powicke did so in his Riddell Memorial Lectures at Durham (published as *History, Freedom and Religion*, 1938) before even the autobiography was published, paying tribute in particular to the crucial 'Human Nature and Human History'. Human intelligence, said Powicke, was the 'soul' of the historical event, informing it 'as a body is informed by a soul'. Historical events were not 'movements' that could be contained within laws like the law of gravity; events could not be separated from 'mind'. This was pure Collingwood (with a theological overtone), for he went on to say that history was the history of ideas, that the thought behind the event is what interests the historian, who has to rethink the thought of the past and to understand events 'from the inside'. Also, like other historians, he emphasised the critical and sceptical nature of historical work and the apparently negative results of much historical inquiry, which he contrasted with the creative achievements in the past of a Gibbon or a Macaulay. History was full 'of intelligence and of human purpose', which was 'an incessant denial of fatalism', but it was an intelligence and purpose which eluded us, and this could give the historians 'a sense of remoteness which we associate with fatalism'. In an unusual flight of fancy, he said:

> Sometimes in the watches of the night, I have seen the whole of human experience, since mankind, as a thinking animal, loosened the hold of matter upon him — human experience with its incessant, ant-like activity, its hopes and fears, its aspirations and its despair — as a giant glacier moving imperceptibly, remorselessly, and myself as a tiny flake of frozen snow upon its lowest edge, explaining the nature and the laws of the vast mass, whence it came and whither it goes.

Whether, like his 'nightmares' about human wickedness and folly, he really preferred to push this sense of fatalism to the back of his mind and concentrate on what could be known it is difficult to say. He did, however, end on a religious and Idealist note: 'What we cannot comprehend, but know to be comprehensible, may be comprehended somewhere, as it occurs'. Was it possible, he asked, that history 'as the very condition of its being', met 'an infinite understanding' and came 'to rest in a divine compassion'.[32] Religious mystery was never far beneath the surface of historical explanation in English historiography.

Norman Sykes, writing in 1945, also acknowledged Collingwood when he claimed that there was a general recognition 'that the particular concern of history is with concrete unique and non-recurrent events, to the understanding of which the category of the particular, even the unique, is appropriate; that the subordination of personality to impersonal forces affords no clue to the interpretation of its record; and that the aim of historiography is to present what Collingwood called "not mere events . . . but actions" . . .'.[33] Sykes had, however, shown his commitment to individualism over ten years earlier, when he too had been critical of Bury: the scientific method, he said, suppressed individual differences in its desire to achieve general laws, but history was 'concerned with the concrete deeds of individual agents . . . The individual fact is the end . . .' He did recognise, though, that even natural scientists had come to recognise and deal in 'epigenesis, emergence, and individual idiosyncrasy'.[34] Unlike some, he felt that the classic scientific method was in retreat or at least changing, and that history was not so much threatened by an implacable scientific enemy as participating in an increasingly influential method; but then, as he later showed acquaintance with Whitehead's works, he may have been influenced by him in this. If so, he did not develop this interesting angle in later years. By 1956 he talked about 'individual personality' having primacy for the historian, whereas 'impersonal categories' were for the scientific method only.

'Indeed', he wrote, 'the attempt to eliminate individual characteristics in conformity with general laws, upon which scientific hypotheses are based, is contrary to the entire genius of historical study, which *per contra* uses generalisation only as a means to the discovery of what is uniquely individual'. He even talked of 'heroes and leaders' and used the life of Christ as the supreme example of 'the influence of individual personality upon history'. He again referred to Collingwood on the inside and outside of the event, and this time referred to Butterfield as well, who he quoted on the 'concrete life of the past' and 'the human and the personal factors, the incidental or momentary or local things', and the circumstantial — all studied for their own sake, not for some 'essence of history'. He ended by referring to Whitehead's presumption, in *Adventures of Ideas* (1933) 'that that religion will conquer which can render clear to popular understanding some external greatness incarnate in the passage of temporal fact'. Christianity, he claimed, could do this. Mere contingency did occur, it is true, as the result of self-determination and human will; so history did contain the unrelated and the inexplicable. But, ultimately, Providence ruled all; and even prayer could affect the course of history. By discovering in the historical process 'the creation of external values' we could be 'assured of the dignity and worth of our own individual share in its pageant or even of purpose in its record'; and Christianity pointed to an end beyond history.[35] Much of this was couched in very allusive language, perhaps necessarily so in the secularised intellectual climate of the fifties. It is strange to see a *deus ex machina* back in business and God's Providence invoked in a manner that J.R. Green had thought *passé* nearly a hundred years earlier. Of course, Butterfield was leading the revival of a religious approach to history in the post-war years (which will be considered later), and chairs of ecclesiastical history, not to mention classical historians, will always keep the Christian approach alive; and the case of Sykes well illustrates the conformity between the Idealist and the Providential approaches.

W.K. Hancock, the economic historian, also claimed Collingwood's philosophy as the basis for his own views on historical knowledge,[36] although he was more sympathetic to the social sciences than his master could have been. R.W. Harris used the pages of *History* to extol Collingwood's virtues, now that *The Idea of History* was available.[37] Eric John used Collingwood's ideas for an assault on Marxism, which we shall consider in the next chapter. The post-war years saw perhaps the peak of Collingwood's influence. He had his critics — indeed it was in defence of Collingwood against an uncomprehending A.L. Rowse that Harris wrote in 1952. Some ignored him, or expressed naïve inability to understand him, seemingly as a result of having heard one or other of his more quotable sayings — such as 'All history is the history of thought' — without bothering to read the philosophy behind the idea. But in a sense this is unimportant; as at least some historians realised, Collingwood was formulating a philosophy that expressed and justified many of the contemporary attitudes towards historical knowledge, ironically including the attitudes of many of those who could not or would not understand his philosophy. The trend away from even lip service to scientific method was clear.

This was not always evident, however, in the related field of economic history. It is often assumed that economic history had always had closer ties with economics that other branches of history had had with their respective bodies of social science theory. The situation was not really that simple. As we have seen, the founders of the subject, like Toynbee and Cunningham, were reacting *against* current economic theory. They were more influenced by Idealist philosophy than by economics. In the inter-war period, however, a determined effort was made to get economic history into a closer relationship with economics and, indeed, with other social sciences, including sociology. The main opponent of this trend was the Cambridge economic historian, J.H. Clapham; his concern was to oppose the application of current economic theory, the other types of social theory being beyond his ken. Significantly, he had come to economic history via mainstream history. In 1922 he launched his attack on Marshall, doyen of neo-classical economists, and on Pigou, who he described as even 'further from the clod and much further from machinery', in other words from the real world of economic activity. It was an imaginative and fierce attack under the now famous title, 'Of Empty Economic Boxes'. The Laws of Returns, proclaimed Clapham, have never actually been applied to specific industries; nobody knew 'under what conditions of returns coal or boots are being produced'. The concepts were empty; economic theory was not useful; even if the theory could be applied it would be of little use, because the real world constantly moves on, and the application would be outdated before any conclusions could be drawn. Economic theory was not universally applicable.[38] Pigou's reply was immediate and scornful: his basic point was telling — Clapham, whilst attacking the supposed inutility of economic theory, was really extolling 'realism', and by implication a pretty naive realism at that; Pigou distinguished between 'pure' and 'realistic' knowledge; mathematics was pure, whilst physics was realistic, for example; though some realistic knowledge was also applied, and some pure knowledge might have implications for realistic knowledge.[39] It is not necessary to attempt a critique of Pigou's epistemology; and Clapham's rejoinder did not add much to the argument.[40] But the debate does illustrate that the old historical realism, so evident before the war amongst mainstream historians, was still alive and kicking. However, there was no danger that this would now be designated a scientific attitude when the basis of Clapham's position was opposition to economic theorists who made their own claims to science — laws, uniformities and predictions. As Court has pointed out, Clapham explained his empiricism in terms of it being what the historian wanted; history was empirical, so it attracted those who delighted in individuality, the passage of time, the lack of clear-cut conclusions or simple patterns. 'The empiricism which led him to distrust theory', wrote Court, 'made him reluctant to discuss aggregates' and perhaps for this reason, he 'doubted whether history is logical' — there was too much left unconsidered.[41] Though critical of Clapham, Court, also a mainstream Cambridge historian by training, betrays the same naïve realism alongside the same scepticism about the logic of history or the historian's capacity to explain it rather than simply describe it: 'A historical situation involves many elements which we cannot explain, as well as those which we can. The historian's business is with the unresolved elements as well as those which are susceptible to rational explanation. This is because his final aim is nothing less than the recreation of the entire situation . . . The recovery of the past . . . is the ultimate aim of his endeavours'.[42] This idea that a whole past situation could be recovered or recreated is the epitome of what we have designated naïve historical realism.

However, the bulk of intelligent comment from economic historians in the inter-war period, particularly from the LSE, suggests that lively opinion favoured taking on board, not neo-classical economic theory especially, but modern social theory; sometimes, though by no means always, this was a very generalised or diluted form of Marxist materialism. This meant that economic history, particularly where its work was on the frontiers with the as yet ill-defined area of social history, was more alert to outside influences than was mainstream history. With the possible exception of international history (itself also best-established at the London School of Economics), which was not, however, methodologically innovative, economic and social history was the most engaged, outward-looking branch of the subject. Ironically, though this brought fruitful contacts elsewhere, it actually increased the gulf between mainstream political history and economic history, as their methodologies and epistemologies grew apart. This would create strains at Cambridge where the historical tripos tried to incorporate economic history into mainstream courses.

As we might expect, Tawney was one of the advocates of less individualism and more science. The individual historical phenomenon, he argued in his inaugural lecture, was not totally unique; it contained elements in common with other individuals; generalisation, therefore, was possible after the manner of the social sciences and, indeed, of ordinary human reaction to social phenomena. He advocated rational analysis of the historical individual (which might be a collective whole such as a nation, an institution or even an epoch) rather than intuitive methods.[43]

The following year, his LSE colleague, Eileen Power, used her own inaugural lecture, 'On Mediaeval History as a Social Study', to make a substantial contribution to ideas about historical methods and knowledge. She pleaded for historians to take seriously social theory and sociology, asking for 'a structural analysis of society', rigorous and scientific method, to replace the perfunctory, 'vague and spineless' social history of the past as typified by Macaulay's third chapter. She praised the Webbs and Tawney. She looked forward to the emergence of 'a social science *par excellence*' out of a co-operation between anthropology, sociology, economics and history which would find 'dependable uniformity and regularity' in society. She was not interested in imaginative reconstruction, in attempts to make 'mediaeval life live again', as in the works of G.G. Coulton; this was of minor importance. The essential purpose of the economic and social historian was to contribute both historical data and expertise to this queen of the social sciences, a true 'science of society'; meanwhile economists and sociologists would look for laws. There would be a grand co-operative effort, involving observation and induction, deduction and comparison.[44] This sounds like a distinctly Positivist programme, very unusual for an English historian and, *pace* Collingwood, unknown amongst academic historians in the Victorian period, but suited to the academic and degree structures of the LSE.

Reviewing the available methodologies, Power rejected the 'artistic' view that historical facts were solely 'concrete' and 'individual wholes' (be they epochs or events), which could be known by intuition. This misunderstood the historical process, which demonstrated the interrelatedness of facts. She was more interested in the Weberian method of 'ideal types', partly because of the work of Werner Sombart, in particular his work on economic systems and epochs and his construction of ideal types of capitalist and pre-capitalist medieval economies. She felt, however, that Sombart had allowed a vital slippage to occur when he identified an economic system (a valid ideal type) with an economic era (a concrete historical reality): 'A useful piece of methodological apparatus has become an historical individual'. His ideal type had 'ceased to be ideal', he forgot that the ideal type accentuates certain aspects of reality, so he misread medieval history. Power felt that such an error was always a risk with the Weberian method which, in any case, was somewhat arbitrary. Her preferred approach was to start with an analysis of an economic system, a phase of civilisation, or whatever, to show its inner connections. This in itself was valuable, but a further exercise gave added value: isolating certain elements within the whole, and then comparing their operation in different places at different times 'to discover whether certain social phenomena are habitual'. Collated with the findings of anthropologists and descriptive sociologists, expanded where necessary by association with approved deductive laws (such as economic theory), these would be the basis for 'laws of social behaviour', less precise perhaps than the laws of natural science, but valid and valuable nonetheless. This looks like a very Positivist programme, but Power herself claimed Marx, not Comte, as the author of the method.[45]

Part of the explanation for Power's attitude might lie in changes that had occurred in the social sciences, and in particular in anthropology. According to a recent account, there occurred round about 1920 a revolution in anthropology and sociology when Malinowski discovered 'field work' as the source of facts, partly because historians had failed to provide the right sort of facts, partly because the newly-professionalised social scientists wanted to be independent and do their own research, and partly because explanation was now sought in terms of function rather than of evolution.[46] So, just as in the past there had been historians who had feared being nothing but the handmaidens of the social scientists, providing facts for theorists, it now looked as if the social scientists were threatening to make history obsolete. One solution was to say that history was a special form of knowledge, not an ineffective social science. Another was to redraw the map of learning and integrate history with the new approach, as Power had done.

If Power avoided open commitment to Positivism, the Cambridge economic historian, M.M. Postan, was more forthcoming. In 1971, when he reprinted some of his essays and lectures from the inter-war period, he said that they were reissued to challenge the automatic and hostile response to anything that smacked of Positivism or scientism in the human studies — a response at variance with actual prac-tice and which left the Marxists as the sole exponents of an explicitly scientific approach to the study of society.[47] His assumption about what constitutes actual practice is highly dubious, but his second assumption is an interesting addition to the motivation for adopting a scientific posture. As we have seen, Postan feared for the intellectual calibre of those attracted to history because of its individualist traditions. In a brief but accurate analysis of the history of English historiography, he saw nineteenth-century scholarship as individualist in character, opposed to laws and scientific method, an individualism which was accentuated by the need to correct or verify in detail the initial theses or outlines of the first generation of researchers, leading to a concern with 'minor blemishes'. He counselled a return to 'social generalisation' and decried the 'neo-Kantian' philosophers who insisted that history was an art not a science. He could not accept that historians had to confine themselves to the 'unique and unrepeatable' or to describing and not explaining. Current practice was not the necessary or desirable practice. There was nothing distinctive about social experience when compared with the natural world. Uniformities *would* be discovered as soon as historians turned away from the unique and unrepeatable. If current sociological tools and categories appeared too crude for the complexities and subtleties of social experience, there was no reason to suppose that they would remain so. Perceptively, he suggested that some of the hostility to social science was derived from a fear of social engineering.[48] That fear, which has been there since Victorian times, was to reach new heights after 1945 with a certain amount of anti-totalitarian hysteria.

Economic and social history was pulled at least two ways, one by Clapham and the 'historian's' economic historians, and the other by those who had more scientific attitudes — though these were a rather heterogenous grouping, especially if we were to include full-blooded Marxists like Christopher Hill in their ranks. The situation was more complex and fluid than in mainstream history, which went on its individualistic, anti-scientific way, largely untouched by those controversies.

Postan did not name his neo-Kantian philosophers who argued that history was an art not a science. He may have had Croce or Collingwood in mind, but the most likely candidate is Oakeshott, whose *Experience and its Modes*, which included an essay on historical knowledge, had just been published (1933). In particular, Postan's insistence that current practice need not be taken as the model of the historian's method seems to be aimed at Oakeshott, for Oakeshott claimed to be taking the actual, known activity of the historians as the only valid concept of what the historical experience entailed. Though he claimed to be describing not prescribing, and all his modes of experience were 'when regarded from the standpoint of the totality of experience, abstract and defective . . . an arrest in experience', he clearly favoured what he described. He seemed to endorse the activities of those historians who were least interested in theory of any kind, whether social science theory or philosophy. He conceptualised the historian's implicit rationale as follows:

> It is presupposition of history that every event is related and that every change is but a moment in a world which contains no absolute *hiatus*. And the only explanation of change relevant or possible in history is simply an account of change. History accounts *for* change by means of a full account *of* change. The relation *between* events is always other events, and it is established in history by a full relation *of* events. The conception of cause is thus replaced by the exhibition of a world of events intrinsically related to one another in which no *lacuna* is tolerated . . . History . . . is the narration of a course of events, which in so far as it is without serious interruption, explains itself . . . And the method of the historian is never to explain by means of generalisation but always by means of greater and more complete detail.[49]

One consequence of this, according to Oakeshott, was that 'accidents are dismissed from history and the contrast between freedom and necessity, free-will and determinism, is made meaningless'. All historical individuals (events, things, persons) were related to each other, so in that sense unfree or determined; but none of them were governed by outside 'cosmic' causes or by 'logical' causes. This was as true for individual will as for anything else. As we have seen, this was not quite right as a description of the actual historical mode of experience in terms of the historian's own opinions: even if they wrote narrative, they somehow thought of the event as discrete and unrelated; and they usually took free will very seriously, unless they were lapsed Whigs who had adopted a world-weary nihilism. But it could be regarded as a logical consequence of their narrative mode, and avoided the dubious task of separating events into causes and effects. The other implication of Oakeshott's thesis was a rejection of 'any notion of a "plot" or "plan" in history, in the sense of an outline skeleton of important events, the abstract story without the details. History and the plot of history, are the same thing, to know one is to know the other'. Now this did represent contemporary historical practice. And, furthermore, argued Oakeshott, any so-called philosophy of history that involved the discovery of general laws also involved 'the complete destruction of history. The moment historical facts are regarded as instances of general laws, history is dismissed'. Therefore, history was not a science. Yet history generalised in its own way: for each historical individual, be it the fall of the Bastille, the Roman Empire, or even Napoleon, was also a generalisation, but a very limited generalisation which should not be taken beyond its limits.[50]

The crucial difference between Collingwood and Oakeshott was that Collingwood believed it was possible to re-enact a living past which was, therefore, relevant to the present and to current questions of ethical and political conduct, whereas Oakeshott believed that 'history is a theoretical undertaking unconnected with, and logically distant from, present practical considerations and the guidance of substantive conduct.[51] Oakeshott maintained this position, basically unchanged, well into the post-war world, where the idea of an ethically and politically mutual discipline met with great favour, partly because the current fear was that it was likely to be a left-wing subversive ideology that was influential if neutrality was not preserved; and partly because nominal neutrality tends to quietism, which is conservative in its effect and, therefore, by no means as neutral in reality as its exponents believe or pretend. Also, just as it has been well said that historians have a professional interest in variety, [52] so it could be said that they have a professional interest in detail, preferably narrative detail.

It is possible that Oakeshott's essay on the historical mode of experience took Butterfield's *The Whig Interpretation of History* as its model: three years separated the publication of the two, and the attitudes expressed by Butterfield are strikingly similar to those described by Oakeshott as the product of a new historical approach to the past: the past had to be studied for its own sake, and it was not directly relevant to the present; selection was anathema, for general outlines were biased or worthless, and general propositions or general truths were not the historian's concern; history was description, which was explanation enough; history was neutral. If so, Oakeshott was merely describing the attitudes of the anti-Whig reaction, of which Butterfield was a rather belated example. Surveying the state of historical knowledge in 1933, R.E. Balfour claimed that, whereas fifty years before, history had been almost universally claimed as a science (perhaps he antedated the 'scientist' attitude), the claim was no longer made. A science of history, he said, had once involved exactitude, a Positivist induction, and a prescriptive intent. But there had been a reaction against this 'excessive optimism' on all but the first of these counts. However, as we have seen, the original 'scientist' claims had involved little more than exactitude in the first place; Positivist induction and prescription had always been a minority interest. So when Balfour claimed that the scientific inductive ambition had been surrendered in favour of more intuitive methods of handling the 'wider processes of history' as an art, he was exaggerating the real changes that had occurred but reflecting current presumptions about what had happened. He himself associated science with 'discovery' and art with 'creation'. The historian discovered his facts through sensory perception, like the natural scientist; but unlike the scientist he was dependent on the arbitrary observations of others, which have chanced to survive. History, therefore, was peculiarly open to abuses; and the historian had to take into account a number of human factors. 'Even at the most favourable, the historian is in the position of a judge who has to decide the truth about a case upon which he has no evidence except the written depositions of witnesses whom he knows to have been untrustworthy and suspects to have been perjurers, with the further disadvantages that large portions of their depositions have been destroyed at random and that their authors are not present to be cross-examined'. We see here, once again, the judicial motif as an alternative to exact science, only this time it is recognised that cross-examination of witnesses is not possible. Having, imperfectly, decided on his facts, the historian then had to 'understand' them. This involved 'sympathetic imagination', and success would depend on the historian's 'innate powers'; the successful historian was born not made. At this stage the historian penetrated beneath the surface of events to show their connection and meaning. This had to be subjective interpretation and would be constantly challenged and replaced. The third and last phase of the historian's activity was exposition and this was purely artistic. In Balfour's model of the historian's activity, one moved from near-scientific method to artistic exposition; in between came the formulation of what corresponded to a scientist's hypothesis, with the difference that the scientist usually went on to test his hypothesis with further experiment, which the historian could not do. So, unable to cross-examine witnesses, dependent on the arbitrary survival of arbitrarily recorded evidence, unable to verify his hypotheses, and unable to keep the three logical stages of his activity temporally separate in practice (selecting in order to interpret and *vice versa*), the historian was a very inferior kind of scientist. Balfour warned against the hypothesis ever being taken as a final truth; it was at best a most tentative conclusion.[53]

The spirit of the time, whether scientist, Idealist, realist or empiricist, was cautious and low-key; only a few had either scientist or Marxist ambitions. Addressing the Historical Association in 1944, and reviewing recent developments in historical study, Powicke reflected on their inadequacy, and recalled the impression that historians of the older generation had made upon him as a young scholar at Manchester at the turn of the century: 'What tremendous fellows these historians were, how sure of themselves and of the world in which they lived! The confidence of the Marxist view of history was tremulous when compared with theirs'.[54] The wistful comparison with Marxism may be significant. History was once again in retreat — not just from a Whig interpretation, but from interpretation itself, particularly at the macro-level of understanding, or giving meaning to, the course of history; the abandonment of scientific pretensions lent added impetus to that retreat, which became one of separate development for history as an independent, if not very useful, form of knowledge — a dangerous sort of epistemological *apartheid*.

NOTES

1. C.P. Lucas, *Op.cit.*, p. 8.
2. A.F. Pollard, 'History and Science: A Rejoinder', *History*, 1 (1916), 25-27, 32-34.
3. *Ibid.*, pp. 35-39.
4. E. Barker, 'History and Philosophy', *History*, 7 (1922), 81-91.
5. B. Croce, *History as the Story of Liberty* (London, 1941), pp. 20-24, 54, 167-168, 301-306.
6. A.F. Pollard, 'History and Progress', *History*, 8 (1923), pp. 81-97.
7. A.F. Pollard, 'An Apology for Historical Research', *History*, 7 (1922), 1622, 165, 175.
8. H.W.C. Davis, 'The Study of History', in J.R.H. Weaver, A. Lane Poole, *Op.cit.*, pp. 74-80.
9. Collingwood Papers, Folder 14: Notes for 'Lectures on the Philosophy of History: written 9-13 January, 1926 for delivery in Hilary Term, 1926, paras 55, 57.
10. Collingwood Papers, Folder 14: paras 26, 29, 59, 64, 72.
11. R.G. Collingwood, 'Oswald Spengler and the Theory of Historical Cycles', *Antiquity*, i (1927), 318-319.
12. *Ibid.*, pp. 319-320.
13. R.G. Collingwood, 'The Theory of Historical Cycles II: Cycles and Progress', *Antiquity*, i (1927), 443-445.
14. R.G. Collingwood, 'Review of *Selected Essays of J.B. Bury*', *E.H.R.*, XLVI (1931), 461-465.
15. Collingwood Papers, Folder 27: 9 January 1931, C. to de Ruggiero.
16. His lecture plans for 1936 show that he lectured on Croce: Collingwood Papers, Folder 15.
17. Collingwood Papers, Folder 27: 25 March 1928, C. to de Ruggiero.
18. R.G. Collingwood, *The Historical Imagination: An Inaugural Lecture Delivered Before the University of Oxford on 28 October 1935*, (Oxford 1935), pp. 5-6.
19. B. Bosanquet, 'The Concrete Universal', in *The Principle of Individuality and Value* (The Gifford Lectures for 1911 delivered in Edinburgh University), (London, 1912), pp. 80-81, XIX-XXI.
20. *Ibid.*, 78-79.
21. R.G. Collingwood, *The Historical Imagination*, pp. 8-9.
22. *Ibid.*, p. 21.
23. R.G. Collingwood, 'Oswald Spengler and the Theory of Historical Cycles', p. 318.
24. R.W. Fogel, G.R. Elton, *Which Road to the Past?* (London, 1983), pp. 12-15, 49-50. His opponent, Elton, denies this, but we must return to Elton in a later chapter.
25. R.G. Collingwood, 'Human Nature and Human History', *Proceedings of the British Academy*, XXII (1936), 97-107.
26. *Ibid.*, p. 108.
27. *Ibid.*, pp. 109, 113-119, 124, 127.
28. Collingwood Papers, Folder 13: Notebooks on Historiography, 'Human Nature or Human History' (9, iii, 36) and 'Human Nature and Human History' (26, iii, 36).

29.　Collingwood Papers, Folder 13: Notes on historiography compiled 1938-9, '(5) The Comparative Method'.

30.　Collingwood Papers, Folder 27: C. to de Ruggiero, 24 July 1938.

31.　Collingwood Papers, Folder 21.

32.　F.M. Powicke, *History, Freedom and Religion*, pp. 5-6, 9-10, 16, 24.

33.　N. Sykes, *The Study of Ecclesiastical History, An Inaugural Lecture given to Emmanuel College, Cambridge 17 May 1945*, (Cambridge, 1945), p. 30.

34.　N. Sykes, 'The Study of History', *History*, 19 (1934), 100-105.

35.　N. Sykes, 'Address to the Historical Association', *Jubilee Addresses 1956* (London, 1956), pp. 8-14.

36.　W.K. Hancock, *The History of Our Times*, Webb Memorial Lecture, 1950, (London, 1956), pp. 18-26.

37.　R.W. Harris, 'Collingwood's *Idea of History*', *History*, 37 (1952), 1-7.

38.　J.H. Clapham, 'Of Empty Economic Boxes', *The Economic Journal*, xxxii (1922), 305-314.

39.　A.C. Pigou, 'Empty Economic Boxes: A Reply', *The Economic Journal*, xxxii (1922), 458-460.

40.　J.H. Clapham, 'The Economic Boxes', *The Economic Journal*, xxxii (1922), 560-563.

41.　Court, 'Two Economic Historians: John H. Clapham', *Scarcity and Choice in History*, pp. 143, 145-146.

42.　*Ibid.*, p. 149.

43.　R.H. Tawney, 'The Study of Economic History', Inaugural Lecture, LSE, 1932, *History and Society*, p. 56.

44.　E. Power, 'On Mediaeval History as a Social Study' in N.B. Harte ed., *The Study of Economic History*, pp. 112-114.

45.　*Ibid.*, pp. 115-119.

46.　P. Burke, *Sociology and History* (London, 1980), p.21.

47.　M.M. Postan, *Fact and Relevance: Essays on Historical Method* (Cambridge, 1971), p. ix.

48.　M.M. Postan, 'History and the Social Sciences' (1935), *Ibid.*, pp. 15-19.

49.　M. Oakeshott, *Experience and its Modes* (Cambridge, 1978), pp. 143, 145.

50.　*Ibid.*, pp. 143-144, 154, 159-160.

51.　D. Boucher, 'The Creation of the Past: British Idealism and Michael Oakeshott's Philosophy of History', *Op.cit.*, pp. 193-214, especially 106, 213.

52.　P. Burke, *Op.cit.*, p. 93.

53.　Balfour, *Op.cit.*, pp. 185-199.

54.　Powicke, 'After Fifty Years', *Modern Historians and the Study of History*, p. 226.

CHAPTER 8

The Marxist Initiative

By the end of the Second World War, English historical thinking was still individualist, still opposed to grand syntheses, interpretations or patterns of development. The bulk of the profession stood opposed to scientific method, thinking history a distinct form of knowledge; the exceptions worked mainly in the field of economic and social history, particularly at the LSE, or were members of a small, partisan sect of Marxists. Opinion was divided as to the normative value of history, but even those who believed in its relevance to society's problems thought its message somewhat allusive, not to say elusive — indeed, that was part of its Delphic attraction. As a positive force, the old Whig interpretation had lost its power and was maintained by a few somewhat unprofessional anachronisms — except where, in its extremely liberal guise it had been internationalised, or given a crusading role by Collingwood. History was usually seen as an alternative to totalitarian ideologies, Marxist or 'Hegelian', just as it had once been seen as the solvent of Comtism; it was, however, easier for historians to say what they were against than what they were for — without sounding trite or old-fashioned. The liberal tradition had become conservative. In this, as in much else, the historical profession mirrored wider political developments. Where there was an underlying philosophy it was usually Idealist in character, though Idealism was about to lose its creative power, and, in any case, had not been the dominant philosophy for some time. Could the old tradition be again revitalised, or would stagnation be the order of the day, or would there be a new departure? Much would depend on the state of rival orthodoxies and the relationship they could establish with the mainstream; and it is to one of these, namely Marxism, that we now turn.

As we have described them, the Marxists have appeared, in the inter-war period, as an isolated group, publishing in *The Modern Quarterly*, discussing issues with each other, occasionally lambasting an unregenerate Whig, and possessing only a few outstanding figures recognised in the mainstream, such as Christopher Hill or Maurice Dobb. In the post-war period, they determined to achieve wider influence and, accordingly, founded the Communist Party Historians' Group in 1946, which became the main vehicle for Marxist history in Britain until 1956, the year of the

Soviet intervention in Hungary and the consequent crisis in the party. A good guide to this phase of the history of Marxist historiography, which ranges widely over the relationships of the Marxists' group to their wider intellectual environment, is Schwarz's essay on the Communist Party Historians' Group (CPHG) in *Making Histories* (1982), produced by Birmingham's Centre for Contemporary Cultural Studies; two essays by McLennan, in the same volume, one on E.P. Thompson and one on 'Philosophy and History', are also useful. In Schwarz's account, Dobb appears as one of the formative influences in the group. A member of the Communist Party since 1921, trained in economics, author of major studies of the Soviet economy and of the development of capitalism which had paid due attention to the theoretical underpinnings of what he wrote, he had great prestige within the Group, albeit located on its 'economistic' wing. Schwarz is concerned to indicate that Dobb, despite his economistic background, was no narrow-minded ideologue or ahistorical theorist. One has to bear in mind that the 'popular front' strategy advocated by the CPHG which sought to locate Marxist historiography within the national radical tradition, and had its parallel in the efforts of the party itself, is again being advocated (though not without opposition). Another influence was identified as that of J.D. Bernal and other Cambridge scientists, who argued the case for the application of the methods of natural science to history, using Marxist concepts and succeeding where inadequate theoretical structures had caused failure in the past. 'From history could be learned the laws of social systems which in turn would guide the reasoned, planned society of the future'. This programme, one must say, seems to owe more to Comte than to Marx. The emphasis, however, was to be on the less rigid application of Marxist theory, on less deterministic or 'economistic' approaches, leaving room for, even emphasising, cultural issues, thus recapturing the 'national-popular' political culture that had briefly belonged to the left during the war years and had led to a radicalisation of political attitudes in 1945. The strength of conservative historiography however, often forced the Marxists into a more defensive role, acting merely as spokesmen for the more radical members of the liberal tradition, such as Tawney or the Hammonds, who were subject to determined attack. This increased their tendency to emphasise personal initiatives in place of economic forces in history. They also turned 'scientism' into 'moralism' said Schwarz: rather than history indicating a socialist future, it was assumed that the people had to be shown their history in order to get them to take the socialist path. This suggests a voluntarist principle. If, wrote Schwarz, 'a single common theme' could be detected, 'it was the desire to demonstrate that the Communist

Party was the inheritor of a long tradition of English popular radicalism' and that the 'working class' was the inheritor of the tradition of 'the people'. E.P. Thompson's *The Making of the English Working Class* (1963) is seen as the classic expression of that ideal, its significance compounded by its author's departure from the Communist Party in 1956.[1]

This interpretation is basically sound. The CPHG did dominate Marxist historical scholarship in this period, and it did adopt a 'popular front' strategy. The key figures before 1956 were Dobb and Bernal; the latter, however, in *Science and History* (1954) seemed more rigidly deterministic than Dobb; but we should also note the roles and increasing status of Hill and V.G. Childe, the archaeologist. Additionally, G.D.H. Cole, a non-Marxist socialist, republished *The Meaning of Marxism*, a sympathetic commentary not out of tune with the Group's refrain. E.P. Thompson, Hobsbawm, and Kiernan were perhaps the leading lights amongst those who provided continuity with the next generation. So the situation was quite complex, and it is worth looking at some of the major statements on Marxism and history as they appeared.

The first major post-war work was *History* (1947) by Childe. In this and a subsequent work (*Society and Knowledge*, 1956) he showed an impressive grasp, not only of Marxism, but of Idealist philosophy, modern science, and the philosophy of knowledge, including the ideas of Bergson and Whitehead; in 1947, however, this had to be topped off with a distasteful homage to Stalin and Stalinism, and the message of *History* was not entirely in tune with that described by Schwarz. He was still concerned to present history as a science, though it was an important part of his thesis that science itself was much changed since the confident day of Comtist Positivism. Though experiment was not possible in social study, and though the empirical method was of limited applicability because the number of instances to be observed was limited and because each instance was not isolable, history could still become a science — 'a science of progress, though not necessarily an exact science'. It should disclose the intelligible order of historical events, the laws of change, and therefore, the 'maxims for action' that derived from them. All scientific laws were recognised now to be only 'statements of probabilities', so the inexactitude of historical science was only a difference of degree from natural science, and individual objects and events could not always be expected to conform to these 'laws'. What we call 'chance' still affected the individual instance, but there was order *en masse* which could be recognised, understood and utilised. Some scientific laws were laws of 'process', like the laws of evolution; it was the historian's purpose to disclose an order in the process of human history.[2]

Though some tried to portray history as a series of accidents, a proper study recognised it as a process of orderly change. Childe recognised several schools of history in the past. There had been the school of 'theological historiography' in which unity and explanation had been provided by the purpose and will of God. There was a school of 'magical historiography', which had produced the 'Great Man' explanatory device, because it had started with kings who could control nature and were thus the cause of history too; secularisation of thought had transformed this into the 'catastrophic' explanation, whereby change was explained in terms of a single act of will, out of the blue. Carlyle was the classic exponent of this version of the 'Great Man' theory, but it lived on in works like Oman's. Then there were what he called naturalistic theories of historical order, which thought in terms of either immutable laws or 'abstract but external' schemes or patterns, the 'geometrical' version of which was couched in terms of immutable cyclical change; these were anachronisms, founded on the borrowed concept of a scientific 'law', which science itself had now abandoned in favour of probability, and on the notion of external concepts and categories, whilst science now thought in terms of evolution and process. Other versions were: geographical determinism, 'anthropological' or racial interpretations; and history as a department of political economy 'subjected to the eternal laws allegedly discovered by theoretical economists'. This last had, however, at least dragged history away from its political, military and ecclesiastical interests, which mirrored the institutional interests of the ruling class; and it had prepared the way for the Marxist Materialist conception of history by concentrating on political economy. Once the Marxist method had been accepted history would become a science through the application of the comparative method.[3] The comparative method, it will be recalled, was anathema to Collingwood, as to all Idealists who believed in the individuality of the historical event or action; the materialist conception of history had no such limitations.

Childe completed this remarkable survey of historical 'schools' by explaining the transition from Hegelianism to Marxism. Hegel had been the first to recognise change 'as a rational and orderly but creative process of the emergence of new values' but he had 'reimported into history, an external theological order under a new name'. 'It remained for Marx and Engels to strip this grand conception of its theological mysticism and to formulate as Dialectical Materialism, a view of history freed from transcendentalism and dependence on external laws'. He was careful to stress that history made its own path as it proceeded; it did not follow a prescribed route to a known terminus. He used organic rather than mechanistic imagery. Additionally, though he outlined a classic base-superstructure model, he allowed that the superstructure sometimes failed to change as and when the base changed, that there were periods of stagnation and delay and that 'economic man' was but an abstraction. Nonetheless, despite these provisos, he sketched an orderly process by which historical change occurred. The question of free will was a metaphysical irrelevance; and human motive in history was both irrelevant and unknowable. Engels, Lenin and Marx were quoted to support the view that 'all "acts of will" are related to, and conditioned by, all previous volitions both by the individual agent and by all other individuals who have contributed to the formation of the historical environment and the society to which he involuntarily belongs'. An isolated act by an isolated individual was not an historical act, not 'socially effective'. He quoted Engels's famous passage about history making itself in such a way 'that the final result always arises from conflicts between many individual wills' and thus 'what emerges is something that nobody had willed. Thus past history proceeds in the manner of a natural process'. He further quoted Engels as follows:

> Men make their own history but not yet with a collective will, in accordance with a collective plan, or even in one definitely constituted society. Their efforts clash and for that very reason all such societies are governed by *necessity* which is supplemented by and appears under the forms of accidents.

If our analysis of the fears that motivated the opposition to the previous great challenge to historical individualism, in the form of Comtism, was corect, and if those fears still existed in the 1940s, then these passages would sound alarm bells in many quarters, with their assumptions that, hitherto, history was a natural process, but that it could be made by a collective will in the future. The promise in Marxism did not appeal. Non-Marxists do not really worry that much about the Marxist interpretation of the past; if they are honest, what worries them is the prospect of a Marxist future; like Bury's liberals who believed in open-ended progress, and like conservatives who could not stomach the concept of progress in the first place, they feared to reach a Marxist goal; they feared the goal itself and the route. Ironically, those who denied the relevance of history to contemporary affairs would have felt most strongly the implicit threat in this Marxist interpretation; they did not worry about the negation of will in the past, but about the implementation of a collective will in the future. Interestingly, Childe was at pains to stress that the ideal society 'would not be static but consciously and intentionally creative. It might be regarded as the true beginning of rational history'. Nor was its attainment inevitable. Unfortunately for the popularity of Marxism, too many people fear an immutable ideal world and are not convinced either by experience or by logic that a world thought ideal by its authors, would be mutable. No doubt the contemporary response to Childe would also have been limited by the homily to Stalin at the end of the book.[4] Despite his impressive erudition and subtlety, Childe's association with Stalinism, his holistic approach to history, his emphasis on Marxism as a complete method for understanding history as a whole and for achieving the classless society, and his emphasis on the parallels between history and natural science, give his work a rather narrow and deterministic, not to say apocalyptic, character.

A year after Childe's *History*, Christopher Hill published a major article in *The Modern Quarterly* which indicated rather more clearly the direction that Marxist historiography was to take. 'Marxism is not determinist', declared Hill. 'This point is so important, and so much misrepresented by ignorant anti-Marxists', he added, quoting the passage from Engels in which the economic base is said to have only an 'ultimately' determining role. Following on from that, he allowed that ideas could influence the course of history — but they had 'an ultimate economic origin' and could not alone alter the course of events. To matter historically, ideas had to reflect or adapt to 'the needs of real historical forces, of classes'. The popular front strategy was most evident when Hill turned to a consideration of the influence that Marx and Engels had had upon the study of history. They had helped towards an awareness of the 'crucial importance' of economic history, which would enable history to become a science. They had forced an awareness of the role of economic classes, which had made individualistic and Whig interpretations at last redundant, despite Trevelyan's antique Whiggery and Butterfield's return to the Whig fold with his wartime *The Englishman and his History*. This prolongation of Whiggism was a political necessity for those who feared the Marxist alternative. Thirdly, Marx's and Engels's influence had led to a general recognition of the 'social origins' of ideas and ideologies; he cited Tawney's *Religion and the Rise of Capitalism* as an example. There was also 'a new relativism'; the absolute moral standards of an Acton could no longer be employed. Fifthly, he made the highly dubious claim that Marxism had played an important part in revolutionising critical attitudes to sources; he qualified this point so much that perhaps he was not convinced himself. Lastly, he felt that 'the modern sense of the unity of history' derived from Marx, who had seen 'the ultimate priority of economic facts' as the source of that unity. It followed that, if history was seen as a whole, then 'the historian himself must have a vision of society and the social process as a whole: he must have a philosophy'. For Hill, of course, only Marxism could meet that need and avoid Fisher's unsatisfying play of the contingent and unforeseen. Hill was struggling to make Marxism appear flexible and influential, already a force in the mainstream of historiography, whilst retaining its own special sense of purpose and conceptual unity.

Additionally, he was trying to make a particular appeal to a broad left opinion schooled in the more individualistic radical tradition. Crude economic determinism was out: Marx himself had said, in *The German Ideology*, that the Marxist interpretation of history, though scientific, had as its first premise 'the existence of living, human individuals'. Hill even allowed a Luther or a Galileo his moment of glory. But individualism was not enough for Hill's appeal; it had to be accompanied by a sense of purpose to replace the old liberal moralism: 'In reaction against the facile liberalism of the nineteenth and early twentieth centuries, many modern philosophers and historians have relapsed into a bleak pessimism. So far from having progressed, man has got progressively worse'; atom bombs threatened the destruction of society; tabloid newspapers threatened its cultural values; humanism was dead; and God was 'the only alternative to suicide'. This pessimism, sense of apocalypse, and even flight back to God, did exist in the post-war period. But Hill claimed that Marxism offered a way out, not with an alternative faith, but because it would 'help contemporary historians to preserve a sense of proportion between social forces and the men through whom they work, between statistics and poetry, necessity and freedom . . . Marxists believe neither that history is made by great men nor that economic changes automatically produce political results'. Though 'ideas are borne in on people by their environment . . . the human mind is one of the factors causing change'. And there was hope for the future: history might have been a tragedy, 'but not a meaningless tragedy', for we were not mere spectators; as participants we could learn and have hope. Though *The Modern Quarterly* itself preached only to the converted, Hill was clearly trying to establish the basis for a bid to, not only replace the Whig interpretation, but, steal the Whigs' clothes, or even, we might add, the Liberal Anglicans'. Marxism, he said, had been largely responsible for the modern scientific approach to history, but in academic hands it had become sterile and determinist. The Marxist wished to retain the right to judge and to choose — in the interests of the class struggle. Choice consisted of choosing the right path for a 'conscious co-operation' with the process of history in hope of a satisfactory outcome from the class struggle. Individual choices had to be made in order to achieve this outcome; there were no blind forces. People, individuals, had to be convinced of the need for action: 'the history of mankind is the history of the growth of freedom of moral judgment', and the Marxist was freest because 'his study of history helps him to learn how to make society and himself freer'.[5] Marxist history, then, had form and purpose; it was teleological; yet the role of the individual was crucial, so long as it was in the service of society; the individual was freest, in a positive sense, if aware of the past and, therefore, of the present and the potential of society — for he would not then mistake the clock. History offered hope but not complacency; it offered a socially responsible role; it was both science and philosophy, but not art. The parallels with the Liberal Anglican view of history are striking; since the long drawn-out demise of the Whig-Liberal tradition, nothing had yet taken its place; the new humanist Marxists were bidding to do so.

Three years later, Dobb, the prestigious doyen of the Group, put the argument before a wider, less partisan audience in the historical association's journal, *History*, which was still faithful to its tradition of airing general and philosophical issues, albeit with qualitatively mixed results. Essentially, he tried to defend Marxism against the charge of using a crude base-superstructure model of society, and employing simplistic economic determinist explanations, which reduced human beings to 'lifeless marionettes' and history to 'a strange automatic march of material factors'. History was meaningful but it could not be reduced to a 'simple formula'. Marxist materialism was an aid to research, a guide to problem-solving, a general hypothesis, not a substitute for true history.[6] Like Childe, Dobb stressed that modern science thought in terms of hypotheses or problem-solving devices rather than laws, and that history was, thus, only different in degree in this respect. This was a deliberately modest overture.

There is some similarity between Marxists' disclaimers, whilst retaining their long-term hopes and ambitions, and the disclaimers and ambitions of the Positivists like Buckle, nearly a century earlier. The Marxists, however, lacking the naïve enthusiasm of the first generation Positivists, and schooled in the hard knocks and disappointments of the previous quarter century, were more insistent in their disclaimers of determinism and anti-individualism. They had one advantage over Buckle: their subject had been professionalised and they were inside the profession; Buckle had been briefly a literary celebrity, but was denied the status of true historian, and branded an infidel.

However, the short-term problem for Dobb and his colleagues was well illustrated two years later in a reply to Dobb by E. John. Though raising some rather standard points of opposition to philosophy of history in general, this article also weighed in with some telling epistemological and methodological points. John started by claiming that if Marxism was more than 'a lifeless *a priori schema*' then it must be capable of proof (or, in the Popperian style, of disproof) by empirical methods — and of this he could find no successful Marxist examples. He also claimed that the 'dualism' of a Marxist like Dobb, who still considered mind and matter, ideas and the material world, to be rival concepts, was now outmoded, citing Collingwood (*The New Leviathan*) and Ryle, Collingwood's successor in the Chair of Metaphysical Philosophy at Cambridge (*Concept of Mind*, 1949) in support. It was Ryle who had criticised the idea of the mind in the body as the 'ghost in the machine'. How far either John or other anti-Marxist historians would have been prepared to go down Ryle's road is unclear; for Ryle believed that attempts to explain free will in terms of human motives (anger, ambition, or whatever) were merely to describe those actions or that behaviour which demonstrated those motives, so that they in turn had to be explained, and so on, *ad infinitum*. In other words, he was a philosophical behaviourist, albeit of a sophisticated type. John most certainly was not a behaviourist, as is evidenced by his criticism of Dobb's dualism; he criticised his ambiguity over the question of 'human freedom', an ambiguity which John obviously did not share. More tellingly he criticised Dobb's imagery: Dobb had talked of ideas as a reflection of social conditions, which nonetheless could be 'complex', 'indirect', not 'a simple mirror image of reality' and not 'purely passive'. This, said John, was then a misleading image which covered up the confusion in Dobb's thought. In more well-worked vein, he also attacked Dobb's minimising of the significance of the 'unique' event or the 'intricacy' of history. 'Scientific' history had always failed: we now read, said John rather cheekily, Stubbs not Comte, and Marx not Hegel, if we want good vintage history. The task of history was to make ideology subservient to 'empirical reality', sitting down 'before the given fact', and the historical fact of human conduct will be seen to be subject to no laws of regularity. The historical event was, therefore, unique. Additionally, the incomplete nature of historical evidence made it impossible to generalise; but the crucial factor was the presence of 'human actions' as opposed to 'inanimate nature'.

However, again acknowledging Collingwood (and Bloch), he challenged the materialism of the Marxists and also the Idealism of the Whig tradition. Human beings were part of nature, but to find out what they were, it was necessary to find out what they do, what they think and feel, for this was part of their nature. In this he was closer to the Idealists. When the Marxist talked of 'material factors', said John, he actually meant 'human appetites and interests'. The task of the historian was to discriminate between the interplay of these appetites, interests, virtues and vices — and reason itself; for man was also a rational being, and could communicate his reasoning to others when the irrational remained private and inexplicable to others. His debt to Collingwood is obvious. Each particular interplay would be unique, and history remained a study of the particular and the detailed, not a generalisation about the operation of material factors. The point about translating material factors into human appetites and interests is a telling one; but if he had followed Ryle's arguments through he might have run into difficulties in terms of whether describing appetites and interests served as any sort of explanation; but, as we have seen, explanation was not always high on historians' lists of priorities. The merit of such individual description, whether it explained or not, however, was that it withdrew 'the sphere of historical interpretation' from 'the ideologues' and put it 'in its rightful place, into the hands of the working historians'. John's article has considerable intellectual power; so much so that one can forget that, however valid his objection to the fudging element in Marxist humanism, however valid his claims against 'dualism', he had switched his attack to the sort of Marxism that Dobb and others were now at pains to deny. Dobb was castigated both for fudging in an effort to accommodate individualism and for having a rigid *schema*.

John's own liberalism was made clear when, just as Mill had argued that all ideas, true or false, were necessary for the preservation of human liberty and unsuitable for censorship, John argued that all human experience, good or bad, was necessary for human liberty and unsuitable for being generalised out of existence. The professional's refusal to generalise had now been given a high purpose. 'How can either the classless society or the British constitution in the heyday of liberalism, be claimed as the *summum bonum* of human wisdom?' asked John. In history, all human life was there! John's historian was rather like the preserver of rare breeds who hopes that their gene pools will one day prove useful; the variety of historical experience was an antidote to societal inbreeding. In a most revealing analogy, he compared the seeker after historical generalisation to the legendary visitor to Oxford who, taken to see the colleges, asked then to see the University.[7] This must tell us something about the life and attitudes of English academics and intellectuals, living in a world of historic individualism, which they refuse to rationalise!

Dobb was unlucky in his antagonist, but John's article illustrates the keenly felt opposition to Marxism and the refusal to take seriously protestations of individualism and denials of determinism. A fairly random selection of articles in *History* during the fifties illustrates the prevalent obsession (which does not seem too strong a term) with individualism. J.E. Neale, the Namier of the Elizabethans, wrote about 'The Biographical Approach to History', in which he declared 'human beings are the stuff of history', and though he was 'almost' prepared to accept abstract generic concepts as having a real, actual existence, group behaviour was always and necessarily studied with reference to individual behaviour.[8] Butterfield weighed in with 'The Role of the Individual in History', a fairly predictable defence of that role.[9] And C. Wilson wrote of 'The Entrepreneur in the Industrial Revolution in Britain', endorsing the interpretations of Ashton and of all those that made the entrepreneur the saviour of the nation.[10]

Meanwhile, J.D. Bernal had demonstrated that the popular front tendencies of the historians, which underplayed the determinist implications of Marxism, were not in sole possession of the field. His *Science in History* (1954) must have confirmed the worst suspicions of people like John. He concluded his book:

> History has in the past been the record of human intentions, of human actions, and of events which were more often than not very different from the ends consciously aimed at. It was the field of action of forces that could only be dimly guessed at, and were far too easily identified with superior beings whose playthings were men. As we come to see more in history than this, as we begin to understand something of these forces and the laws they must obey, the events of history will become the results of conscious planning and achievement. With the discovery of the science of society, as Engels said, the true history of mankind begins.[11]

There is an interesting ambiguity in the use of the term 'history' in this passage. With an obvious echo of Engels, past 'history' is first portrayed as a 'record' of intentions, actions and events, which were not usually the product of anybody's intention or will. Here he refers to history as historiography, in which explanations had been vague, confused and, as likely as not, theological or magical. But as social forces and laws come to be understood, 'the events of history will become the results of conscious planning and achievement'. By now he is talking of the events themselves. The way history is written will alter; so will the way history is made. Bernal's thinking seems to be confused here; a slippage of the meaning of 'history' has occurred. But, by implication at least, written history will not only change to accommodate the actual change that will occur, but will change prior to the actual change, and will, indeed, be instrumental in creating the actual change by helping to create the necessary understanding of the forces of history in place of the inadequacies of previous forms of explanation. It is precisely this use of history (as historiography) to change the course of history, as events, that non-Marxists found so alarming. They could stomach chance; they could even stomach impersonal forces, so long as they remained hidden and there could be retained an illusion, at least, of will. But they could not face man controlling his destiny through understanding of the forces of history, even though this suggested a hitherto undreamt of use of will, because it would be a collective will, not an individual one.

Bernal's book contained a mixture of perceptive insights into the way history had been written, a wildly inaccurate or simplified chronology of the changes that had occurred, and some crude and naïve judgments, especially about the Societ Union, where (for example) science had progressed untrammelled by the needs of military research. Basically, he had seen Victorian historians as 'justifying by default' their own economic and political system by their refusal to theorise and by being satisfied with collecting facts: 'it was an episodic and meaningless history corresponding to an individualist and unregulated economic system'. This was a half truth, in that the individualist mode was supplemented by the 'Whig' national story and overlaid by a sense of Providence; it was, however, a half truth that fitted perfectly with a base-superstructure view of society. Bernal seems to have equated 'Victorian' attitudes with those of Fisher in the nineteen thirties; by muddling his chronology, he missed the Whig and Providential characteristics of the former. He did, however, recognise the Victorian commitment to Progress and the significance of the loss of that belief. He also recognised the failure of professional historians either to engage the interests and sympathies of readers or to understand society, which, he felt, left the field open to 'propagandists of nationalism and imperialism', 'ignorant fanatics', and 'downright reactionaries with race theories and prophetic fulfilments'.[12]

His account of the impact of the Vienna School of Logical Positivism is quite interesting. Vienna, before the First World War, he said, produced a culture of an élite of uprooted and disillusioned intellectuals, mainly dependent on the old imperial administration. It was, therefore, a culture of 'intellectual pessimism', especially in terms of its two greatest creations, psycho-analysis and neo-Positivism, both of which had a profound effect on twentieth-century bourgeois thought. The pessimism of the latter, in particular, seemed to justify an acceptance of the status quo: 'by stressing in the most learned terms the intrinsic irrationality and meaninglessness of the Universe, the inevitability of bias in our interpretation of it, and the irresponsibility of the individual psyche at the mercy of its complexes, they confused and paralysed attempts to reform it. By insisting on the rights of the individual to remain detached from society, they furnished a haven for those who wanted to justify their own ineffectiveness'. Though Bernal wrote of the past, Popper's ideas, which have some similarity to those of the Vienna circle, reached a wider audience in the fifties than in the thirties; and Bernal was overly optimistic when he assumed their demise and the imminent triumph of his own principles. Instead of this pessimism, Bernal offered 'a new science of society', which alone would save history from being reduced to 'personal trivialities' or the action of divine providence, this latter being a completely outmoded concept.[13] With a polemicist's licence, Bernal exaggerated the strength of his own position and minimised the strength of his opponents, but he did correctly identify the nature of the opposition.

Marxists did seem to be pulling in two directions in the fifties; some, like the Historians' Group, trying to integrate with the radical tradition, so minimising the doctrinaire and determinist traditions of Marxism; others still insisting that history was a science, that it worked according to laws, that it could be predicted. Not all non-Marxists reacted in the way John had done. G.D.H. Cole, veteran labour historian and Guild Socialist, did see the liberal potential in Marxism, whilst severely criticising the more scientific or schematic traditions. His *What Marx Really Meant* (1934) was updated and republished as *The Meaning of Marxism* in 1948. Cole claimed to be influenced by Marx without being an obedient 'Marxist'. He distrusted 'systems' and 'Marx's system hits right up against my conviction that it is a profound error to attribute to "classes", of things or of men, any reality distinct from the individuals which compose them, or to regard the classes as distinct from the individuals, as active forces shaping the course of history'. All action and all consciousness were attributes of the individual; groups or classes never acted, except in the sense that the individuals of which they were composed acted, individually in the same or related ways. Cole's nominalism, though typical of historians, is striking in that he was the leading exponent of Guild Socialism, yet in this remained untouched by holistic ideas. Other of his writings suggest such an influence, but in the face of Marxism it is nominalist individualism that comes to the fore. Cole, who claimed to have come to Marx through Hegel, reckoned that when Marx talked of classes, as real things acting for themselves, he had failed to rid himself of Hegel's metaphysics, especially when he talked of individuals, rather than groups, as abstractions. The logic of Cole's insistence that only individuals, not groups, acted, was that group behaviour was unpredictable.[14]

More sympathetically, Cole tried to relocate Marx as a 'realist' rather than a 'materialist'. Marx took things as they are — changing, living, growing, and concrete, not abstract. To study these things historically was to interpret them, not in terms of searching for their origins, but 'by the whole active force of which their entire history is the expression'. Marx was a realist opponent of Idealism; to call him a materialist, in the twentieth century, was misleading. Marx always accepted the power of mind, as when he acknowledged that man's power over nature lay at the root of history or when he included mind-affected objects in his powers of production. Marx accepted that men made their own history. In other words, Cole was suggesting that the twentieth century notion that the dichotomy between mind and matter was false, had been anticipated by Marx. Cole concluded: 'the worst enemies of Marxism are those who harden it into a universal dogma, and thus conceal its value as a flexible method of social analysis'. Dominating Cole's treatment of Marx and Marxism was the belief that the 'free wills of men form part of the chain of causality', and that nothing was predetermined.[15] Cole's treatment, nonethelesss, was in many ways closer to that of the Historians' Group than were some Marxists. The Marxist problem remained, however: they wanted to provide more than 'a flexible method of social analysis'; they wanted to provide a sense of purpose; but how could they do that whilst retaining the flexibility of the method! A sense of purpose suggested a sense of destiny; a sense of destiny suggested determinism.

By the mid-fifties, the ground had been prepared for a new initiative by Marxist historians, almost irrespective of the formation of the 'New Left'. If they were to become something more than an isolated sect, like latterday Comtists, then they needed to adapt to mainstream traditions. In the next twenty-five years they did just this, through works of original scholarship which have had an influence beyond the Marxist circle itself (such as Thompson's *The Making of the English Working Class*, 1963), through the influential 'normal science' of textbooks (as in Hobsbawm's *Industry and Empire*, 1968), and through what they have written about historical knowledge itself. Their flexibility has been tested recently by the growth of feminist history but, despite tensions, they have largely stood the test. A great deal has been written about the Marxism of the New Left from the inside, so we need not attempt a full-scale review of its ideas, quarrels and impact. From the historiographical point of view, however, two main initiatives demand attention: the examination of the meaning of Marxism for history, especially in relation to the question of free will; and the attempt to relate Marxist historiography to a wider historical tradition.

The problems revolving around the first of these issues were well illustrated by Gordon Leff's *The Tyranny of Concepts* (1961; revised 1969). Leff, a former Marxist and one-time member of the Cambridge University Communist Party, who had become increasingly disillusioned first with Communist practice and then with Marxist theory, developed a sophisticated critique of Marxism during the sixties. The preface to the second edition (1969) of *The Tyranny of Concepts* states that: 'Marxism has become one more closed system, imprisoning its adherents in its categories', and there was a conflict between Marx's two central premises, namely 'that the mode of production is the ultimate determinant in man's life and outlook, and that men are their own agents in changing their history and themselves'. Neither Marx nor his successors had succeeded in resolving this conflict. For Leff, this seems to have become the central issue, as it had been for others so often in the past. Revolutions, for example, occurred, not out of the predictable movement of social forces, but as a result of contingent circumstances 'when individuals refuse to accept the present'. He objected to Marx's teleology when Marx said 'mankind sets itself only such tasks as it can solve'. He took a nominalist position when he objected to the idea of 'society as a whole'. He felt that Marx had simply 'inverted' Hegel when he saw historical change as a 'necessary and autonomous revolutionary sequence'; most history was neither necessary nor revolutionary. Marx's teleological vision of what man could, should, and would be, was 'substituting a belief in necessity for human agency and destiny for humanity'. The use of 'destiny' as an antonym for 'humanity' is striking. Leff could see that recent emphasis on the 'early Marx' might reinstate 'man' in place of 'history', but had no faith in the Marxists' ability to adopt this Marxist form of humanism.[16]

Like John, Leff suggested that the old dualism of mind and matter, Idealism and materialism, was an anachronism; Leninist dialectical materialism was a blind alley, and a continued obsession with this kept Marxists intellectually isolated. However, he argued the paradox that 'through historical materialism we are able to see the fallacy of dialectical materialism', the former dissolving the 'false scientism' of the latter. The argument went as follows. For Marx, what distinguished man was his role in society; man as social being was indistinguishable from man the individual;' thus 'society' and the 'individual' were a false dichotomy. So for Marx, 'the truth about man was not to be found in his consciousness but in his existence; and his existence was not timeless but rooted in a specific set of circumstances', past and present. The determining element in those circumstances was, in the words of Marx and Engels, 'the mode of production of material life'. This materialist conception of history was 'an historical interpretation of society' based on a recognition that men and their ideas are products of circumstances, and thus we go to history, rather than to 'human nature' or philosophy, to understand them; 'this entails considering men as active members of society engaged in the pursuit — or the rejection — of a given mode of life'. In this way it was possible to pass beyond an understanding of subjective ideas to reality itself, historical materialism being 'the strongest antidote to self-delusion, fatalism and obscurantism'. This was realism of a sophisticated kind, though it was also the classic defence of historicism: man, as an Ideal-ist would have put it, had history not nature; history rescued us from the tyranny of concepts and temporal provincialism; we needed to understand past and present in order to achieve objectivity; history was a powerful sol-vent, because it was about real people in real situations.

Having argued this case, however, Leff drew back. As well as a history, man did have a nature, which could not be subsumed under economic determinism, and had to be studied through psychology and sociology. The conjuncture of historical change and man's nature, however, rules out determinism, for Leff conceived human nature in a highly individual-ist way. The individual personality was not to be explained solely in terms of social conditioning: 'he may have digestive trouble, his parents may not be compatible, he may be bullied or terrorised, he may feel unloved, he may not respond to school discipline, he may be hypersensitive, or introspective, or in some other way unable to adjust himself to his surroundings'. We have speculated on the private motivations for an individualist attitude, from Froude (who suffered from at least half of the above torments) onwards. Such confessions of weakness would not have been popular in Victorian times. But, in the twentieth century, the individual is no longer the hero but a victim; he does not change society; he is threatened by it. One might, of course, doubt if Leff is correct in positing such a clear distinction between social conditioning and private grief; there are, doubtless, socially-conditioned digestive troubles, types of incompatibility, bullying and the rest.

The Marxist interpretation of history, then, was not a science. Leff, like others before him, argued that historical events could not be subsumed under general laws, that verification by experiment was impossible, that selection of evidence was arbitrary, as was histori-cal reconstruction from the evidence. So-called historical laws were generalisations from tendencies, subjectively arrived at; they were not falsifiable — a Popperian point (and Leff had quite a lot to say about Popper). The extent of Leff's epistemological individualism is evident when he stressed the 'personal' nature of the historian's own interests and perceptions. Moreover, 'to observe is not the same as to understand'; in other words, mere observation and induction was no substitute for human recognition; as we shall see, in a later book Leff turned to Dilthey for epistemological guidance. The Marxist, attempting to formulate causal laws of economic determinism, found too many exceptions to the supposed rules or became hopelessly vague, or fell back on parallels, metaphors and analogies. Society was composed of individuals; and individuals change. Marxism was as teleological, anachronistic and presentist, as ever the Whig interpretation had been.[17]

Of all these themes the most persistent was: 'A man's consciousness is not just the product of social values; it is the outcome of all the experiences that have been registered by him as an individual'. For it was the necessary starting point for Leff's argument that, beyond any social or economic dynamic in society, was the motor force of the individual's search for power, a search that sprang 'from the need of every individual by virtue of being an individual to establish his individuality and not, to be, metaphorically, trodden under foot'. He has to 'establish his place in the sun' like 'any living thing, vegetable or animal'. With its imperialist imagery and biological simile, this looks dangerously imbued with Social Darwinism — or maybe it is Nietzschean, for this is a psychological will to power: 'just as we are born with certain instincts indispensable for survival, so we are endowed with capacities and bents that we desire to realise and that are equally indispensable to our personalities. In seeking to gratify these we are asserting ourselves'. Should we fail to assert ourselves we should do nothing — and *be* nothing; reciprocal assertiveness amongst individuals leads to the desire for power and even the abuse of it; out of the clash of wills powerful individuals emerge, a Luther or a Robespierre, who are more than the personification of social forces.[18] So Leff's threatened individuals assert themselves, and become little big men, and some even go on to become heroes and change history!

Similarly, changes in the superstructure of ideas were not always dependent on changes in the base, sometimes preceding the latter, 'when men are no longer prepared to accept the existing forms', when there is 'a revulsion against the prevailing outlook or institutions', or from the 'sheer logic of internal development whereby one concept leads to another'. This last is dialectical Idealism; the rest is voluntarism or it is nothing. Explicitly on free will, however, Leff simply refused to accept a dichotomy between free will and necessity; in this he is typical of modern social theorists.[19]

Finally, and perhaps most importantly, we should note Leff's criticism of what he regarded as the absence from Marxism of any distinct theory of ethics, beyond the necessity of submitting 'to the ineluctable forces of history'. As he put it: 'there is no guarantee that what is held to be necessity is necessary', and the argument for necessity is an argument for tyranny. Moreover, such an argument means 'jettisoning any principles of moral conduct other than the pragmatic one of expediency (with what result can be seen from the changes and purges in the Communist states)'. That Leff argued that these ideological convictions had such practical consequences suggests that he had forgotten his own words about the inevitable search for, and abuse of, power, but this does illustrate the political, as well as the intellectual, concerns of those who feared or disliked Marxism, concerns of which those who desired to change the world, as well as study it, could hardly complain. The Marxists' lack of a code of ethics beyond that of recognising necessity was, for Leff, a fatal flaw, excluding 'anything that can be called moral choice and with it personal morality. The effect has been to efface free will . . . Since personal freedom cannot be conceived in its own right, conscience, intention, motive, volition, are all disregarded, or when acknowledged, as with conscience, derided as bourgeois'. Even if 'personal morality was essentially the product of bourgeois society', it was a great achievement and not to be wantonly destroyed. 'This individualist ethic has its epigraph in Luther's cry of defiance. "Here I stand" is an appeal to man's power of choice; it is a recognition of individual responsibility in the face of which any other authority is of no avail'. In comparison, Marxist ideas of morality were a reversion to a 'medieval ethic', discounting 'men themselves'. It seems that if you scratch an individualist, you still find a Protestant standing firm on his conscience — even if he is a medievalist. But Leff's position was explicitly humanist: ethics were about men, not history; 'true socialism' could only be founded on humanism.[20]

Leff's position was that of an intelligent critic of a once-admired ideology, very different from the knock-about anti-Marxism of some, who had got their Marxism from *The Communist Manifesto* and nothing else.

However, those within the Marxist camp were concerned with the very same issues — but concerned to adapt the Marxist tradition, in the manner of the CPHG, rather than write it off.

In the sixties the main organ for the expression of these liberal views was the 'new' New Left Review, *The Socialist Register* (edited by Miliband and Saville), in which V.G. Kiernan, in 1968, issued a plea for less rigidity in Marxist doctrine and a recognition of its defects as well as its virtues. As its footnotes show, he tried to deal with some of Leff's points.[21] He tried to explain Marxist emphasis on the 'masses' as a product of a particular time and a particular (by implication, continental) society; 'Communism has on the whole talked too much about "the masses", too little about individual men. Its formative years were those of the huge conscript armies, today being dismantled. In England the looseness of left-wing politics paralleled the freedom from conscription, and had some good as well as bad consequences'. So we see that individualism was again a thing to be proud of; and if, as a consequence of its own individualist history, England lacks a rigorous socialist philosophy then this is nothing to be ashamed of. Kiernan was well aware that the radical upheavals of the sixties, which peaked in 1968, contained a great deal of a typically romantic emphasis on self-discovery, even to the point of a drugged loss of contact with external reality. He offered Marxism as an alternative to self-indulgence, which could, nonetheless, 'help the individual to expand as an individual, without losing contact with social reality'. Marxism could offer an effective framework for the application of humanist principles: in effect, he was offering Marxism as a rational alternative to the 'hippy' movement, whilst pledging his fellow members of the 'new' New Left to broad-minded tolerance, looking forward to a free market in ideas in a way that Mill would have appreciated. Also he wanted historians to write well in order to reach a large audience, and to become engaged in the problems of society, regretting their narrow-minded professionalism and political quietism, and mourning the passing of Marx, Carlyle and Macaulay, whose competing visions had offered the reading public real choice. Marx, he said, had had to stress economic determinism to redress the balance against 'abstractions, religions, great men, as the directing forces of history'. One of the things that worried Kiernan, in 1968, was that economic determinism seemed to have become a tool in the hands of conservative as well as Marxist historians, the former being well satisfied with a form of explanation 'very close to a literal mechanical rendering of economic determinism', in which 'men and parties have no motivation beyond their own immediate material interest or that of their class. It can go comfortably with a conservative bent of mind, because if all politicians are mercenary self-seekers they can all be written off, leaving private property where it is'. This suggested cynicism about politics and politicians was fashionable at the time, and is, in any case, something of a British habit of mind, fostered no doubt by the Namierite approach to politics, to which Kiernan was clearly alluding.

More fundamentally, Kiernan aired doubts about the course of history being divided into sequences or stages marked by different modes of production, which gave birth to the next. Moreover, revolutions were

made, not by 'the solid men in the ruck of any class' but by 'skirmishers
. . . young men, adventurers, idealists, intellectuals' or in short, one
might say, individualists; all revolutions were made by vanguards: or
so it looked in 1968. Additionally, revolutions created periods of greater
individualism than usual, by breaking down existing structures. As for
determinism: 'by foreseeing the future we alter it, and thus falsify our
prophecies'. Thus voluntarism and individualism reasserted themselves
within Marxist thought. Marx, said Kiernan, had dealt exclusively with
collective problems, just as Freud had thought entirely in terms of an
individual's problems; both had a touch of monomania. The modern
Marxist had to take more account of the individual, and allow room for
psychology in history. In historical change, 'ideas and moral feelings' had
their role alongside changes within the productive system, indeed ideas
had their own autonomy; and if ideas were important, then so was the
individualistically-inclined intelligentsia.[22]

These new emphases were not confined to the 'new' New Left,
nor even the old New Left. Hobsbawm, one of the few to remain
loyal to the Communist Party, was to write in similar, though more
restrained, vein. His essay, 'Karl Marx's Contribution to Historiography', though perpetrating some of the conventional errors about the history of historiography in Britain which we are attempting to correct, drew
a useful distinction between the influence of what he called 'vulgar Marxism' and true Marxism. The former, not necessarily derived from Marx,
consisted of crude economic determinism, a simple base-superstructure
model of society, a view of history as simply a story of class interest and
class struggle, a penchant for historical laws, and a presumption of historical inevitability — hence the preoccupation with the problem of
how to accommodate the individual and the accidental in history. Such
vulgar Marxism would tend to be interested only in a limited range of
historical topics, such as industrialisation or revolution. It would seek to
explain away, by *explaining* in base-superstructure terms, the supposedly
objective, professional scholarship of mainstream historians. Hosbawm's
intention, whilst he recognised the power of vulgar Marxism, was to help
prepare the ground for a more sophisticated Marxist influence, which he
felt was now possible. The social sciences had been for some while subject
to 'historisation', and were now more concerned with tension and change
than with order, with dynamic rather than static social situations; their
own models of social change were unsophisticated, and they had turned to
Marxism for guidance. Simultaneously, for a number of reasons, Marxist
historians had come to the fore. Consequently, functionalist models of
society, based on a presumption of stability, were being replaced by a

more sophisticated Marxist model which accommodated both stability and disruptive tendencies, indeed was virtually dependent on both. We might note that one consequence of what Hobsbawm claimed was happening, would be to bring history and the social sciences together. He made it clear that a sophisticated Marxist model was not crudely determinist in terms of base and superstructure: elements of the superstructure, such as the state, had the capacity to neutralise or even utilise disruptive elements under some circumstances and not in others; history would still need writing for it would not always fit a simple formula. Societies could not simply be described in terms of their productive relations; each society had its own dynamic and, therefore, followed its own history. Most of these arguments could be ascribed to Marx himself; they did not represent a weakening of the Marxist impulse — on the contrary.[23] In some respects this essay makes less concession to traditional English radicalism than others we have looked at: history and the social sciences were as one in their application of an, albeit sophisticated, Marxist model of society; historical individualism was limited to the individualism of each social formation; Hobsbawm said little of the humanist concept of individualism that had occupied Kiernan. However, if each society was an individual, if each state could sometimes control its disruptive forces and sometimes not, independently of any economic determinants, then human agency was at work.

If the Hobsbawm of 'Karl Marx's Contribution to Historiography' was a little less fluid than, say, Kiernan, the exigencies of the 1980s brought a change of heart. Writing now in the *New Left Review*, he eschewed the prospect of prediction altogether and opted for more probability. The Marxist historian had to become fully engaged in the task of assessing the probable, 'discovering what human beings can and cannot do' about the future, establishing 'the settings and consequently the limits, potentialities and consequences of human action', and distinguishing 'between the foreseeable and the unforeseeable and between different kinds of foresight'. Thus, let us say, man makes his own history, and though not in the circumstances of his own choosing, the historian can tell him about these circumstances and assess their potential. An interesting feature of Hobsbawm's later article was his attack on 'those absurd and dangerous exercises in constructing automata for prediction, popular among seekers after scientific status', and on the new manipulators, the social engineers, 'statistical extrapolators' and technocrats who attempted to use such spurious predictions.[24] The scorn was mixed with anxiety; just as so often with vehement *anti*-Marxists (or anti-Positivists), there was the fear that these exercises are dangerous, not because they are false, but because they do, indeed, threaten individualism and choice; to a large extent, one's reaction to this challenge will depend on who seems to be making it, friend or foe.

It would be wrong to over-schematise our treatment of the Marxist diaspora in the years after 1956, but Leff, Kiernan and Hobsbawm are representative of different reactions to the problem of how to relate the liberal and Marxist traditions. Within that diaspora, the most widely influential figure has been E.P. Thompson. So much has been written about his role, [25] that it seems almost superfluous to add anything here. Perhaps a few indications will suffice, for the unititiated or unconverted. According to Thompson in his first really influential work, the English working class *made itself*: it was not made, as a self-conscious body of men and women with their own social and political attitudes and ideals, by the industrial revolution or the capitalist class; it made itself, and amongst the ingredients were popular culture, and traditions of liberty that would not be out of place in some Whig histories. In general, the only acceptable definition of class is that used 'by men as they live their own history', and class is always an historical category. Classes do not exist without class struggle; indeed, struggle is the prerequisite of classes — they exist because they struggle.[26] As for Law, which he tackled in *Whigs and Hunters*, and which had been another key ingredient in Whig history as well as part of the superstructure in the classic base-superstructure model, it was not solely or simply a means of class oppression; it was a cultural achievement with its own autonomous standards; it was capable of defining and defending individual rights, even when at its most oppressive — in the heyday of Whig rule in fact, a heyday Thompson found totally repugnant.[27]

In general, he attacked structuralism, which he saw as an enemy in both its conservative form, and its Althusserian Marxist form which was, for Thompson, the Stalinism of the intellect; structuralism tried to remove the historical process from our view of society. He went so far as to condemn the notion of Marxism as a science, neatly reassessing the usual presumption that those who advocated science sought to enlighten and those that avoided science sought obfuscation:

It is in the very notion of Marxism as a 'science' that we find the authentic trade-mark of obscurantism, and of an obscurantism borrowed, like so much else, from a bourgeois ideology of great longevity. Utilitarians, Malthusians, Positivists, Fabians, and structural-functionalists, all suppose(d) themselves to be practising a 'science', and the most unabashed centre of brutalised capitalist ideology in contemporary England acclaims itself as the School of Economics and Political Science.

The contrast with earlier Marxist calls to establish a 'Science' is striking. Thompson would have no truck with such mysteries, and clearly divided the Marxist tradition since 1956 into the rigidly authoritarian, doctrinaire, Stalinist and Althusserian brand and the libertarian or humanist kind. He even said that he would rather be a radical Christian than an Althusserian; as such, he would at least retain a vocabulary that permitted 'the defence of human personality'; failing that choice, he would opt for being an 'empirical, liberal, moralistic humanist'. But, pretending to think out loud, he pulled himself together and rejected these 'spurious choices' and determined to fight false Marxisms from within the 'communist' camp, ignoring the old slogan, 'no enemies to the Left!' Echoing elements of inter-war and post-war anti-totalitarian arguments which had linked Stalinism and fascism, he identified 'the generation of the anti-fascist struggle and the resistance, . . . the generation most possessed still by the illusions of voluntarism (that they were "makers of history")' as the most dedicated anti-Stalinists. Having suffered a close loss in that fight, he was, perhaps for that reason, particularly bitter about the theorists who indulged in extremism till the presses reeked 'with ideological terror and blood', without fear of dangerous political involvement. Not only the free-born Englishman, but the freedom-fighter, lurk behind Thompson's vivid prose; and the ambiguity of his reference to the 'illusions of voluntarism' is patent.[28]

This libertarian stance has been potent, particularly as it has been frequently coupled with dire warnings against the false objectivity of those who seek to exclude committed, politically-engaged and radical history from the professional debate and are, thereby, guilty of the very crimes of which they accuse the Left — namely duplicity, intolerance and blind adherence to a narrow and exclusive epistemology.[29]

Moreover, the attempt to locate the 'humanist' Marxist tradition within the wider national radical tradition continued unabated, not only by the way major historical works treated sympathetically of a variety of working class and radical movements, and of the working class itself as in Thompson's own work, but in historiographical essays with that explicit intent.[30] Additionally, it is only within the Marxist tradition that there is a continuous and serious effort to popularise the consideration of the relationship between history and theory as a valid exercise;[31] otherwise, theory is left largely to the Americans, for it is part of the conservative commitment to realism that theory is unnecessary, epistemology and methodology being simply a matter of commonsense. The brief boom in university courses in theory or in critical studies of historiography appears to be over.[32] This may have left the Marxists in possession of the field, but they would, no doubt, prefer to cross swords with somebody in order to publicise their ideas. Many mainstream historians continue to ignore the Marxists and would not take seriously their claims to be the heirs of the Whig-liberal tradition.

NOTES

1. B. Schwarz, '"The people" in history: the Communist Party Historian's Group, 1945-56', in R. Johnson, G. McLennan, B. Schwarz, D. Sutton (eds), *Making Histories: Studies in History-Writing and Politics* (London, 1982), pp. 44-95.
2. V. Gordon Childe, *History* (London, 1947), pp. 2-5.
3. *Ibid.*, pp. 34-62.
4. *Ibid.*, pp. 67-68, 70, 83.
5. C. Hill, 'Marxism and History', *The Modern Quarterly*, N.S. 3 (1948), 52-64.
6. M. Dobb, 'Historical Materialism and the Role of the Economic Factor', *History*, 36 (1951), pp. 1-11.
7. E. John, 'Some Questions on the Materialist Interpretation of History', *History*, 38 (1953), pp. 1-10.
8. J.E. Neale, 'The Biographical Approach to History', *History*, 36 (1951), pp. 193-203
9. H. Butterfield, 'The Role of the Individual in History', *History*, 40 (1955), pp. 1-17. Reprinted in H. Butterfield, *Writings on Christianity and History* (New York, 1979), pp. 17-36.
10. C. Wilson, 'The Entrepreneur in the Industrial Revolution in Britain', *History*, 42 (1957) pp. 101-117.
11. J.D. Bernal, *Science in History*, second edition (London, 1957), p. 933.
12. *Ibid.*, pp. 745-746.
13. *Ibid.*, pp. 755-756, 858-859, 901.
14. G.D.H. Cole, *The Meaning of Marxism* (Ann Arbor, 1964), pp. 11-12.
15. *Ibid.*, 14-19, 28-29, 49-50.
16. G. Leff, *The Tyranny of Concepts: A Critique of Marxism*, second edition (London, 1969), pp. 1, 9, 14-16.
17. *Ibid.*, pp. 75-77, 81-91, 107-112, 127-139, 152-153.
18. *Ibid.*, pp. 156-159, 163.
19. *Ibid.*, pp. 183-187.
20. *Ibid.*, pp. 196, 202-204, 208-209, 211, 213-218, 249.
21. V.G. Kiernan, 'Notes on Marxism in 1968', *The Socialist Register* (1968), pp. 213-214; also pp. 149-151.
22. *Ibid.*, pp. 180-185, 189, 198, 204, 206-207, 209-210.
23. E.J. Hobsbawm, 'Karl Marx's Contribution to Historiography' in R. Blackburn ed., *Ideology in Social Science: Readings in Critical Social Theory* (London, 1972), pp. 265-268, 270-271, 279-283.
24. E.J. Hobsbawm, 'Looking Forward: History and the Future', *New Left Review*, 125 (1981), pp. 12-13, 18-19.
25. For example: F.K. Donnelly, 'Ideology and Early Working-Class History: Edward Thompson and his Critics', *Social History*, 2 (1976), pp. 219-238; references in G. McLennan, 'E.P. Thompson and the discipline of historical context', and B. Schwarz, '"The people" in history: the Communist Party Historians' Group 1946-1956', both in *Making Histories*; T. Eagleton, A. Assiter, G. McLennan, 'E.P. Thompson's *Poverty of Theory*: a symposium', *Literature and History*, 5 (1979), pp. 139-164; also, of course, E.P. Thompson, *The Poverty of Theory and other Essays* (London, 1978); and MARHO, Interview with E.P. Thompson, *Visions of History* (Manchester, 1984), pp. 5-25.

26.   E.P. Thompson, *The Making of the English Working Class* (Harmondsworth, 1975), pp. 9-12; also, E.P. Thompson, 'Eighteenth-Century English Society: class struggle without class?', *Social History*, 3 (1978), pp. 146-150.

27.   E.P. Thompson, *Whigs and Hunters: the Origins of the Black Act* (London, 1975), pp. 258-269.

28.   E.P. Thompson, 'The Poverty of Theory: or an Orrery of Errors', in *The Poverty of Theory*, pp. 265-271, 321-323, 326, 360, 377, 380-382.

29.   See, for example: Editorial Collective, 'The Attack', *History Workshop Journal*, 4 (1977), pp. 1-4.

30.   R. Samuel, 'British Marxist Historians, 1880-1980: Part I', *New Left Review*, 120 (1980) pp. 21-96.

31.   Most recently: G. McLennan, 'History and Theory: Contemporary Debates and Directions'. *Literature and History*, 10 (1984), pp. 139-164.

32.   J.M. Bourne, 'History at the Universities', *History*, 71 (1986), 60. In 1977, 50% of university single-subject history degrees included a compulsory or option course in Historical Method; in 1985, only 38.6% did.

CHAPTER 9

Liberalism without Liberals

Although in some respects Marxism can be seen as the heir of the Liberal Anglican and Whig tradition, adapting to its more radical individualist tendency and providing, at last, an alternative basis for generic concepts and an overall pattern in history, conservative historians appear in other respects as the true heirs. Though scornful of the Whig *schema*, they relished the individualist tradition, both social and epistemological, the hostility to scientific methods, and the refusal to see patterns or laws, or to predict. Strengthened by the association of conservatism with professionalism since the days of J.H. Round and his ilk, they continued to press with vigour the sort of arguments that had been common for a century or more. In sometimes uneasy alliance with this supposedly hard-headed realism and professionalism was a reborn Christianity which looked anachronistic and inappropriate to sceptics but which was very much part of the English historiographical tradition; and, in the form of God's Providence, it topped off an otherwise formless and rather pointless type of historical explanation.

The leading exponent of the Christian approach was Butterfield, atypical perhaps in his Methodist background and in the prominence afforded religion in his writings, but influential. Much of his influence was due to his access to public lecture series, including talks on the BBC; repetition conceivably heightened rather than diminished this influence. His best known work in this connection was his 1948 series of lectures, published in 1949 as *Christianity and History*. The tone was set immediately: the principal challenge to Christianity in the modern world was Marxism, a dangerous and intellectually formidable foe; the challenge had to be met by the West in a positive way, not with a negative, Metternichian defence of the status quo[1] — he had the centenary of the 1848 revolutions in mind, no doubt. In the post-war world, however, Butterfield had apocalyptic visions: apocalypse had been narrowly averted with Hitler's defeat; but western civilisation was now threatened by Marxism and the Bomb. The only way this could be explained was as 'God's chastisement' of sinful man. Historians did not need to make moral judgments, for history itself did that. German militarism from Frederick the Great onwards had now been judged by its recent defeat. But the victors were not virtuous, merely the chosen instrument of God's punishment; in fact, not just Germany, but the whole of western civilisation was still under judgment; its survival was still an open question. Catastrophes were always somehow related to moral defects. He jibbed at saying outright that moral defects caused catastrophes, but they were related in some vague but undeniable way: 'the processes of time have a curious way of bringing out the faultiness that is concealed in a system which at first view seems to be satisfactory'. It is difficult for us to comprehend how Butterfield could adopt such a naïve perspective, ignoring the long-term successes of wicked systems, the tragedy of failed benevolence, the ultimate mutability of all social systems, and focusing on the moment of truth for the wicked; but the world must have looked very different in the aftermath of the Nazi defeat. The judgment of history was always on systems, not individuals: 'the very things which provide the neat developing patterns in history books — provide the supra-personal edifices like state, culture, capitalism, liberalism — and which are associated with the idea of progress, are the things which are shattered when the judgment falls on men'. The 'meaning' of history, therefore, did not lie in progress or the development of 'systems'; generations were not mere stepping stones for later generations, but ends in themselves. For each individual exists for the glory of God; and 'one of the most dangerous things in life is to subordinate human personality to production, to the state, even to civilisation itself, to anything but the glory of God'. He had faith only in God.[2] Thus, he explicitly rejected the Whig view of history once again (despite his wartime apostasy) and, by implication, rejected materialism, Idealist statism, and Toynbee. But he shared the Liberal Anglican's view of God's Providence, if not their view of how it manifested itself, for Butterfield's God was a vengeful God who destroyed 'systems'. Butterfield took the realist-Fisher view of history as without pattern or meaning for man, but resurrected God as the mysterious force that gave it supernatural meaning, comforting himself with a Rankean faith in the immediacy of each era, each person, to God.

Progress and order in history were, he believed, spurious and transient modern concepts, born in the seventeenth century, and reaching their apogee in the nineteenth. As the ancients had realised, history had a 'risky, cataclysmic character'. If progress occurred, that was purely providential, not guaranteed; stripped of its complications, history was God's Providence. Yet he did allow that man had an improving instinct, that he sought to co-operate with Providence, and rebuilt after the destruction of a system. If this seems to be a tortuous alternative to progress, it was also a defence of short-term objectives, of pragmatic (or Popperian?) tinkering with the system in normal times; messianic or 'arrogant' Communists and Nazis, in contrast, sacrificed the present for a possibly unattainable future, risking all on mad ambition. Man could not control nor foresee Providence, but he could instinctively co-operate with it in a limited and unambitious way. Butterfield's view of history was a curious compound of pragmatism and cataclysm; but, having stared the possibility of immediate holocaust full in the face, he decided that Providence would somehow protect us after all — so even that prospect required no man-made initiative. However, as God had no stake in any particular system, 'the existing order' could well be swept away: there was only one sure principle — 'hold to Christ, and for the rest be totally uncommitted'.[3] This seems to be a very negative and passive attitude, consisting of political agnosticism and abdication of responsibility. Butterfield stoically contemplated the end of civilisation as he knew it, confident that it would somehow serve God's Providential ways.

Elsewhere, Butterfield showed that he was, in fact, committed to the defence of individualism against collectivist or holistic ideologies, as well as taking refuge with the methodological individualism implicit in the notion of the immediacy of the individual to God. He regarded the conversion of the Christian principle of loving one's neighbour, as an individual, into collectivism, as a perversion of the original message, from 'love thy neighbour' to 'serve the state'. The exponents of collectivism failed 'to notice that, instead of actual people, some abstract noun or political-science concept has been inserted as the real end, and to this more artificial object human beings are regarded as subservient. The Hitlers of the world do carry a certain plausibility sometimes, when they call upon young men to sacrifice their private egotisms and immolate themselves for the good of Germany'. It is easy to understand why Butterfield felt oppressed by the monstrosities committed in the name of collective nouns; the post-war world lived with the memory of the Third Reich and the cold-war presence of Stalinism. It led him and others to a strict nominalism and individualism, which was loaded politically, despite his renunciation of all faith except in Christ. Human personalities were the only reality. Unable to accept that social wholes were creations of God and immediate to Him, indeed His highest form of creation, as the Idealists would once have argued, Butterfield held that 'actual live human beings are to be taken as the values in the world because they are souls meant for eternity'.[4] This had been a popular argument in Victorian times, and it suggests a Protestant lineage. But if the nominalism and individualism of history were to be based on theological arguments in the 1950s, they would run the risk of intellectual isolation and anachronism. There is a contrary view: C.T. McIntire, editor of Butterfield's *Writings on Christianity and History*, has argued that Butterfield's Christian faith was part of a revival of religious influence amongst the intelligentsia in the post-war years, claiming that a 'very diverse collection of people were united around the theme that Christian faith offered hope for the revitalisation and reorientation of a distraught civilisation', people like C.S. Lewis, T.S. Eliot, Tolkein and Dorothy Sayers, to mention only a few of the more popularly known, and historians like Christopher Dawson, Dom David Knowles, Tawney, Gordon Rupp, and Arnold Toynbee.[5] However, the English, in the twentieth century at least, find religion slightly embarrassing, not really for polite company; it has a touch of the fanatical or odd-ball about it. In a sense, though, Butterfield catered for this distaste: the advantage of his philosophy of history was that one could indulge in empirical research without bothering one's head about how the subject of one's study fitted into God's providential world, for that was unknowable.

Of course, Butterfield's nominalism need not have been based on his theology — though all that we know about his life suggests that to him personally Christianity was fundamental, not just a convenience. In subsequent essays, however, he concentrated on a nominalist explanation of his individualism rather than the Christian explanation of his nominalism. For example, he attacked Marx thus: 'the genesis of historical events lies in human beings. The real birth of ideas takes place in human brains. The real reason why things happen is that human beings have vitality'. McIntire has seen this as the most important part of Butterfield's thought, present in his earliest writings.[6] It was the basis for his rejection of simplified or 'schematic patterns' in history, and his insistence on 'the elasticity of ordinary narrative history' in all its detail and complexity. Although we have echoes here of the naive realism of the early Butterfield in *The Whig Interpretation of History*, the enemy was no longer the Whig interpretation, but the Marxist interpretation, which was too rigid and monocausal, and ignored the human factor. In general he warned against 'the idea of process in history' unless it be balanced by 'a doctrine of personality'.[7] Like others before him, he was convinced that Communism and Fascism were 'twin forms of the same revolutionary and totalitarian menace' rather than 'authentic antitheses'.[8] His hostility to Communism dated back to the days of student Marxism at Cambridge in the thirties, but whether we can accept that there was something peculiar to Cambridge about his historical individualism,[9] is questionable; the tradition seems to be more widespread.

McIntire reckons that 'God in History', a lecture delivered in 1952, comes close to being a synopsis of his views.[10] If he had earlier given the impression that his God was remote and mysterious, requiring nothing of his creatures other than passivity, he dispelled this now: he did not want an 'absentee God'; he wanted to 'recover the sense and consciousness of the Providence of God . . . working at every moment, visible in every event'. Three different levels of explanation were needed to explain the historical event: the willed actions of individuals, which required a biographical approach; the operation of certain laws, akin to natural laws, these being reconcilable with free-will, and thus producing true historical explanation; and embracing the other two, 'the providence of God', Butterfield's preferred alternative to blind chance. God provided both free-will and regularities or laws; God was in everything. 'The Providence of God is at work in the downfall of Nazism, in the judgments that come on the British Empire for its own sins, in the present prosperity of the United States, and in our own individual daily experiences'. He was convinced that the current state of the nation betokened national sin. Add his constant worries about Marxism, and we have here his world view: Britain fallen on evil times as the result of evil ways; other powers and creeds triumphant — also part of God's mysterious purpose; but at least Nazism had been vanquished — shades here of the Liberal Anglicans' detection of the hand of God in the defeat of Napoleon. Whereas, for Arnold, England had been entering on her maturity, there was no such optimism for Butterfield, living in an age of national decline. The Christian interpretation of history required all three of these levels of explanation: free-will was necessary to establish individual moral responsibility; knowledge of circumstances was necessary for the exercise of Christian charity when judging moral responsibility; and the Christian was bound to choose Providence above Chance. Acts of judgment punctuated history (the Jewish exile, the fall of Rome, the Norman Conquest) but these judgments were providential, good coming out of disaster. Past sins served future purposes. Old worlds were judged, and made way for new.[11] This is nothing but a pessimistic version of Liberal Anglicanism a hundred years on.

Butterfield certainly saw himself as within the English tradition of historiography, which, he said, had tended to the narrative form, to be about personalities, particular episodes and periods, and to be concerned with recovering the past 'in its concreteness and particularity'. It directed its attention to 'what is free, varied and unpredictable in the actions of individuals', including art and spiritual life, leaving that which is reducible to 'law and necessity' to more materialistic scholars. The play of personality was its prime concern; and its importance was its ability to show every individual 'that it does really matter to the world what decision he makes on a given issue here and now'. This approach was, he felt, peculiarly congenial to the Christian tradition. Furthermore, he said, the English historical tradition 'insists that the story cannot be told correctly unless we see the personalities from the inside, feeling with them as an actor might feel that part he is playing — thinking their thoughts over again and sitting in the position not of the observer but the doer of the action'. Unlike Collingwood, to whom nevertheless his debt is obvious, Butterfield thought this was an impossible aspiration, but one that had to be attempted;[12] and he stressed the intuitive, empathetic, artistic way of knowing somebody from the 'inside', using appropriate thespian imagery, as against Collingwood's more rational, cerebral method. (Some people seem to have taken their Collingwood from Butterfield.)

One final point about Butterfield needs to be made clear. He did not think that academic history itself could provide the material for a Christian faith; faith had to be acquired elsewhere and brought to history. Academic history could not aspire to be the basis for any *credo*, materialist or spiritual. It was not the queen of the sciences.[13] Typically of historians, therefore, Butterfield took low ground in defining the possibilities of his subject, despite his insistence on a Christian interpretation. Here was none of the grandeur of Stubbs's sense of religious purpose in studying history as the work of God. The sole difference between Fisher's despairing cry and Butterfield's stoicism was the latter's presumption that God's purpose was hidden in the play of the contingent and the unforeseen.

Whether or not Butterfield's Christianity was part of a general post-war ethos, a sort of Christian Democrat movement of the intelligentsia, is arguable. Whether or not he has had successors is also open to question. Cowling seems to be prepared to argue for an Anglican vision, and his Anglicanism is avowedly conservative, not liberal, but his idiosyncratic approach seems to be confined to assembling a motley crew of academics and politicians as a sort of Cambridge-based, right-wing front[14] — to what purpose it is difficult to say. In any case, no disciple of Butterfield, he has been staunchly opposed to seeing a divine purpose, or indeed any purpose, in history, refusing to see anything more than 'fortuitous accident' in the course of history, and indeed refusing to see anything ideological in his insistence that history is a field of study with only limited capacity for understanding strictly limited phenomena.[15] In that sense he is more closely akin to the 'professionals'.

The hallmark of most of the conservatives who have sought to defend their individualist methods and assumptions was a strong sense of professionalism coupled with naive realism. Foremost amongst them, in fame and output at least[16], must rank Elton. In Elton's view professionalism is the safeguard against bias or misunderstanding,[17] the evidence should be approached without preconceptions or even questions in mind, 'all the available and potentially relevant evidence must be seen', and 'no evidence must be constructed additional to that which is found extant in its own right'. Thus Elton fondly imagines an exact fit between the potentially relevant evidence and the evidence that the working historian is likely to consider, as if no personal judgment was involved, and assumes a mind wiped clear of ideas. He also believed that the historian had to identify, initially, a 'dominant archive', which did not, apparently, create the same risks of bias as a prejudice might! Working in this *ad hoc* but impartial way, the historian, perforce, argued from effect to cause because he knew of the event that he needed to explain (having happened upon it?) but did not yet know of its causes; it followed that he was totally unable to 'argue forward' or predict, as he had to know of the effect before the cause. This seems a very naive presumption that causal chains can be broken cleanly into absolute causes and absolute effects and that we know only the effect and have no prior knowledge of probable causes; that one man's 'effect' will be another's 'cause' is clear enough. Elton's supposed method is a reversal of Gardiner's, which worked forward assuming no prior knowledge of what followed; Elton's ideal investigator had to be naive about what went before. This is the basis of Elton's assertion that the historian's experience teaches him 'how powerful the contributions are of the unexpected, the unforeseen, the contingent, the accidental and the unknowable'. How do we ever know the contribution of the unknowable? All the factors are unknown to us, initially, according to Elton. Does this mean they were unknown to others? There seems to be considerable slippage here from one meaning to the other, as there is from the concept of 'the unknowable' to that of the 'unforeseen' and of 'the contingent'. These are three different concepts which muddle history in the sense of the events that occurred, and history in the sense of that which is written; the sharp distinction between the three is blurred by the repetition of the first and second concepts — the 'unexpected' and 'unforeseen', 'contingent' and 'accident'. According to Elton, proper history was 'empirical or thesis-free', allowing for no generally applicable 'scheme of interpretation' such as 'Marxist-Leninist' history. Proper, empirical history could never answer all the questions posed; our understanding would always be incomplete, always be in the form of hypothesis, unlike that of the natural scientists who could solve some questions once and for all. (As we have seen, not a view of natural science generally accepted at that time.) Yet, having muddled the two concepts of history earlier in his argument, and made the incompleteness of historical knowledge an essential part of the conservative approach, he insisted that relativism was 'frivolous' or 'nihilist' for 'there is a historical reality'. Elton fails to grasp the simple point, evident to Bradley nearly a century earlier, that there *is* no such thing as historical reality, even though there *was* an historical reality which has now gone. Additionally, even that reality never existed as a knowable corpus of fact. It cannot, therefore, be free from interpretation if it is to be given any meaning at all; history has, in this sense, to be 'critical' history. Elton's view of historical knowledge as necessarily limited and particular, yet objective and testable against a finite corpus of information that fits with an extant historical reality, is not only naive but is as much 'a norm for the society studied' as any of the other research methods that he rejects and condemns.[18] Not only is it 'part of the conservative style to emphasise that history is studied for its own sake', as Pocock had pointed out in the context of a critique of Oakeshott,[19] but it also fits the conservative purpose to suggest that aspirations are unlikely to be fulfilled and that society can only be understood a little bit at a time. But Elton has many followers, and perhaps we should leave further consideration of his views to his admirers.

At a more sophisticated level, two philosophical approaches to the epistemology of history also supported the conservative position. The first of these, as indicated by Pocock, was the Idealism of Oakeshott. As we have seen, Oakeshott's *Experience and Its Modes* had already provided a justification of the detailed narrative style as an end in itself, the only properly historical form of explanation. Oakeshott had claimed to take the historian as he was, for his subject, justifying the professional, conservative realism that had been replacing the Whig approach since the 1890s. There was no plot or plan to history beyond that revealed by the minutest details. However, a further consequence of Oakeshott's position was a holism that in no way corresponded to the standard form of historical explanation that he purported to be describing: 'accidents', he said, 'are dismissed from history', all events being part of a sequence which was autonomous, having its own inner connection. For Oakeshott, the question of free-will was an irrelevance. Actually, the abandonment of free-will might have suited the more hard-line conservative realists had they only but realised the strength of their own illiberalism, but the removal of the accidental would not have suited their ironic mode. In general, however, we have seen that Oakeshott's early essay appeared to support conservative realism. He reinforced his position, after the war, with 'The Activity of Being an Historian' (1955). Again he claimed that 'activities' emerged naively, that is, without prior epistemological or methodological consideration; and his intention was to describe not prescribe. Yet it is notable that he straightaway said, in particular, that he had no intention of prescribing that the intelligibility of past events be sought 'by revealing them as examples of general laws'. Hitherto, he said, the three most important ways of looking at the past were the 'practical', the 'scientific' and the 'contemplative'. The practical way was to see past events in relation to ourselves, as lawyers did: 'We read the past backwards from the present or from the more recent past'; we search for origins; we make moral judgments about past conduct; and we expect the past to speak to us about the present. Though he does not refer to this explicitly as Whig history, we can recognise the genre; one of his examples is the evolution of parliament. The scientific view of the past saw the past, not as the origin of the present, but for its own sake, in the sense that it was evidence for general laws — a specious view, therefore, according to Oakeshott. The contemplative attitude regarded the past as a mere storehouse of images, mere vehicles for present understanding, after the manner of an historical novelist like Tolstoy. Oakeshott, however, argued that the historians had recently acquired their own mode, the genuinely historical mode — not practical, not developmental, not the basis for laws, not in any way related to, or useful to, the present. Nothing in history needed to be discarded, therefore; there was no such thing as a 'non-contributory' fact. Historian's history did not justify, criticise, or offer an explanation beyond its own terms — the actual course of events; it was neutral. According to Oakeshott, the historian 'collects for himself a world of present experiences (documents, etc.) which is determined by considerations of appropriateness and completeness. It is from this world of present experiences that the historical past springs.[20] It is clear that this emphasis on evidence as present experience separates Oakeshott from the most naive of the realists; but it is equally clear that the result of both approaches would be the same and that both emphasise the sovereignty of the (mainly documentary) evidence. This was not accidental, for Oakeshott described professional practice as he saw it.

Oakeshott had pertinent comments to make about the approaches to history in the past as well; of particular interest to us are his comments about the long-term confusion between the 'scientific' and the professional or 'historical' approaches which we ourselves have spent some time examining. His explanation for the confusion bears some resemblance to Whitehead's, in that he said that the truly scientific method (for studying the natural world) developed almost simultaneously with, but slightly in advance of, the development of true historical study; both methods were characterised by a lack of practical content, and were, therefore, seen as an advance on the 'primordial' practical attitude. Because they shared this characteristic, it was assumed that where one, the senior partner, or the elder twin, led, then the other should follow; indeed that one should be subsumed under the other. Science led to 'general causes' and 'necessary and sufficient conditions', and it was assumed that history had to follow, forgetting the crucial difference between the two, namely that science dealt with hypothetical situations, whereas history, by its very nature, did not. For a while the historian was intoxicated with the idea of science.[21] As a statement about the confusion that had existed over the question of scientific and historical knowledge this was perceptive, though of course it suffered from the same fault as had Collingwood's analysis — the presumption that a lot of historians had actually believed in their Positivist or inductive scientific role and wanted to provide generalised explanations of historical change and social behaviour. As he recognised in the case of contemporary historians, their detailed narratives were, not bad and incomplete science, but an end in themselves; what he failed to recognise was that they always had been.

In conclusion, Oakeshott claimed that this 'historical' thinking about the past, though a new (as he thought) and perhaps fragile achievement which would not necessarily be recognised as being of interest or value, was a 'severe and sophisticated' manner of thought, dealing in complexity rather than pattern or purpose, with 'a world composed wholly of contingencies and in which contingencies are intelligible.[22] Though there are obvious similarities with Collingwood, as one would expect, the great difference was Collingwood's commitment to an engaged role and Oakeshott's presumption of quietism and lack of relevance to the present. Although Oakeshott professed to be describing, not prescribing, he was, to say the least, ambivalent about this; and in any case, a later piece explicitly prescribed a non-political and non-vocational role for the academic study of politics and indeed a non-relevant role for the 'academic' mode of thought in general.[23]

Oakeshott was not without critics; Postan who, it will be recalled, had criticised 'neo-Kantian' philosophers in the 1930s, and accused them of confusing what *was* done by historians with what *ought* to be done, now explicitly attacked Oakeshott's ideas as being a mistrust of reason.[24] Postan was a renegade Marxist,[25] who thought that attacks on the 'scientific' method were anti-Positivist in character, but were in danger of leaving the Marxists with the sole claim to scientific history. Oakeshott's significance, however, lies not so much in whether or not practising historians endorsed his opinions, but in his endorsement of historian's practices.

The other philosophical approach that approved much current practice was associated particularly with Karl Popper, an adopted son of liberal England. He had been developing his ideas for some time, but his wide influence dates from *The Open Society and its Enemies* (1945) and *The Poverty of Historicism* (1957), the former being reissued four times by 1966 and a second edition of the latter coming out in 1961. *The Poverty of Historicism* is the most succinct and relevant to our purposes. Its genesis, he claimed, began in 1919; its thesis was first propounded in an academic paper in 1936; and it was first published in three parts in *Economica* (1944-1945). But its publication in book form was well-timed, catching the post-war mood, as *The Open Society and Its Enemies* had already done. Oakeshott and Namier, both of whom had propounded their ideas earlier, also came into their own in the fifties. The mood was caught by Popper's dedication: 'In memory of the countless men and women of all creeds or nations or races who fell victims to the fascist and communist belief in Inexorable Laws of Historical Destiny'. This belief was 'sheer superstition'. Such a belief he denoted as the 'historicism' of his title, though this was far removed from the traditional usage of the term. His refutation of this historicism was that 'the course of human history is strongly influenced by the growth of human knowledge', that by the nature of the situation we could not predict the growth of knowledge, and that, therefore, the course of human history could not be predicted. He also argued that as it was not possible to construct a valid 'historical social science that would correspond to theoretical physics', there could be no theory of development that would serve as a basis for prediction.[26]

Of the academic subjects his real target was inductive sociology, not history as it was practised. He was not particularly interested in the question of the role of individual personalities in history, merely noting that the issue had been much debated,[27] but he insisted that the concrete individual event could never be understood as part of a hypothetical whole. He was completely opposed to the inductive method, in any case, regarding its use in everyday matters as a myth and its scientific use as wrong-headed.[28] Holists, he said, overlooked the fact that all the constituents of the whole can never be studied; 'they insist that the specialist's study of "petty details" must be complemented by an "integrating" or

"synthetic" method which aims at reconstructing "the whole process"',
yet were unable to cite an example of 'a whole, concrete social situation'.
'Yet', he expostulated, 'holists not only plan to study the whole society
by an impossible method, they also plan to control and reconstruct our
society "as a whole"'. This is central to Popper's concern, for his work
is a work of politics as well as epistemology. As with the Tory realists at
the beginning of the century, there were no grand syntheses and no valid
grand projects of social engineering — only limited understanding and piecemeal reform. History was to do with 'concrete individual
events' and 'individual personalities', not with 'abstract general laws';
and the concrete individual was not to be confused with the idea of a concrete whole. History had to be selective; it could never purport to write
about the whole social organism, the changing state of 'society' or 'all the
social and historical events of an epoch'. The intuitive view that there was
a *history of mankind* as a vast and comprehensive stream of development
was false; such history could not be written. The terrible temptation to
simplify had to be resisted, particularly when the centralisation of power
led to the assumption that knowledge about society as a whole could also
be centralised, and that it was then possible to embark on holistic policies
of social engineering, never daring to question the epistemological basis of
the enterprise for fear of undermining the entire edifice; true knowledge
was being threatened.[29] The shadow of totalitarianism always loomed
large over Popper's work.

Equally, he denounced the pseudo-scientific search for a law of social
evolution, after the manner of Comte, because the evolution of human
society was 'a unique historical process'. It may have proceeded according to certain causal laws (of mechanics, chemistry, heredity, etc.) but
its description was not a law, 'only a singular historical statement'. So
Popper added to his nominalist position a presumption that description,
rather than any generalised form of explanation, was all that it was possible to attempt in what, at that time, was often called meta-history; the
course of history in general had no meaning and could not be explained.
Popper even quoted, with approval, the famous passage from Fisher
about there being no plot, no rhythm, only a sequence of emergencies,
a unique sequence, about which it was impossible to generalise. On
this point, he also made reference to Hayek, that terrible individualist,
ferocious exponent of economic laissez-faire, much favoured by Popper,
and now seen as the prophet of our resurgent individualism. It was, said
Popper, a mere 'holistic confusion', 'to think that society itself', 'like a
physical body' moved '*as a whole* along a certain path and in a certain direction'. There were no 'Newtonian' social laws. As for statistical trends,

which had so impressed the nineteenth-century Positivists, 'trends were not laws'; statements about trends were 'singular historical' statements. He defended the traditional view of historical knowledge as 'characterised by its interest in actual, singular, or specific events, rather than by laws or generalisations', and thought this quite compatible with a scientific method: historical sciences assumed the existence of the universal laws that the theoretical sciences sought and tested; these historical sciences were 'mainly interested in finding and testing singular statements'. Essentially, history was interested in a 'causal explanation of a singular event'.[30] Unlike Oakeshott, then, Popper allowed for more than description at the micro-level, even prepared to employ *genuine* scientific laws.

Also, unlike Oakeshott, he was prepared to consider whether existing historical practice should be reformed, and whether sociology could not become 'a theoretical history', dealing in wholes such as 'periods', the spirit or style of an age, 'movements', irresistible tendencies, and so on. He reckoned that historicism met a real need, as when Tolstoy's vision of the course of history being determined by countless unknown individuals provided a deterministic reaction to the immature Great Man view of history. But Popper was contemptuous of the historicism of both the Idealist and materialist alternatives to Carlylean history. There was a need for something better, for a sociology that really did analyse social movements, but it had to have an individualist methodology starting with an analysis of 'the logic of situations'. As for historians, they also needed to meet a demand for meaningful history. But causal chains stretching back to remote posterity were not the answer, 'for every concrete effect with which we might start has a great number of different partial causes; that is to say initial conditions are very complex, and most of them have little interest for us'. At first sight this looks rather like Carlyle's hostility to causal chains or Bosanquet's 'complete ground', despite the inimical philosophical position of Popper. For Popper, of course, such holism was neither possible nor interesting, so 'a preconceived selective point of view' was necessary, quite simply in order to write 'history which interests us'. So, in Bradley's terminology, Popper accepted 'critical history', or, if it be preferred, subjective history. It is often forgotten that Popper accepted these 'historical interpretations' so long as their authors did not claim for them the status of scientific hypotheses. They could not be falsified, which was Popper's test for the status of scientific hypotheses, but they were still interesting points of view — some more fertile than others. The 'classical historians', by which he meant traditional historians, rightly suspicious of the false claims made for these interpretations, aimed at objectivity, which was impossible because of the need to be selective, so ending up with an unconsciously held point of view, which they mistook for objectivity; the result was, of course, an even greater degree of subjectivity. Perhaps this aspect of his critique of historical knowledge has received less attention that it deserves, because attention has focused on his attack upon the grand, predictive 'theories' of history and his insistence on methodological individualism. He concluded with this very point: 'the human or personal factor will remain *the* irrational element in most, or all, institutional social theories'. Yet what he called 'methodological psychologism' did not help; it was not the corollary of 'methodological individualism'. Psychology was simply one of several social sciences; human 'nature' changed, affected by different social institutions; and like other social sciences, psychology was not concerned with human intention. So the 'human factor' in history could not be measured by psychology; it was *'the* ultimate uncertain and wayward element in social life and in all social institutions'. Popper was as opposed to psychology as Collingwood had been, as sure of the impenetrable nature of the 'human factor' as ever Kingsley or Froude had been. The need to protect that mysterious citadel of will, or to leave, for ever, a gap in our understanding of human society and, therefore, in our potential to control it, was very strong. Popper insisted that the 'wayward' human element could never be controlled by institutions, even by tyranny — for tyranny elevated to paramount power the human factor itself, in the person of an arbitrary ruler. Nor could the human element be controlled by science, for science itself would need dictatorial control for the task to be attempted, and the objectivity of science would thus be destroyed, along with the free market in thought, and science would be destroyed as an efficient force; the system of control would perish. Meanwhile, disaster would have struck, for evolution depended on the 'freedom to be odd and unlike one's neighbour' and 'to disagree with the majority, and go one's own way'.[31] This was a classic liberal position, reminiscent of *On Liberty*, though with overtones of a sort of intellectual Darwinism — not just in the sense that the fittest ideas need to flourish, but in the sense that the 'sport' has a vital role. Not that Popper was a relativist; he regarded intellectual and moral relativism as a 'malady'.[32]

Popper thought that historicism fulfilled an emotional need occasioned by loss of faith in an unchanging world; it provided prediction of change through the discovery of an unchanging law — the next best thing.[33] There may be some truth in his analysis of this emotional need; but his own fears of prediction, so like those of his predecessors, are very evident. His argument was exhortatory as well as epistemological.

His individualism was not an attack on existing historical practice, of course; far from it. Though critical of naïve realists' claim to objectivity, his fire was concentrated on the sociologists and, in the post-war world, the Marxists. He differed from some of the defenders of professional practice in that he did not believe that history or any discipline for that matter, had qualities peculiar to it,[34] but this would have been in accord with the tradition that historical practice was simply common sense and was the only viable way of handling social evidence under any circumstances. Like Collingwood, Popper, for all his philosophical sophistication, and whatever the implications of his philosophy for other students of society, merely reinforced existing historical attitudes.

Of course, most historians concerned themselves not at all with either Oakeshott or Collingwood, nor would Butterfield's Christianity appear very relevant in the later fifties and sixties. For those not entirely satisfied with Elton's common-sense professionalism, new approaches to the study of society did challenge some of their preconceptions, and required a response. Issues like the use of generic concepts and generalisation, induction and the employment of models, would not go away; and the institutional rise of the social sciences kept the whole issue of their relationship with history in the academic eye, especially as the new universities of the sixties provided the opportunity for pedagogical experiment.

One of the more thoughtful responses was that of Kitson Clark in *The Critical Historian* (1967). In any given social situation, he argued, all 'factors' were interdependent; they created 'a complex situation which controls what happens and which cannot be resolved into its component parts'. This was very like the Idealist approach of 'complete ground' — each social situation was a complex whole, but it could not be fully analysed in terms of constituent causes or elements. Moreover, because there was a connection between events (in the sense that some elements of one situation would survive into the next, into 'changed worlds', and therefore would themselves change in the new situation, necessitating further change, and so on and so on), each situation was unique in its complexity, and every action or event was significant. There was infinite diversity in Kitson Clark's world of history, diversity within the Unity that was history; history definitely had an inner connection, but each situation was unrepeatable. A general science of history would therefore be either impossible or superficial. He adopted a more or less nominalist position, treating most generic concepts with suspicion, but making exceptions for certain established concepts which were 'independent' of history in that, though they appeared at particular times, they survived into new eras; examples he gave included ideas, like Christianity or Mohammedanism, institutions, like a Church or a nation, and economic habits. But most generic concepts about people ran into the difficulty of the quirkiness of individual human behaviour. What he seems to be doing here is accepting, albeit with caution, low-level historically limited generalisations which have appeared as concepts in the minds of participants and which have not been invented by historians or other students of society, who might be tempted to turn them into higher-level and potentially anachronistic generalisations. With this degree of caution about such, as it were, autonomous generic concepts, it is no wonder that he was highly suspicious of anything like a collective personality, preferring, for example, to think in terms of states rather than nations. As for method, he entirely rejected induction, and was in favour of an impressionistic, intuitive approach, which at its best, at the level of 'genius', was true 'historical imagination', which could reveal more than the most painstaking historical research. This was especially true when looking behind the actions and the words of history and into the minds of the actors and speakers. One is tempted to suggest that if as successful a work of synthesis as Kitson Clark's *An Expanding Society* is a product of this method then it must be a good method; but the question is — to what extent *is* it a product of such methods? The 'historical imagination', and, one might add, empathy, had to play upon something, and what it played upon was a knowledge of Victorian society painstakingly acquired by research. Not that he professed to doubt the value of research; it would take a very bold iconoclast to do that today; detailed research, even quantification, was often very useful. He admired the myth-breakers, Round, Tout and Pollard, and Namier and his emulators in the study of nineteenth century parliamentary history and electoral reform, and Clapham's use of statistics in economic history. The point of course is that they had challenged the Whigs and the Hammonds. Research is admired for its destructive capacity. In the last resort, the most important of the historian's principles was that 'what happened in the past has a unique significance because it happened. It may have demonstrated the working of some observed law or the secular application of some eternal principle, and a knowledge of the law, or of the principle, may have helped the historian to understand what happened', but the key point was its uniqueness as a happening.[35] Though by no means a naïve view of the historian's task, the aptly named *The Critical Historian* is everywhere sympathetic to the conservative tendency in historiography.

More combative and showing explicit hostility to both Marxist theory and sociology, which he came close to identifying with each other in a way that was to become common in the sixties and remains with us today, despite the variety of social models and, indeed, the empirical methods employed by most British sociologists, was Alfred Cobban. Perhaps because he launched his attack on a narrow front, the specific issue of the Marxist interpretation of the French Revolution, it was enormously successful, revolutionising the study of French history in the late eighteenth century. Until recently, Cobban's assault upon Lefebvre has been the starting point for virtually all discussion of the origins of the French Revolution — this side of the Channel at least. *The Social Interpretation of the French Revolution* (first delivered as a lecture series in 1962, and published as a book in 1964) was unusual in that, though about a specific historic event and not a general work on methodology or theory, its first chapters were devoted to a discussion of method and epistemology. Significantly, most historians assume a paradigm and get down to business, to normal science, straightaway — a highly efficient business, if you know what are you doing. Accepting Oakeshott's explanation of this, namely that being an historian was 'a naïve, un-selfquestioning activity', he nonetheless rejected Oakeshott's own 'admirable' description of that activity as being at all desirable as a model of behaviour. To think in terms of studying past events for their own sake required self-deception. To avoid discussion of origins or causes and confine oneself to narration was naïve and defeatist; in any case, a full narration of all events, Oakeshott's ideal, was impossible. Nor was it possible to avoid shaping historical facts into some form of explanation that went beyond sequential narrative. The historian could avoid ideas, even ideas of what constituted 'good and evil'. He decried the naïve realism of his colleagues. So he was prepared to accept Oakeshott's description of historians' activity, but refused it as a prescription. However, and here we come to the nub of his argument, if some historians had taken the meaning out of history, Marxists like Lefebvre or Soboul had put too much back into it. They had reduced the French Revolution, 'the greatest happening in modern history to the determinist operation of an historical law'. There we have it: two irreconcilable approaches! A great 'happening', majestic, important in its own right, unique — or the demonstration of an historical law? Never mind that Cobban's explanation of the Revolution was decidedly unheroic; the point was that it was the product of specific circumstances and not repeatable. Cobban saw his task as doing for the French Revolution what, so he believed, had already been done for the English Civil War, namely, ridding it of the Marxist interpretation.

His argument was as follows. A philosophy of history, such as Marxism, was both a secular religion and a theory of sociology —

and any theory of sociology was likewise a philosophy of history. Any philosophy of history was based on the assumption that 'the evolution of humanity is a single process'. But, and here he followed Popper, no scientific law could be deduced from a single example. Moreover, the 'sociological historian' selected his facts on the basis of his theory, and then tried to use his facts to prove his theory; success, therefore was 'built-in'. Additionally, if a sociological law predicated a basic determining social factor, then that was equally free from the danger of falsifiability. Sociology, alone of the supposed sciences, refused to abstract or isolate its data 'from the total world of experience'. In practice, therefore, argued Cobban, unconsciously (as I suppose) echoing Stubbs a century earlier, general laws of sociology turn out to be either platitudes or so qualified as to fit only a single case — unless they be mere dogmatic assertions. Having disposed of sociological theory, he refused to fall back on 'naïve history . . . the belief that the facts will speak for themselves, and presumably even select themselves, that all historical events are unique, and that generalisation is the crime against history'. Though 'a general sociological theory' was 'incompatible with critical history', there was a need for a social vocabulary to match the successful, well-established vocabularies of political science and economics; new social concepts were required. The historian had to find these by 'the process of dealing with actual difficulties presented by specific periods or subjects'. In other words, new concepts would have to emerge, even if not naïvely, from the exigencies of empirical research. Why this method was necessary, and why it was necessary to avoid the terminology of general sociological theory, when the acceptable terminology of political science began (as he admits) with Aristotle and was, presumably, devised for a particular type of political theory, and when the vocabulary of economics originated in classical economic theory, is not clear, though it has something to with limiting the generalisation. Professing himself dissatisfied with terminology derived from 'nineteenth-century sociological thought and present-day social conditions', he counselled avoidance of 'traditional sociological clichés' and 'large omnibus classes', and, in their stead, the use of 'social distinctions and classifications based on historical actualities'.[36] Though he did not believe in the unique event, his method was clearly empirical; he wanted to break down conventional generic concepts into smaller categories which might be applicable to only one society, in one place at one time.

The empirical method was at the heart of Cobban's argument. Evidence, even if gathered to support a particular theory, had its own autonomous power and could even be used to discredit that theory

— which is precisely what Cobban believed he was doing with Lefebvre's evidence. History could not be deduced from a rigid theory derived from the circumstances of a later age; only the empirical approach was acceptable.[37] He ignored the fact that the economic concepts which he found acceptable had been devised to suit the rigid theory of an earlier age, and that economic historians of an earlier generation had attacked it in terms similar to those he used in assaulting sociological theory. The only difference was that Toynbee, Cunningham and the rest were disciples of T.H. Green, and Cobban seems to be essentially Popperian in his argument.

Cobban's hope for a new set of concepts, historically and empirically based, generic but more time- and space-specific than those of social science, was similar to the arguments of the economic historian, W.H.B. Court, also first expressed in 1962. Like so many others, he located his argument within the context of post-war ideological controversy:

> European experience in the last half century has tended to undermine the faith in general explanations which seem to achieve unity and system at the expense of truth, and has reinforced the caution of historians. Whenever men have been free to reflect on their experience they have found it disillusioning and perplexing in the extreme.

Bloodshed and 'atrocious deeds' had been justified by appeals to philosophies of history. The worst mistake was 'to substitute theory for life, to take the abstract for historical reality, and to act accordingly'. There is a fundamental weakness in this argument, a basic philosophical error common to all naïve realists: the description of something is confused with the thing itself. When he contrasts 'theory' and 'life', the 'abstract' and 'historical reality', he forgets that even the most detailed narrative or precise empirical study is not 'life' or 'reality', but a description — a description, what is more, that is a more complex construction, in some ways, than any general 'theory'. Both, in their own ways, are explanations, not life itself, nor 'reality'. Nonetheless, having made this distinction between theory and 'reality', Court went on to identify Marxism as the one great nineteenth-century theory of history to have flourished in the twentieth century. Wishing to combat both Marxism and scepticism, he advocated the 'pursuit of the concrete and analytical truths of history' which recognised the limits of historical explanation, which might seem 'laborious and unsatisfying' when compared with grandiose theories but which would turn out to be 'no less philosophic' and a guide to action.[38] Like Cobban, Court recognised that history could not remain isolated from either political concerns or the challenge of social theory; whilst wishing to retain an individualist method, they both sought ways of rejuvenating the subject and giving it a purpose. In this they were in sharpest contrast with Oakeshott.

The theme of bloodshed and 'atrocious deeds' as the outcome of systematising and what Popper had called 'historicism', which had been common since the First World War, reached a rather hysterical peak in the post-war years, often couched in cold-war terms. One of the noted controversialists of the period, Hugh Trevor-Roper, exhibited these attitudes very clearly. Apart from his attack upon Tawney's thesis on the rise of the gentry, one of several demolition jobs for which English historians were acquiring something of a reputation, he wrote numerous short pieces along these lines. All the forces in history were determinable bar one — 'the human mind which sometimes triumphs, sometimes destroys, sometimes flounders'. The heroic-tragic tone is quite typical of the time. Hitler and Stalin had been harbingers of the threat of a modern dark age that was inimical to the freedom of the human mind. Their influence had to be combated 'by Western methods' of free thinking: 'ideologies are only applicable when night has already fallen. That, no doubt, is why Hitler and Goebbels preached a gospel of destruction, and Stalin hungrily scans the future for unemployment, misery and slumps'. He said he understood the public hunger for philosophies of history and the impatience with painstaking, detailed research that carried no message. The modern prophets, Spengler (Hitler had been 'in some ways the disciple of Spengler'), Toynbee, and especially Marx, appealed to the layman's sense of general crisis in the West since 1945. It is very noticeable that Trevor-Roper, by no means untypical in this, constantly talked of the post-war world in crisis; there seems to have been very little sense of the West having *survived* its greatest crisis by 1945. The cold war and Stalin, and for many no doubt the Labour Government, appeared to threaten traditional values just as much as Hitler had done; the shadow of 'the bomb' no doubt also loomed large. Complacent Victorian England had produced relatively few prophets of doom — Carlyle was a rare exception. Trevor-Roper claimed to see, in Nazism, Carlyle's 'terrible legacy'. One suspects he would have been at a loss to explain the exact nature of the relationship between the Victorian sage and the Third Reich, but he felt that (in some obscure way) doom-ladened fatalism had led to a flight into authoritarianism, for he argued that Toynbee, something of a *bête noir* for Trevor-Roper, had created the sort of pessimism about the future of western civilisation that drove men to seek refuge with Marxism, which told them what to think and offered hope for a new future, and which would grow in popularity now that Hitler's attempt to halt the decline of the West *vis à vis* Russia had failed. Consequently, the Marxist interpretation of history, though disproved 'by all intellectual tests', and maintained only by the fact of Russian power, posed a challenge to the western tradition of free thought.[39] This was just knockabout stuff, but it was taken seriously at the time.

More intellectually satisfying than Trevor-Roper, and more informed by the real spirit of old liberalism, was the work of Isaiah Berlin. His 'Political Ideas in the Twentieth Century', first published in the American journal *Foreign Affairs* in 1949 is a classic of its times, a typical view of the intellectual history of the first half of the century. The nineteenth century, said Berlin, had produced 'two great liberating political movements' — 'humanitarian individualism and romantic nationalism', both optimistic, but one predicated on man as naturally free and good, corrupted only by corrupt institutions, and the other predicated on man as needful of an institutional environment in order to fulfil his potential. They reached their distorted apogees in the Communism and Fascism of the twentieth century. The new element, in the present century, overlaying both traditions, was a sense of the irrational nature of man, creating a new dichotomy between the old belief in rational processes and the new obscurantism. Carlyle and a few others were dismissed as isolated thinkers, admired as writers, but whose irrationalist ideas were without influence in the nineteenth century. As we have seen, this was by no means the case, and the nineteenth century was far less committed to rationalism and enlightenment than Berlin claimed. The onset of irrationalism, according to Berlin, came (not with Marx), with Lenin in 1903: Lenin's commitment to a vanguard role for the Social Democrat Party was a turning point in the history of ideas, said Berlin; it was based on authoritarianism and a low opinion of humanity. This linked up with the right-wing anti-rationalist tradition of Nietzsche, Pareto, De Maistre and Maurras. The anti-rationalist tendency was further emphasised by Bergson and Freud. Berlin's twentieth century was a nightmare world of thought control, tyranny and enforced ideological conformity, of *1984* and *Brave New World*. Berlin differed from Popper in that he saw both forms of modern authoritarianism as products of twentieth-century irrationalism overlaying the more rational philosophical systems of Marx and Hegel. Marx himself was 'a typical nineteenth century social theorist', comparable to Mill or Buckle, rationalists all.[40] Modern social conditioning was the enemy. Berlin seems blissfully unaware of the alarming pressures for conformity and acceptance of authority that attitudes like his own were already engendering, especially in America. If the generation of the 1860s, Kingsley, Acton, Froude and the rest, were obsessed with the free-will issue as a philosophical problem, and were in danger of seeking refuge in obscurantism as a consequence, the cold war generation of the late forties and fifties was in a similar danger of panic over brainwashing and enforced loss of will. Berlin thought liberal individualists were an endangered species in the modern world; the mysterious citadel was under siege.

It was in this context that Berlin wrote 'Historical Inevitability', ironically for the Auguste Comte Memorial Trust Lecture at the London School of Economics in 1953 (published in 1954). He attacked those who saw 'large patterns or regularities' in history, who used holistic causal concepts whether of a material, generic kind (race, nation, class) or of a metaphysical or spiritual kind — anything impersonal, 'trans-personal' or 'super-personal'. This was nominalism of the strongest kind, and highly individualist in the personal sense. The idea that 'History' obeyed laws had unacceptable metaphysical origins. He did recognise that historians could and should judge both individuals and the course of history. Relativism, as much as determinism, was unacceptable. The individual was responsible for his actions. The very language the historian used was value-laden: he could not pretend to be neutral; he had, therefore, to judge.[41] Berlin himself was unashamedly didactic, a spokesman for the old liberal tradition: history was without form, but it was possible to be optimistic about man's potential because history was about individuals; these individuals were morally responsible human beings, who were judged by the historian; the historian used value-laden terms, the language of ordinary society devised for social intercourse and description. Relativism and determinism were the enemies. Acton would have approved.

When these established assumptions, and others like them, were challenged by the publication of E.H. Carr's *What is History?* (1961) there was a furore. The best-selling success of this book, and the reactions to it, must make it the publishing event of the entire post-war era as far as the philosophy of historical knowledge is concerned, and on a par with Buckle's *History of Civilisation in England* or with the Bury and Trevelyan debate as a source of historiographical controversy. It excited hostility partly, no doubt, because it sold so well and was regarded, rather naïvely, by some, as a textbook answer to the question posed by its title, and partly because Carr, a distinguished historian of Soviet Russia, was regarded by his critics as little better than a fellow-traveller. The vehicle for this controversial contribution to the post-war debate was as unlikely as Berlin's August Comte Lecture — the 1961 Trevelyan Lectures at Cambridge. They were not Carr's first statement on the subject. He had already, in a series of BBC Third Programme broadcasts in 1951,

attacked Butterfield, Spengler and Toynbee for their pessimism, and the
two latter for their cyclical views of history, which attitudes had replaced
the once dominant Victorian belief in progress. He thought Butterfield's
approach was a primitive and superstitious view of history as governed by
God's Providence and judgment. He also rejected Fisher's 'patternless'
history — not on the grounds that the past had a pattern, but
that the historian had to create one: 'for me the pattern in history is
what is put there by the historian'. This was a direct challenge to current realist attitudes. Without a pattern, imposed by the mind of the
historian, there could be no history. Part of the appeal of history was
that it showed how the past was linked to the future and how the past
had created the conditions of our own lives; also, because it gave us that
knowledge, it helped us to avoid being totally conditioned by the past or
unquestioning about current fads, be they for 'progress' or 'decadence'.
To accept the idea of total conditioning would bring 'moral and intellectual bankruptcy'. He was also outspoken in his criticism of the fashion for
'neutrality' amongst intellectuals like Oakeshott. He recognised that 'to
denounce ideologies in general is to set up an ideology of one's own', for
'neutrality' meant burying heads 'not in the sand, but in the graveyards
of dead ideologies'.[42]

Despite his denunciation of Spengler and Toynbee, which would have
met with professional approval, one wonders why it took *What is History?* to bring so much criticism upon his head, criticism which has now
followed him to the grave, particularly as the context of these thoughts
was a survey of the decline of individualism *vis à vis* collectivism, and of
the passing of the European age, for neither of which he wept many tears,
but which were dear to the hearts of most historians. In part, the answer
must lie in the sales of the later book and perhaps in the generally jittery
air of the establishment in the radical sixties.

Ironically, *What is History?* received a welcome in *Encounter*, of all
journals. W.H. Walsh, author of *An Introduction to Philosophy of History*
(1951), welcomed Carr's book because it raised 'fundamental questions
about the nature and possibilities of the subject in a way which is quite
new among British historians in the present century'. He added: 'It is to
be hoped that Professor Carr's colleagues will recognise these questions
as being important in themselves, and not merely dismiss them out of
dissatisfaction with Carr's own answers'. A vain hope, that all too correctly anticipated the hostility of Carr's fellow academics! Walsh referred to
Carr only incidentally, for his article was already in proof when *What is
History?* was published, but an examination of Walsh's thesis, on the
relative sterility in Britain of methodological or epistemological debate

about the nature of history, tells us quite a bit about why his own hopes for a constructive debate were dashed. 'A subject develops a philosophy', said Walsh, 'only when it is a matter of more or less acute controversy', but in Britain such controversy did not exist for reasons 'connected with certain striking, and perhaps not wholly admirable, features of British intellectual life'. British historiography, like so much else in Britain, had become an institution: it was worked at in an 'unreflective' way. British historians tended to be narrow specialists, obsessed with detail; he cited Oxford's medievalists as cases in point. He lamented the failure of the political science courses, which had been a part of the more traditional undergraduate history degrees, to awaken historians to the importance of 'ideas in the abstract' or to equip them to deal with the analysis of ideas. This was an interesting point: the failure of political science courses in history degrees is one of the unexplained aspects of the history of history courses up to the 1960s, when they were largely abolished or relegated to minor options. Walsh thought there was an absence of serious doctrinal disputes amongst British historians, which would have forced them to examine their assumptions. In this he ignored the Marxist initiatives that we have chronicled; but, in a sense, he was correct, in that non-Marxists all too often indulged in mere denunciation or ignored Marxists in the hope that they would go away, so little effective debate occurred. He felt that intellectual life in Britain was handicapped by much unthinking acceptance of empirical methods and by a distrust of 'intellectuals' as a group, even amongst intellectuals themselves. This was a perceptive point: British intellectuals respond very badly to the idea that they constitute an 'intelligentsia', and the historians amongst them perhaps most noticeably so. This would need explaining in sociological as well as intellectual terms, and that would be well beyond the scope of this book. But Walsh claimed that, as a consequence, there was constant pressure on 'a left-wing party in politics, or a moral or religious movement which advocates principles to which it claims there can be no exceptions, to abandon its "dogmas" in favour of practical compromise'. He contrasted this with, for example, the disputes between clericals and anti-clericals, Marxists and anti-Marxists, that have enlivened the intellectual life of France, and he reckoned that, in contrast with America, the behavioural sciences had made such little headway in Britain that British historians had not yet been forced to justify their methods and concerns *vis à vis* sociology. He seemed to regard Toynbee, the subject of so much hostility from the historical establishment, as an unworthy challenger of orthodox opinion — and in this we follow Walsh, who wanted worthier challengers to awaken historians 'from their dogmatic slumbers', to an awareness of their public duty to debate 'the point and purpose of their studies'.[43] Remarkable for its setting in *Encounter*, its perceptive analysis, and its plea for debate, this article can only be endorsed here. But the plea for constructive debate arising out of Carr's initiative fell on deaf ears. Vilification was, and remains, the commonest response to Carr's intellectual challenge.

In what ways did Carr offend? He accused British historians of being unthinking about the historical process not because they believed that history had no meaning, but because they believed that its meaning was implicit and self-evident. The Liberal nineteenth century view of history had a close affinity with the economic doctrine of *laissez faire* — also the product of a serene and self-confident outlook on the world. They assumed a 'hidden hand' of Providence that led to progress. Since then had come the Fall; the age of innocence was lost, 'and those historians who today pretend to dispense with a philosophy of history are merely trying, vainly and self-consciously, like members of a nudist colony, to recreate the Garden of Eden in their garden suburb'. This was not so different from Walsh; but it stung, perhaps because of the style, most probably because of who delivered the rebuke. He attacked the 'cult of facts', accepted that all history was contemporary history, and denounced Trevor-Roper's 'cliché' that the historian 'ought to love the past', counselling him instead 'to master and understand it as the key to the understanding of the present'. He also attacked 'the cult of individualism' which denied the obvious truth that the individual and society were inseparable. Such a cult had been the dominant habit of thought, 'the ideology of a particular epoch' from which the western world was just emerging; it had been closely associated with capitalism; but it no longer constituted part of a common ideology, being but the ideology of one particular group that used it to bolster its own claims upon society and to counter competing ideologies. It had become, in its obsolescence, 'a barrier to our understanding of what goes on in the world'. He denounced the 'Great Man' approach to history, and less provocative forms of individualism as well. It had been one of Collingwood's 'serious errors' to place 'the conscious thought or motive of the individual actor' centre-stage.[44] This constituted an attack on the traditionalists' individualist mode that was unforgiveable; it attacked them on the same ground that they attacked others — for allowing their ideology to dictate their interpretation of history, for being, as a consequence, ineffective guides to historical understanding, and for serving the needs of a small self-interested group. The charge of hypocrisy was only just below the surface. As Carr's sales grew so did the resentment.

Furthermore, Carr did not accept that history was a distinct form of knowledge. Not only did science no longer think in terms of inductive laws, more in terms of hypotheses (a common theme amongst the more enlightened commentaries on epistemology), but conceptions of history were changing, or should be changing. The historian was not really interested solely in the unique, as was so often claimed, but 'in what is general in the unique', even though he believed it was necessary to study each individual phenomenon rather than apply a general theory. So we are back with the question of what is general in the individual, an issue first raised for us by the Idealists with their concept of the concrete universal. Carr looked forward to a period of co-operation between historians and sociologists, which would abolish the false distinction between a generalising science and a concrete history. Moreover, though oddly sceptical of the modern physicists' belief that they too affected their data and the subject of their study simply by studying it, he believed that modern theories of knowledge in general had made the old idea, that the interrelationship between the known and the knower was one-way, largely out of date. History, as a human study, was not unique. Neither the putative religious ingredient in world history nor the supposed requirement for moral judgment on individuals (which Isaiah Berlin championed) made history distinct. He wanted history to accept its role amongst the 'sciences' (in the broad sense of the term), become more rigorous, acquire a higher academic standing, and rid itself of the 'literary intellectuals' in its ranks.[45] This was strong stuff!

Worse was to come. Popper and Berlin came in for some disrespectful treatment — Popper for his hostility to what he called 'historicism', and Berlin for his influential championing of free-will and ethical judgment. The tone was mocking, jocular, but combative:

> It is perhaps unfair to hold Sir Isaiah responsible for his disciples. Even when he talks nonsense, he earns our indulgence by talking it in an engaging and attractive way. The disciples repeat the nonsense, and fail to make it attractive. In any case there is nothing new in all this. Charles Kingsley, not the most distinguished of our Regius Professors of Modern History, who had probably never read Hegel or heard of Marx, spoke in his inaugural lecture in 1860 of man's 'mysterious power of breaking the laws of his own being' as proof that no 'inevitable sequence' could exist in history. But fortunately we have forgotten Kingsley. It is Professor Popper and Sir Isaiah Berlin who between them have flogged this very dead horse back into life; and some patience will be required to clear up the muddle.

His efforts to clear up the muddle involved dismissing 'the human being whose actions have no cause' as a mere abstraction, in terms that could have been used by Bradley or Bosanquet. By no means everything was possible in human affairs, said Carr. The concept of causation was crucial to the very notion of rational understanding: Berlin was elevating the human will to an almost divine position so that inquiry into how human beings acted was as sacrilegious as it had been in the days when everything was ascribed to God's Will. This, said Carr, 'perhaps indicates that the social sciences are in the same stage of development today as were the natural sciences' when the argument of sacrilege was used against them. We may well feel a sense of *déja vu* at this point, for Carr's evocation of Kingsley was perhaps even more apt than he knew; his own speculation has clear Comtist overtones. This is no accident: the rationalist or 'scientist' tradition of the Positivists has many links with the modern Left. For Carr, as for Buckle, 'the logical dilemma about free-will and determinism does not arise in real life', and determinism and moral responsibility were not mutually exclusive. All actions were both free and determined, depending on one's perspective; but one of the determinants was the personality of the actor. Fear of determinism, he recognised, was politically motivated, arising out of a desire to reverse some recent events, such as the Russian Revolution. As for accident in history, Carr reiterated (and acknowledged) Bury's contingency thesis, ascribing the popularity of accident theses to post-1914 psychosis or 'intellectual laziness'. For Carr, the historian, being interested in the causal relationships within human society in human terms, had to select the rational and real, or historically significant, causes of events, leaving the irrational and accidental, and those necessary conditions which could and should be taken for granted, to take care of themselves. To illustrate this point, he enacted the now famous drama of Jones and Robinson, in which Professors Popper and Berlin appear, as bit-players, in a comic interlude.[46] This was as hard-hitting as the most knockabout stuff, but more dangerous by far.

Finally, Carr asserted that the return to obsessive individualism and voluntarism, so apparently anachronistic, was the result of the modern presumption that the exercise of reason could lead not just to an understanding of the world but, in Marx's terms, to changing it — an exercise of reason that caused irrational fears.[47] Our own study of the well-springs of modern voluntarism suggests the truth of this assertion. He castigated some of the 'voices of the 1950s', such as Namier, Trevor-Roper and Oakeshott, who, with varying degrees of sophistication, spoke with conservative caution and a dislike of reason. Though praising Popper for his attachment to the rationalist cause, he attacked him for conservative and cautious ideas about the opportunities for social engineering. He worried about 'the waning of faith in reason' and issued a call for optimism and faith in the future.[48]

Since *What is History?* few writers on the subject have avoided mentioning Carr or his book. Berlin devoted a large part of his lengthy Introduction, in effect a fifth essay, for *Four Essays on Liberty* (which included a reprint of 'Historical Inevitability'), to refuting Carr and like-minded critics. Leff took up some of Carr's points in critical but measured terms; whilst Sidney Pollard, in his inaugural lecture, weighed in in support. To Leff and Pollard we will return for other purposes; but Berlin must be allowed his right of reply.

Berlin disclaimed any attempt to disprove determinism, saying that he only meant that the arguments were inconclusive and that nobody *acts* as if he believes in determinism; he felt, however, that it was Carr who ducked the issue when he said that people 'are both free and determined'. In general, he called Carr the last exponent of the Age of Reason, 'more rationalist than the rational', writing with 'enviable simplicity, lucidity, and freedom from doubt . . . a late positivist . . . *un grand simplificateur*', and (a rather neat turning of the tables) 'respectful towards Marx, but remote from his complex vision; a master of short ways and final answers to the great unanswered questions'. He reasserted his belief in the inherently ethical and judgmental character of history, and pleaded guilty to the charge 'of supposing that history deals with human motives and intentions, for which Mr Carr wishes to substitute the action of "social forces"'.[49] There was a lot of exaggeration of the opposing position from both men; but Berlin was not entirely out of order in identifying the tradition within which Carr worked, in the way he did. Their dispute indicates the rift between the rationalists and the exponents of the irony of history and the glorious unpredictability of social behaviour. Carr's reputation has been savagely mauled by conservative-minded historians, especially since his death.

Perhaps before leaving the dominant conservative faction we should mention again the tendency to see social individualism, in the broadest sense, not so much as a fundamental feature of all social formations, but as peculiarly true of English society. Macfarlane's *The Origins of English Individualism* (1978) has already been mentioned: it seems to revert, albeit in economic terms and despite the claims of its author, to the old Victorian Whig perspective. It could be argued that this is not even a straw in the wind, but there has always been a tendency to see economic individualism as, at one and the same time, a prescription, an economic law, and an ideal most closely approximated to in England, with the industrial revolution as the high point for an individualistic society. This was a prevalent attitude amongst economic historians after the last war; its doyen ws T.S. Ashton, who claimed to be a disciple of Unwin, but represented the extent to which liberal ideas had become conservative in effect. He proclaimed it 'the duty of economic historians to point to those spontaneous forces of growth in society that arise from ordinary men and women and find expression in voluntary associations as well as in the state'. He criticised *Zeitgeist* concepts and teleological forms of explanation. His purpose in the post-war context was clear: 'if, by the grace of God, we managed to cast out the devil of Teutonic mysticism from the house, of what profit would it be if we let in seven more demons under the name of Economic Determinants?' His prescription for avoiding such errors and his view of society were both methodologically and socially individualist; like his mentor, Unwin, he did talk of groups in a pluralist way, but the main thrust of his argument was about individual initiative, as the concluding passages of his inaugural lecture make clear; 'the best antidote' to materialist teleology and *Zeitgeist* mysticism was 'detailed work on the records of some one merchant, manufacturing concern, banking house, trade union or other organisation. The sense of the individual or group overcoming obstacles and building some fragment into the social fabric is heartening'. History, he said, told us about people, not the spirit of the age. Business history, in particular, could do this: 'for it is in the business unit that economic forces can be seen in operation, as it were in the front line. Business history may serve as a reminder that demand and supply, the various elasticities and multipliers, the determinants and stabilisers, are all generalisations, useful indeed, but causal factors at one remove; and that it is the wills and choices and acts of men and women that are the ultimate data for economists and historians alike.' In Ashton's historical works the frugal self-made entrepreneur receives special treatment.[51]

Throughout the English-speaking world such attitudes were strengthened, it has been suggested, by the influence of Schumpeter's individualist *The Theory of Economic Development* (translated into English, 1934), after the establishment of a research centre at Harvard and a journal, *Explorations in Entrepreneurial History*, both based on Schumpeter's approach, and under the guidance of A.H. Cole. For Schumpeter, it was said, the entrepreneur was 'the "unmoved mover" of economic growth, the active agent of change'.[52]

The ideological slant of this type of economic history was freely admitted by many. For A.J. Youngson, economic history was 'an important weapon' in 'the struggle between communism and the free nations of the world'. He wanted to deal with 'persons and intentions' rather than 'quantities and averages', and knew that 'explanations in economic histo-ry must . . . be detailed . . . lengthy . . . personal'. He advised against squeezing 'the juice of humanity out of the subject. The past in which the economic historian is interested is not just a repository of economic problems. It is also an ever-changing society comprised of individuals'.[53]

J.D. Chambers, a popular 'character' in the world of economic history and at his native Nottingham University, saw a link between economic individualism and material success on the one hand, and Western intellec-tual traditions on the other; the West's success in developing its economic potential was, perhaps, due to the western tradition of the pursuit of truth for its own sake and by the scientific method, and to the preference for down-to-earth investigation rather than 'contemplation of the abstract and the eternal'. Empiricism, not *apriorism*, was the basis of an inquiring mind and, consequently, of economic advance. Moreover technological advances occurred when and where corporate authority was weak. Only a free society could be progressive. All this required a relatively *laissez faire* state and the absence of any strong collectivist or holistic ideal. In liberty under the law, especially, England had led the way, permitting the creation of a society of social movement and economic differentiation. The high point of individualism had been reached in England in the ear-ly nineteenth century with the concept of enlightened self-interest. But, and this is where Chambers's doctrine ceases to be merely a reworking of old shibboleths and shows itself to be on the liberal, progressive wing, economic development itself, not Christian Socialism or Marx-ism, showed the way to further progress through the development of new progressive ideas – new wealth, political democracy, welfare and education, all of which have embodied, and allowed for continual development of, the ideals of western civilisation.[54] This presumption that western civilisation was based on individualist values, and that therefore the survival of western society in more or less its current form, was essential, was very common, and had been since Victorian times, since when it had shed its original racial basis; it was the wider variant of the English individualist myth. Thus G.N. Clark, committing himself to 'the freedom of the human will', and defending the concern of the diplomatic historian with the role of decision-making by individual statesmen, said: 'to work thus, in terms of individual minds and wills, of freedom and responsibility, is to adhere to the main tradition of western thought'.[55]

We could continue to illustrate this general theme from the economic historians of the period, almost indefinitely, but with Chambers we left the entrenched and often pessimistic conservatism with which we started and moved to sunnier, more liberal climes. It is time to ask if, apart from the continued optimism of some economic historians, who believed in material progress and attendant benefits therefrom, and the almost Positivist rationalism of Carr, there are any survivals of the true liberal spirit. In the inter-war period, as we saw, international affairs, in the League of Nations spirit, had provided a field for the old liberalism, carrying a national, progressive myth into the international sphere. Did the post-war period provide any similar opportunities, or was the pessimism engendered by the failure of those international ideals the dominant feature of once-liberal attitudes? E.L. Woodward provides us with a typically pessimistic view. During the war, whilst denouncing 'manifest destiny' theories and finding Marxism too much of a simplification, in fairly standard terms, he had nonetheless seen a 'wisdom in history' that would act as 'a warning and a steadying influence, a mirror of the strength as well as of the frailties and waywardness of human beings'.[56] After the war, however, this somewhat muted defence of historical 'wisdom' turned into something more pessimistic. Free historical writing, the very touchstone of freedom itself and of a liberal culture, could only be achieved in a certain type of society, he felt. Victorian Britain had been such a society; but the modern age was sick, and the freedom of the enquiring mind, upon which historical study depended, was threatened; 'one of the signs of disintegration in our own culture is an unwillingness to consider that man has dignity and that his acts may be noble'. Though the historian should continue to take 'a high view of human kind', he could not reverse the disintegration.[57] Both moral and methodological individualism were thus identified with history as a particular type of knowledge, and Britain as a particular type of society; one grew from the other, and if one was threatened so was the other. Could anything or anybody counteract this mood?

The most notable plea for a resurgence of faith in progress was J.H. Plumb's *The Death of the Past* (1969). His main purpose was to distinguish between, on the one hand, 'the past' as 'a created ideology', sanctioning the present and a future destiny, and on the other hand, critical history. The influence of his old supervisor, G.M. Trevelyan, the opponent of Bury's scientism,[58] may be discernible here; though this attitude was, of course, typical of the period. Whether such a clear-cut distinction is possible is more than doubtful, not only from the point of view that 'critical' history is also highly selective history (as Bradley had argued), but also in that a sense of 'the past' (as in Plumb's usage) had gone hand-in-hand with a desire for objective knowledge of the past: in the nineteenth century, the formative era for modern scholarship and historical thinking, a greater historical awareness had led to contemporary developments, from Rankean research to historical novels, which were not so much antagonistic as complementary.[59] However, as we have seen, to make this distinction is crucial to a certain type of justification of history – as *the* ideology-free, liberal study. Unlike some, however, Plumb was keen to give history a role, a social purpose. Alongside the professional, critical role, the historian had to tell the story of progress, achieved through the rational action of men, and leading to international and intra-social peace and goodwill.[60] It is a heartening prospect, but how could he be sure that 'Progress' is not just the liberal 'past'?

The internationalist theme has been taken up with more vigour by Barraclough in *History in a Changing World* (1955) and *An Introduction to Contemporary History* (1964). He urged the redirection of hitherto Anglo-centric and Euro-centric history into a new world-wide study of cultures relevant to the 'contemporary' world. Perhaps because of other historians' inertia, perhaps because of his departure for America in 1965, and most certainly because his books were a response to Toynbee's comparative study of the rise and fall of civilisations, which was regarded with great suspicion or hostility, his impact was slight. Also, although there was a typical liberal relativism and internationalism about Barraclough's approach, which was designed in part to create a greater understanding of other societies, and he looked to the future, he assumed that western European civilisation was past its peak; spiritual decay, which preceded economic decline, had already set in.[61] This was neither optimistic nor calculated to appeal to cold-war warriors.

Apart from some of the economic historians, then, the optimistic, progressive liberal presence was pretty slight. Most historians reacted in the same negative way to any organising principles or new ideas as generations of historians had reacted since the first challenge to their *ad hoc* methods had been mounted by the Positivists in the 1850s and 1860s. Apart from Marxism, what were the sources of new challenges perceived in the 1950s and 1960s? Spengler and Toynbee came in for some predictable criticism, and they were often seen as the heirs of Hegelian Idealism and German 'mysticism'. But, despite Barraclough, they posed no more of a threat to established academic practice than had H.G. Wells. Most non-Marxist philosophy buttressed and justified the most ossified historical practices. It is evident that the real fear was of social science (sometimes coupled with Marxism in a simplistic way); and it was from social science that the main academic challenge came. Although the pervasive religious element in the Victorian response to Comte was largely (though by no means wholly) lacking, the arguments bear a remarkable similarity to those of a century before. Individualism of method and epistemology, and social individualism in its various forms, were always cited in defence of history. With God's Providence largely missing, however, and with half a century of European folly and destruction behind them, they no longer believed in progressive liberalism; there was no lasting twentieth-century successor to the Whig interpretation of history, largely because the secularisation of thought took away God's Providence, and then the disasters that seemed to overtake European civilisation destroyed the humanism that had initially replaced God's Providence – hence the tortured and tortuous reasonings of Butterfield. When all that folly and destruction were laid at the door of authoritarian régimes and their determinist and holistic ideologies, there was no acknowledgement of the original Liberal Anglican influence with its biographies of nations, an influence which had been so long submerged under the individualist tradition, which in turn has been confused by the issue of 'science' at the turn of the century. The holism of the Idealist influences apparent before the First World War, which had been quite efficacious in dealing with a variety of social phenomena (like churches, gilds and unions) had likewise been forgotten in a mood of patriotic insularity, not to say obscurantism.

An apparent exception to this rule was the so-called 'Leicester School' of local history, associated in its early years, from 1947 onwards, with W.G. Hoskins and H.P.R. Finberg.[62] Here we find the idea of an organic community, at the sub-national level, alive and well – the idea, that is, but not the community itself. For herein lies the secret of the Leicester success: the organic local community posed no threat, for it was dead or dying. For Hoskins, in the 1950s, acknowledging Maitland as his mentor, the central theme was 'the organic growth, and (often) the decay of the local society'; a theme that allowed the local historian to discard the miscellaneous and the insignificant (a notion reminiscent of Bury's developmental principle or selection, but with decay as the final 'development'). In the past century, 'modernity' had eaten away at 'the heart and spirit' of the local 'community', leaving only a hollow shell. In most places the 'community' had disintegrated and dwindled. The 'sense of place, of belonging somewhere' had gone, especially where the 'social cement' of hereditary ties had been broken up. Why then had local history, seemingly obsolete, boomed since 1945? Hoskins thought it was probably a reaction to 'the growing complexity of life, and the growth in size of every organisation with which we have to deal nowadays', and because 'so much of the past is visibly perishing before our eyes'. He reckoned that only 'shallow-brained theorists' would call this escapism

– just because we could not all cope with internationalism or the 'complexity and size of modern problems'. 'We belong to a particular place and the bigger and more incomprehensible the modern world grows the more will people turn to study something of which they can grasp the scale and in which they can find a personal and individual meaning'. Thus, only in the small-scale (though organic) local community could true individuality be realised – a traditionally Idealist line. At the risk of being labelled a 'shallow-brained theorist', one has to say this looks very escapist; and Hoskins portrayed local historians in a distinctly romantic and nostalgic way, mapping their villages or their country towns in the shortening days of autumn, studying in country parsonages, writing in humble school exercise books and so on. The truth was that, for Hoskins, the post-war era was 'a bad time' of social revolution which was sweeping away much that was good.[63]

In 1952 Finberg had argued along similar lines, noting Toynbee's attempts to direct historians' attention away from the nation state and towards larger, supra-national societies or civilizations, he (like Hoskins faced with large problems) fled in the other direction, towards the 'hundreds of rural and urban communities which have possessed a spiritual and economic vitality of their own, and their own organs of local government'. But he, too, found these largely in decline, except in remoter, isolated parts like the Forest of Dean, which he romanticised somewhat. Like Hoskins, he stressed that local communities had a natural 'life-span' and could be studied in vigour and in decline. If the death had already occurred, so much the better, despite the loss of immediacy, for the purpose was 'to tell a story, and every story is more readable, more shapely, if it has an end as well as a beginning'. So, for artistic purposes, the dead were preferred to the living; and the individualist method *par excellence*, the narration, was invoked for the history of social wholes, as the biography of local communities (rather than the biography of nations). The narrative was such a natural mode of historical exposition that, when tracing the history of a local community, it took shape 'as a block of marble takes shape under the sculptor's chisel'. In a clear echo of Collingwood, Finberg said that the local historian had 'to re-enact in his own mind, and to portray for his readers, the Origin, Growth, Decline, and Fall of a Local Community'. If re-enactment suggests an individualist approach, rather than social holism, it is noticeable that, despite believing that the historian should 'reconstruct' (a touch of naive realism here) social life 'in its entirety', Finberg (like Hoskins) thought that the small scale of the local community allowed it still to be about 'the commun run of chaps' – 'social beings' indeed, but real 'flesh and blood' ones, not (and here he cited Butterfield) a vast agglomeration to be generically labelled as 'villeins, Puritans, the lower middle-class, or what you will'. History, once again, was the solvent of 'isms – feudalism, protestantism, capitalism', or indeed Whiggism. Thus the naive realist is discovered to be a Tory historian at heart (despite the hostility of conservative governments in the 1980s to local government), and the local holist is seen to be nothing but a strict nominalist in every other sense, explaining best with more details and fewer concepts. Examples are sometimes revealing; 'you may execrate the landed gentry and everything they stand for', suggested Finberg, 'and yet freely recognize that the present squire's grandfather was adored by his tenants and reared the finest herd of Ayrshires in the county'.[64]

All this was really rather comforting. The local community was a device, despite some holistic presumptions, for getting at the 'flesh and blood' of individuals, for avoiding generalisations; it threatened nobody — particularly as it was becoming defunct! And the typically Idealist natural history model (as opposed to the natural science model) adopted by the Leicester school, testified to its place in the English historical tradition.[65]

Elsewhere the influence of Idealism lingered on in an atrophied way when it was used as a form of historical explanation without rigour or consistency, as 'ideas' fluctuated and caused things to happen after the manner of Fisher's method of writing history. In an equally vague way, history had come to be regarded as a special form of knowledge by virtue of its individualism, and as a special safeguard against statist holism and authoritarian habits of thought, which were increasingly associated with Marxism and social science-cum-engineering.

Associated with the predominant fear of social science was a rather more circumspect reaction to the cross-Channel influence of the *Annales* School, itself influenced by social science methods and concepts. *Annales* has had its friends, and it did not seem to arouse the same fear engendered by Marxism or social science. At first sight, this is puzzling. *Annales* history had little room for the individual, and it challenged the supremacy of the traditional field of individual decision-making, namely, political history. It was not event-oriented, so it took no account of the individuality of the event, nor much of narration. It borrowed concepts and sometimes methods, quite deliberately and explicitly, from social sciences. Sometimes it introduced controversial concepts such as Braudel's three time-scales (which may have owed something to Bergson and disturbing notions that challenged common sense linear views of time, the essential medium of the traditional historian). It often had distinctly structuralist tendencies which minimised the role of free individuals; and it sometimes seemed to be more interested in studying, as it were, cross-sections of the past *in toto* than in change over time. It risked taking the movement out of history. For all these reasons, and no doubt more, including sheer insularity, *Annales* met with a minimal response in Britain. Yet it did not arouse a great deal of outright hostility; indeed, though not much copied, it was often praised. The reason is that if it did not move, it did not threaten. It was not 'historicist' in the Popperian sense. The vexed question of causal explanation, which some historians and philosophers counselled abandoning outside of either narration or getting into the 'inside' of the event, in other words into the mind or thought of the actor, did not greatly concern the *Annales* school. In their native France they often seemed ranged against politically-engaged Marxists. There was something of the fatalistic about *Annales*, with its functional and serial approach and its geographical determinism; not a vision of wave upon wave of crises and the play of the contingent and unforeseen, but a series of systems changing only slowly in their important particulars – but the effect could be similar, albeit heroic stoicism in one case and merely quietism in the other. When *Annales* has had its emulators, this may be partly due to the veins of traditional research becoming worked out in medieval and early modern history, where the impact has been greatest, and so the widening spheres of the *Annales* approach have had their attractions.

Trevor-Roper wrote sympathetically about *Annales* in general and Braudel's *The Mediterranean and the Mediterranean World in the Age of Philip II* in particular. He recognised the holistic, organicist tendencies of the *Annales* approach, and recognised that *Annales* was a philosophy of history, not just a compendium of new ideas and approaches, but interestingly, he was particularly concerned with its implications for individual freedom, describing the philosophy of the school as one of 'social determinism limited and qualified by recognition of independent human vitality'. What precisely that means is another matter. He also welcomed *Annales* historians as fellow rationalists who had turned their backs on Germany mysticism with its *Zeitgeist* and manifest destinies, and who were employed in pushing forward the frontiers of man's understanding.[66]

As we have seen, Trevor-Roper himself was classed as an anti-rationalist by E.H. Carr, but the rationalist motif, so important to Carr, is also important when considering the appeal of social science. Those that responded well to the challenge of social science did so largely because they had a rationalist's optimism about the possibility of understanding human society. This was coupled with a belief, sometimes Marxist, sometimes Positivistic, in the possibility of historical knowledge being scientific. This optimism was most common amongst the economic historians.

As we have seen, Postan was particularly outspoken, bravely risking the Positivist label, and in 1948 criticising Oakeshott's conservative anti-rationalism, linking this 'distrust of reason . . . a perennial feature of conservative thought' with the sort of German mysticism which produced Nazism,[67] thus neatly turning the tables on those who sought to tar all attempts to develop theories of social change, with the totalitarian brush. This theme was taken up Sidney Pollard in his inaugural lecture (1964), which was entitled 'Economic History – A Science of Society?'. Referring to Fisher's now famous pessimism, he quoted Camus by way of reply: 'Those who rush blindly to history in the name of the irrational, proclaiming that it is meaningless, encounter servitude and terror and finally emerge into the universe of concentration camps'. He also claimed that nobody actually lived their lives according to Fisher's precept, that even von Mises and Popper thought it necessary to act on the presumption of regular and rational occurrences. Pollard took the view that arguments abut the role of the individual were misplaced, it all depending on the 'scale of magnification' employed as to whether individual caprice or 'the laws of change of society as a whole' caught the eye. Pollard declared himself a student of the latter, because he was interested in making sense of history. 'The fortress of holistic determination', he declared, 'has been for so long under siege by Professor Popper's heavy guns . . . that few have the temerity to entrust themselves to its walls'; but he believed that 'it is precisely at the level of whole societies that we can use the laws of the social and the natural sciences to make sense of history, just as it is precisely at the points at which the material needs of society enforce a violent political change, that the political historian is most inclined to accept the validity of historical determinism'. As for the implications of this approach for free will, the whole debate was 'trivial' and Isaiah Berlin was misguided: 'The responsibilities of the individual are not impaired by the fact that societies as a whole obey social laws'. We simply have a limited freedom of choice – limited by the social and legal conditions of our society and by its partial conditioning of our expectations. With changing ideas as to the meaning of a scientific law, with it being seen as much more conditional and relative than was once thought, there was no difficulty in coping with the 'accidents' of history. Prescriptively, Marx's ideas, though not infallible, were excellent guidelines, and the scientific method was the great hope for the future, enabling us, as E.H. Carr had said, to understand the society of the past and to manage it better in the future. 'If I did not search for reason in history', said Pollard, 'I should have no subject to teach'. Even if all past efforts at understanding society in this holistic way had been unsuccessful, they had still contributed something to our understanding of social processes, and we should not give up the search for better methods; the rational methods of the social sciences offered the best hope. Moreover, 'all social sciences seek their purpose and find their logic in active intervention in social life, in social melioration'. The study of how society changes was essential — and the key to understanding this was held by the economic historian.[68] This was a clearly materialist position; and, even allowing for the need to adopt a high profile in an inaugural lecture, it was a bold statement of the historian's task, and it was not unique amongst economic historians.[69]

The diffusion of materialist presumptions does a lot to explain the prevalence of such attitudes amongst economic historians as opposed to traditional political historians.

Not that all economic historians even were so bold, many drawing a sharp distinction between social science and history as forms of knowledge. For some, like Mathias, this attitude went no further than wanting to bring *fellow social scientists* to 'the stubborn test of the empirical'.[70] For others, like Court, the roles of the two, though mutually beneficial, were distinct, the historian being concerned with the unique, the concrete, and the 'particularity' of events, whilst the social scientist was concerned with uniformities, abstracting from society in order to emphasise the common qualities of the situations he studied.[71]

This sort of basic distinction, between history and, specifically, sociology, was accepted by Peter Burke in *Sociology and History* (1980), even though he was exploring the links between the two. Burke acknowledged the influence of Dilthey and Windelband in Germany, and of Collingwood in England, in providing a justification of history's individualist approach. But he went on to suggest several holistic, structural, or generic sociological concepts that could be adopted by historians and would make them abandon their old individualist ways: structure and function; social role, 'defined in terms of the pattern or "norms" of behaviour associated with a particular status or position', which allows for explanations in structural rather than personality terms; kinship and family; socialisation, deviance and social control; social class and social stratification; bureaucracy; patrons, clients, and factions; 'mentality' and ideology.[72] On the face of it, it seems absurd for historians to continue to ignore these sorts of concepts as an aid to explanation. Such obscurantism could be justified in two ways. If it is felt that history is simply a distinct form of knowledge and *cannot* employ these sorts of generic concepts, which is a dangerous line because it effectively distinguishes, not between the individual in a strict nominalist sense, and the generic, but between the unselfconscious, arbitrary and everyday use of generic terms, and the regulated use of relatively new social scientific generic concepts — an arbitrary distinction. And, secondly, if each concept, after careful examination, is found to be wanting; such dismissals have been attempted, as, for example, with the idea of social control,[73] though it might be felt that a study of the use of history over the years could, in itself, make any historian think again before dismissing the concept from the historian's vocabulary.

The idea that history and sociology have been different but are converging is not uncommon. Dilthey, Oakeshott, Rickert and Croce, have been cited as justifying history being concerned with the 'concrete and individual', as being an 'idiographic' study, in contrast to 'nomothetic' social science, whilst at the same time it has been argued that the way forward lies in combining the two methods, in the sense that history explains the present in terms of the past and sociology can adopt a functionalist way of explaining the present in terms of existing social relations.[74] Such a bold commitment to functionalism is rare today, but convergence is still often thought to be both possible and desirable.[75]

The most serious lengthy examination of the opposing view has been by Leff. Having, as it were, laid to rest the ghost of his Marxist past in *The Tyranny of Concepts*, he had turned to consider, amongst others, Dilthey and his impact upon historical thought, in *History and Social Theory* (1969). In his first work he had anticipated this interest. Criticising the scientism of Marxism, he had stressed that all knowledge begins, though it does not end, 'with the knower' and the act of knowing has to be a 'relationship between knower and known'; there were no 'series of truths simply to be found, grasped, and utilised', as Marxists believed. Knowing was qualitatively different from merely sensing. All social knowledge was 'value-charged', and understanding social phenomena 'entails going beyond the object or event itself to the meaning that it held at that time. It is this dependence on meaning that sets the procedures of the humanities and social sciences apart from the natural sciences'. Only history could locate the 'meaning' of the event in time and place; therefore, the social sciences needed history. Leff, himself, did not argue that history and social sciences were distinct, only that *science* and the *human* studies were distinct, and that history had a special contribution to make to those human studies.[76]

In *History and Social Theory* he took his argument further. In terms reminiscent of the attacks by the early economic historians upon classical economic theory, he accused Popper and Talcott Parsons of leaving social theory 'a-historical to the degree where it seems often to be without relevance to the world of men'. But: 'as Dilthey and Weber long ago recognised, the study of nature is different from the study of society'. Natural sciences were deterministic, dealt in regularities and 'general laws at once causal and predictive'. Whereas 'social beings' were diverse, irregular, value-ladened, unpredictable and forever changing; the human world, as Dilthey said, was 'mind-affected'. Leff continued:

> The interplay of individuals with distinctive and often conflicting attitudes and inter-ests, acting singly or in groups, is the irreducible element of history and society. Since the forms that it takes are not reducible to universal laws, they can only be grasped through the sequences and contexts in which they have occurred — i.e. historically. History accordingly consists in the reconstruction of events, not inherently necessary in themselves, in the light of their outcome.

There seems to be some slippage here into naive realism with talk of 'reconstruction', but the basic point is sound: the meaning of the event has to be understood in the light of its outcome as well as in terms of its contemporary meaning for the authors of the event. Although he referred to Dilthey in this passage, there seems to be some Collingwood influence here, with the addition of a developmental causal concept, as in: 'history, as the record of man in society, constitutes the totality of human experi-ence; it alone enables us to comprehend what men are through showing us what they have been and how they have become what they are'. Indeed, later we find Leff quoting Oakeshott and Collingwood, along with Weber and Rickert as well as Dilthey, in support of his views. But Dilthey seems to have been particularly important to him as, in a sense, humanising or demystifying Hegel, replacing the Absolute Spirit as the inner connection of history with the 'lived experience' of man; only man could give history unity. The method to be employed was, of course, that of 'understanding' and 'interpretation', but this involved not only comprehending the individual but 'the context of his whole life and epoch'. The individual could only be understood in relation to the whole. Leff seems to have become something of a disciple of Dilthey, but felt it necessary to emphasise the social and cultural context *vis à vis* the individual. The historian's purpose was understanding, not causation: Leff attacked Carr on this point. 'The justification of history', according to Leff, 'lies in man's own nature. It gives him antecedents and so a place in time . . . Men define themselves through history as an individual does through memory. They turn to the past for an understanding of what they are or what they might become . . .'[77] It is not possible to deal with all the points made by Leff in two lengthy books which draw on many ideas and criticise many others; but he was clearly placing history amongst the *Geisteswissenschaften* of Dilthey, the past of human society being part of the *geistige Welt* or mind-affected world which required understanding, not scientific analysis. Here then we still have the great divide between the 'scientists' and, as it were, the pure historians. It is probably no accident that the most ardent and informed advocates of both traditions were all, in different ways, influenced by contacts with Marxism, in one sense or another the most potent source of historical thinking in the twentieth century, because it forces a reaction — for or against.

Throughout the century and a half of historical thinking that we have considered the basic issues have been: the relevance of the scientific method to the historian's purpose — this is an unresolved issue, though majority opinion still seems to be unscientific; the individuality of the past event or action or person — an issue inextricably linked with the question of science; the course of history, and whether such a holistic concept is valid, and if it is, whether or not it can be known. Much else flows from this: the questions of moral judgment and individual responsibility; the questions of determinism and of forecasting; and indeed, therefrom, the whole purpose of historical study. From a practical point of view this affects the historian's perception of his own social and pedagogic role, his approach to methods of research, even his attitudes to political decisions about the place of history and related subjects in the educational system. The historian cannot, therefore, afford to ignore these issues; he must study them and confront them. He must always know something of the history of his own subject or he cannot understand the process of his own historical thinking. He has a duty to understand historical ideas. He cannot afford to be naive.

NOTES

1. H. Butterfield, *Christianity and History* (London, 1954), pp. 4-5.
2. *Ibid.*, pp. 47, 50-51, 64-65, 67.
3. *Ibid.*, pp. 68-92, 95-96, 98-99, 1-3-105, 145-146.
4. H. Butterfield, 'Christianity and Human Relationships', *History and Human Relations* (London, 1951), pp. 44-45, 50.
5. C.T. McIntire, Introduction to: H. Butterfield, *Writings on Christianity and History*, ed. C.T. McIntire (New York, 1979), p. xviii.
6. *Ibid.*, pp. xi-xii, iii.
7. 'Marxist History', *History and Human Relations*, pp. 66-67. 80-94.
8. 'Official History: Its Pitfalls and Criteria' (1949), *Ibid.*, p. 216.
9. C.T. McIntire, Introduction to: Butterfield, *Writings on Christianity and History* pp. xl-xlii.

10. *Ibid.*, p. xlv.

11. 'God in History', *Ibid*,. pp. 3-16.

12. 'The Christian and Historical Study' (first published in *History and Human Relations*), *Ibid.*, pp. 161-163.

13. 'The Christian and Academic History'. *Ibid.*, pp. 172-175.

14. M. Cowling, *Religion and Public Doctrine in Modern England,* especially pp. 453-454.

15. M. Cowling, *The Nature and Limits of Political Science* (Cambridge, 1963), pp. 150-151.

16. G.R. Elton, *The Practice of History* (Sydney, 1967); *Political History: Principles and Practice* (New York, 1969); 'The Historian's Social Function', *TRHS*, 5 (1977), pp. 197-211; 'Two Kinds of History', in R.W. Fogel, G.R. Elton, *Which Road to the Past? Two Views of History.*

17. Elton, *The Practice of History,* p. 68.

18. Elton, 'The Historian's Social Function', *TRHS*, 5 (1977), pp. 201-210.

19. J.G.A. Pocock, 'Time, Institutions and Action: An Essay on Traditions and Their Understanding', in *Politics and Experience: Essays Presented to Michael Oakeshott,* ed. P. King, B.C. Parekh (Cambridge, 1968), p. 237.

20. M. Oakeshott, 'The Activity of Being an Historian', in *Rationalism in Politics and Other Essays* (London, 1962), pp. 137-138, 147-155.

21. *Ibid.*, pp. 155-156.

22. *Ibid.*, pp. 167.

23. 'The Study of Politics in a University', *Ibid.*, pp. 301-333.

24. M.M. Postan, *Facts and Relevance,* pp. 17-19, 1.

25. E. Hobsbawn, 'Marx and History', *New Left Review*, 143 (1984), p. 49.

26. K.R. Popper, *The Poverty of Historicism* (paperback edition, London, 1961), pp. iii-vi.

27. *Ibid.*, p. 12.

28. T.E. Burke, *The Philosophy of Popper* (Manchester, 1983), pp. 43-45.

29. Popper, *Op.cit.*, pp. 78-81, 88-90.

30. *Ibid.*, pp. 105-115, 143-144.

31. *Ibid.*, pp. 147-160.

32. T.E. Burke, *Op.cit.*, p.82.

33. Popper, *Op.cit.*, p. 161.

34. Burke, *Op.cit.*, p. 2.

35. G.K. Clark, *The Critical Historian* (London, 1967), pp. 23, 25, 135-138, 158-160, 169-170, 177-178, 197-198.

36. A. Cobban, *The Social Interpretation of the French Revolution* (paperback edition, London, 1968), pp. 3-4, 6, 8-9, 11-13, 15-17, 21-24.

37. *Ibid.*, pp. 52, 168-169.

38. W.H.B. Court, 'What is Economic History?', *Scarcity and Choice in History,* pp. 177-179.

39. H.R. Trevor-Roper, *Historical Essays* (London, 1957), pp. v-vi, 12-17, 285-288.

40. I. Berlin, 'Political Ideas in the Twentieth Century', *Four Essays on Liberty* (paperback editions, London, 1969), pp. 5-7, 13-14, 16-28, 38.

41. I. Berlin, 'Historical Inevitability', *Ibid.*, pp. 43, 45, 51, 96, 114-115, and generally pp. 41-117.

42. E.H. Carr, *The New Society* (Boston, 1957), pp. 1-18.

43. W.H. Walsh, 'History and Theory', *Encounter*, XVIII (6) (1962), pp. 50-54.

44. E.H. Carr, *What is History?* (London, 1961), pp. 14-15, 20-21, 27-29, 39-41, 46-49.

45. *Ibid.*, pp. 51-80.

46. *Ibid.*, pp. 85-99. Jones and Robinson (and Popper and Berlin) appear on pp. 98-99.

47. *Ibid.*, pp. 129-141.

48. *Ibid.*, pp. 147-151.

49. I. Berlin, 'Introduction', *Op.cit.*, pp. x-xix, xxiii-xxxiii.

50. T.S. Ashton, 'The Relation of Economic History to Economic Theory' (Inaugural Lecture at the London School of Economics, 1946), *The Study of Economic History,* ed. N.B. Harte, pp. 163, 166, 178-179.

51. See, for example, the story of the Walker brothers of Rotherham in T.S. Ashton, *The Industrial Revolution 1760-1830* (second edition, London, 1962), pp. 95-95.

52. P. Mathias, 'Living with the Neighbours: the Role of Economic History', *The Study of Economic History* ed. Harte, pp. 376-377.

53. A.J. Youngson, 'Progress and the Individual in Economic History', *Ibid.*, pp. 223-226.

54. J.D. Chambers, 'The Place of Economic History in Historical Studies', *Ibid.*, pp.6, 237-240.

55. G.N. Clark, *The Cycle of War and Peace in Modern History* (Cambridge, 1949), pp. 6, 25-27.

56. E.L. Woodward, *Short Journey* (London, 1942), pp. 141, 144.

57. E.L. Woodward, 'Some Considerations on the Present State of Historical Studies', *Proceedings of the British Academy*, xxxvi (1950), pp. 110-112.

58. J. Kenyon, *The History Men* (London, 1983), p. 232.

59. For an elaboration of this theme see: S. Bann, *The Clothing of Clio* (Cambridge, 1984).

60. J.H. Plumb, *The Death of the Past* (Pelican edition, Harmondsworth, 1973), pp. 16, 109-115.

61. G. Barraclough, *History in a Changing World* (Oxford, 1957), pp. 15-19, 233-238.

62. Hoskins was Reader in Local History at Leicester Univgersity from 1947 to 1951; Finberg succeeded him and, some years later, assumed the professorial title. The term 'Leicester School' was invented by Asa Briggs in 1958, according to Finberg. H.P.R. Finberg, V.H.T. Skipp, *Local History, Objective and Pursuit* (Newton Abbot, 1967), p. 32.

63. W.G. Hoskins, *Local History in England* (London, 1959), pp. 20, 12, 25-26, 28, 4-5, 15.

64. H.P.R. Finberg, V.H.T. Skipp, 'The Local Historian and his Theme' (1952) *Op.cit.*, pp. 3-7. 10. 22. 12. 14, 18. Ten years later he made similar points: see 'Local History' (1962), *Ibid.*, pp. 25-44, espec. 30-33,35; and again in his 1964 Inaugural lecture, 'Local History in the University', *Ibid.*, pp. 45-70, espec. pp. 58, 62, 63; and in his 1964 'Postscript' to these earlier pieces, *Ibid.*, pp. 128-130.

65. I am grateful to Dr. Jonathan Barry of The University of Exeter for suggesting that I look at the Leicester school of local history in terms of holism and individualism. My conclusions are my own.

66. H.R. Trevor-Roper, 'Fernand Braudel, the *Annales*, and the Mediterranean', *Journal of Modern History*, 44 (1972), pp. 469-471. Peter Burke has also attempted to popularise the *Annales* school: see *A New kind of History: from the Writing of Febvre*, ed. P. Burke (London, 1973).

67. M.M. Postan, *Fact and Relevance*, pp. 1-4.

68. S. Pollard, 'Economic History — A Science of Society?' *The Study of Economic History*, ed. Harte, pp. 296-309.

69. For example: W.A. Cole, 'Economic History as a Social Science' (Inaugural Lecture, Swansea, 1967), *Ibid.*

70. P. Mathias, 'Living With the Neighbours: the Role of Economic History' *Ibid.*, p. 382.

71. Court, 'What is Economic History', *Scarcity and Choice in History*, p. 152.

72. P. Burke, *Sociology and History*, (London, 1980), p. 13, 18, 42-79.

73. F.M.L. Thompson, 'Social Control in Victorian Britain', *Economic History Review* 34, second series (1981), pp. 189-208.

74. S.W.F. Holloway, 'Sociology and History', *History*, 48 (1963), pp. 154-155.

75. For example: G. Barraclough, *Main Trends in History* (New York, 1979), especially chapter 3 'The impact of the social sciences'; G. McLennan, 'History and Theory: Contemporary Debates and Directions', *Literature and History*, 10 (1984), pp. 139-164.

76. G. Leff, *The Tyranny of Concepts*, pp. 81-84, 101-102.

77. G. Leff, *History and Social Theory* (London, 1969), pp. 2-3, 5, 25-31, 34-43, 68, 128.

Selective Bibliography

R.C. Richardson, *The Study of History: A Bibliographical Guide* (Manchester, 1988). Recent and comprehensive.

Lord Acton, *Historical Essays and Studies*, ed. J.N. Figgis, R.V. Laurence (London, 1907).

T. Arnold, *Introductory Lectures on Modern History with the Inaugural Lecture* (seventh edn., London, 1885). Most accessible of the 'Liberal Anglicans'.

S. Bann, *The Clothing of Clio* (Cambridge, 1984). A wide-ranging study of nineteenth-century attitudes to the representation of the past.

G. Barraclough, *History in a Changing World* (Oxford, 1957).

I. Berlin, *Four Essays on Liberty* (pbk. edn., London, 1969). Includes 'Historical Inevitability'.

P.B.M. Blaas, *Continuity and Anachronism: Parliamentary and Constitutional Development in Whig Historiography and in the Anti-Whig Reaction between 1890 and 1930* (London, 1978). Turgid, but important.

F.H. Bradley, *Collected Essays* (Oxford, 1935). Contains his 1874 essay, 'The Presuppositions of Critical History', now largely forgotten, but worthwhile.

H.T. Buckle, *History of Civilization in England* (London, 1902). First published in two vols., 1856, 1861. A classic Positivist piece.

J.W. Burrow, *A Liberal Descent* (Cambridge, 1981). Useful study of Whig-'Liberal' Victorian historians, including the Tory, Stubbs.

J.B. Bury, *Selected Essays*, ed. H. Temperley (Cambridge, 1930). Contains his famous inaugural lecture, but generally of interest.

J.B. Bury, *The Idea of Progress: An Inquiry into its Origins and Growth* (New York, 1955). First published in 1920.

H. Butterfield, *Christianity and History* (London, 1954). Influential in its time.

H. Butterfield, *History and Human Relations* (London, 1951).

H. Butterfield, *The Whig Interpretation of History* (Harmondsworth, 1973). First published in 1931. Overrated but influential.

T. Carlyle, 'On History' and 'On History Again', *Critical and Miscellaneous Essays* (London, 1869). First published in 1830, 1833.

T. Carlyle, 'Lectures on Heroes' I–VI, *Sartor Resartus, Lectures on Heroes, Chartism, Past and Present* copyright edition, (London, n.d.).

E.H. Carr, *What is History?* (London, 1961). The bestseller that annoyed the historical establishment.

V. Gordon Childe, *History* (London, 1947). Vintage Marxism, including an interesting study of different schools of history.

G.D.H. Cole, *The Meaning of Marxism* (Ann Arbor, 1964). First published as *What Marx Really Meant* (1934); revised under present title, 1948. Sympathetic treatment from the best-known Guild Socialist.

R.G. Collingwood, *An Autobiography* (Oxford, 1939). Key work by Britain's best-known philosopher of history.

R.G. Collingwood, *The Idea of History* (Oxford, 1946). Along with *An Autobiography* the most convenient way of discovering his historical thought.

R.G. Collingwood, *The New Leviathan or Man, Society, Civilisation and Barbarism* (Oxford, 1942).

W.H.B. Court, *Scarcity and Choice in History* (London, 1970). Essays by a leading economic historian.

L. Creighton, *Life and Letters of Mandell Creighton* (London, 1904). Fascinating account of the life of an historian who crossed the Oxbridge divide at a formative time for the subject.

O.D. Edwards, *Macaulay* (London, 1988). One of a new 'Historians on Historians' series.

G.R. Elton, *Political History: Principles and Practice* (New York, 1969). Trenchant stuff from the guru of 'Tory' professionalism.

G.R. Elton, *The Practice of History* (Sydney, 1967). More of the same.

R.W. Fogel, G.R. Elton, *Which Road to the Past?* (London, 1983). Heavyweight contest; some blows, some clinching.

D. Forbes, *The Liberal Anglican Idea of History* (Cambridge, 1952). A study of the historical works and thought of Thomas Arnold, A.P. Stanley and co. Very important to the present book. Probably little known today.

E.A. Freeman, *The Growth of the English Constitution from the Earliest Times* (third edn., London, 1876). An example of classic Whiggism allied to racialism.

J.R. Green, *Letters of John Richard Green*, ed. L. Stephen (London, 1901). Green was a younger contemporary and friend of Stubbs and Freeman: together they made up the first Oxford 'school' of historians.

F. Harrison, *The Meaning of History and Other Historical Pieces* (London, 1906). By a follower of the true Comtist faith.

N.B. Harte, *The Study of Economic History* (London, 1971). Inaugural lectures since the beginnings of the subject in British universities.

T.W. Heyck, *The Transformation of Intellectual Life in Victorian England* (London, 1982). Chapter on the development of history.

G.G. Iggers, *The German Conception of History* (Middletown, CT., 1968). Seminal work on German historical thinking; provides a useful contrast to the English tradition.

R. Jann, *The Art and Science of Victorian History* (Columbus, Ohio, 1985).

R. Johnson, G. McLellan, B. Schwarz, D. Sutton, *Making Histories: Studies in History, Writing and Politics* (London, 1982). Marxists on Marxists.

J. Kenyon, *The History Men* (London, 1983). Mainly about great British historians.

W.R. Keylor, *Academy and Community: the Foundations of the French Historical Profession* (Cambridge, Mass., 1975). Useful study of pre-'Annales' French school; useful for comparative purposes.

C. Kingsley, *The Limits of Exact Science as Applied to History. An Inaugural Lecture Delivered before the University of Cambridge* (London, 1860).

W.E.H. Lecky, *Historical and Political Essays*, second edition (London, 1910).

G. Leff, *History and Social Theory* (London, 1969). A sequel to *The Tyranny of Concepts* (see below).

G. Leff, *The Tyranny of Concepts: A Critique of Marxism*, second edition (London, 1969). An ex-Marxist comes to terms with the loss of his old ideology.

P. Levine, *The Amateur and the Professional: Antiquarians, Historians and Archaeologists in Victorian England, 1836-1886* (Cambridge, 1986).

L. Namier, *Personalities and Powers* (London, 1955). Representative sample of Namierite attitudes.

M. Oakeshott, *Experience and its Modes* (Cambridge, 1978). First published 1933; contains Oakeshott's first and ultimately influential piece on historical knowledge.

M. Oakeshott, *Rationalism in Politics and Other Essays* (London, 1962). Contains 'The Activity of Being an Historian'.

J.H. Plumb, *The Death of the Past*, Pelican edition (Harmondsworth, 1973). First published 1969. Once described as the Whig Interpretation on a slow wicket.

K.R. Popper, *The Poverty of Historicism*, paperback edition (London, 1961). First published 1957. An attack on the notion of historical laws by a well-known opponent of Marxism.

F.M. Powicke, *History, Freedom and Religion* (London, 1938). Venture into theory by a noted mediaevalist.

P. Slee, *Learning and a Liberal Education. The Study of Modern History in the University of Oxford, Cambridge and Manchester, 1800-1914* (Manchester, 1986).

W.R.W. Stephens, *The Life and Letters of Edward A. Freeman*, 2 vols., (London, 1895). A revealing study of one of the first 'Oxford School' historians.

W. Stubbs, *Select Charters and Other Illustrations of English Constitutional History from the Earliest Times to the Reign of Edward the First* (sixth edn., Oxford, 1888). There have been several subsequent editions. The preface is a classic piece of Whig history, well-known to medievalists.

W. Stubbs, *Seventeen Lectures on the Study of Mediaeval and Modern History and kindred subjects*, (third edition, Oxford, 1900).

R.H. Tawney, *History and Society: Essays by R.H. Tawney* ed. J.M. Winter (London, 1978).

E.P. Thompson, *The Making of the English Working Class* (Harmondsworth, 1975). First published 1963. Classic example of adaptation of Marxism to English habits of thought.

E.P. Thompson, *The Poverty of Theory and other Essays* (London, 1978). Important to an understanding of effects of left-wing quarrels on English historiography.

A. Toynbee, *Toynbee's Industrial Revolution* (Newton Abbot, 1969). Reprint of lectures by one of the founders of Economic History.

H. Tulloch, *Acton* (London, 1988). Another in the new 'Historians on Historians' series.

G. Unwin, *Studies in Economic History: The Collected Papers of George Unwin* (London, 1927). Unwin was a key figure in the early days of Economic History.

A.N. Whitehead, *Science and the Modern World* (London, 1948). First published 1925. Reshaping attitudes to the nature of scientific knowledge.

D. Wormell, *Sir John Seeley and the Uses of History* (Cambridge, 1980). Useful study of this Cambridge professor during the early years of the modern history tripos.

H. Wright (ed.), *Cambridge University Studies: Cambridge 1933* (London, 1933). Contains 'History' by R.E. Balfour: representative of interwar attitudes.

Index

Acton, Lord, 24-25, 31, 57, 86-87, 89, 94-96, 148.
Annales school, 236-237.
Arnold, T , 1-2, 4, 44, 45, 66, 91.
Ashley, W.J., 46-47, 63-64.
Ashton, 187, 230
Austin, 70.

Balfour, R.E., 130-131, 148-149, 173-174.
Balliol (College), 57, 58, 63, 134, 141.
Barker, Ernest, 75-78, 154-154.
Barraclough, G., 233.
Belloc, H., 93-94.
Berlin, I. , 28, 41, 222-223, 227, 229.
Bernal, J.D. , 178-179, 187-189.
Bernhardi, 104-107.
Blaas, P.B.M., *Continuity and Anachronism*, 9-13, 14, 18, 41, 98.
Bosanquet, B., 51, 54-56, 66, 69, 76, 108-109, 160.
Bradlaugh, 23.
Bradley, F.H., 51-54, 83-86, 157, 214.
Braudel, F., 236-237.
British Academy, 88.
Brogan, D., 126.
Browning, Oscar, 68.
Buckle, H.T. , 21-41.
Burke, P. , 239-240.
Burrow, J.W., *A Liberal Descent*, 13.
Bury, J.B., 13, 39-40, 83, 89, 94-96, 99, 100-101, 159-160, 181.
business history, 230.
Butler, Bishop, 35, 79.
Butterfield, H., 126, 146-148, 173, 182, 187, 202-207.

Caird, E., 57, 160.
Cambridge historians, 68, 131-132, 148-149.
Cambridge Modern History, 95-96.
Carlyle, T., 1, 4-9, 14, 15, 17, 28, 36, 38-39, 51, 63-64, 180, 214, 221.
Carr, E.H., 110, 223-229, 237.
Centre for Contemporary Cultural Studies, Birmingham, 178.

Chambers, J.D., 231.
Charity Organisation Society, 54-55.
Childe, V.G., 179-182.
Clapham, J.H., 167-168, 171.
Clark, G.N. , 231.
Clark, Kitson, 216-217.
Cobban, A., 139-140, 217, 220.
Cole, G.D.H., 179, 189-190.
Coleridge, 1, 46, 51.
Collingwood, R.G., 83, 86, 119-126, 153, 156, 164, 173, 211.
Collingwood, influence of, 156, 164-167, 185, 207.
Collini, 78, 98, 107.
Communist Party Historians' Group (C.P.H.G.), 177-189.
Comte, Comtism, 21-41, 61, 90, 181, 213.
concrete universals, 160-161.
constitutional history, 10, 11-12, 42-45, 68, 74.
contingency thesis, 160, 228.
Coulton, G.G., 169.
Court, W.H.B., 131-132, 168, 220.
Creighton, M., 14, 25, 57-58, 68, 148.
'critical history', 83-86, 214.
Croce, 84, 112, 153-143.
Cunningham, W., 59-63.

Darwin, 35, 68-69, 100.
Davis, H.W.C., 104-105, 110, 137, 155-156.
de Ruggiero (correspondence with Collingwood), 121-122, 157, 159.
Dilthey, 3, 76-77, 86, 89, 97, 153, 239-242.
diplomatic history, 109-115.
Dobb, M., 177-179, 184-187.
Durkheim, 97.

economic history, 58-66, 167-171, 229-231.
Elton, G.R., 208-209.
Encounter, 224-226.
Engels, 180-181, 182, 187.

249

English Historical Review, 25, 88.
entrepreneur, 187, 230.
Expansion of England, The, 67.

Feiling, K., *A History of England*, 13.
Figgis, J.N., 68-72, 95.
Finberg, H.P.R., 234-236.
Fisher, H.A.L., 84, 88, 93, 109,
    126-131.
Fogel, 161.
Forbes, D., *The Liberal Anglican Idea of
    History*, 1-4, 39.
Foreign Office, 110-111, 115.
Fraser's Magazine, 5.
Freeman, E., 4, 9, 10, 20, 44-45, 47, 55,
    91, 137.
Free will (Will), 3, 14-15, 20-41, 52-53.
French Revolution, 23.
Froude, J.A., 23, 28-31, 34, 36, 90-91,
    137.

Gardiner, S.R., 94.
George, Henry, 58-59.
Germany, reactions to, 56, 67, 104-109,
    111, 114-116, 119-127, 132, 138, 142,
    152-153, 202, 212.
Gierke, 64, 68-69, 75.
Gladstone, 33.
Glasgow University, history at, 74.
God, God's Providence, 2-3, 12, 13, 14,
    24-25, 28, 30-31, 32, 39, 48, 73-74,
    107, 148, 202-207.
Goldstein, D., 13, 87.
Gooch, G.P., 109, 113-117, 138-139.
'great men', great men theory of history,
    5, 6-9, 27-28, 155-156, 180 214, 226.
Green, J.R., 4, 14, 20, 32, 38-39.
Green, T.H., 30, 51-52, 58, 59, 78, 121.
group mind, 108, 75-77.

Hacking, I., 21.
Hancock, W.K., 156, 166-167.
Hare, J., 1, 3.
Harrison, F., 23, 29, 90-92.
Hayek, 213.
Hegel, Hegelianism, 32, 56, 66, 78, 87,
    114, 119, 120, 156, 177.
Heyck, 87.
Hill, C., 129-131, 171, 177, 179.
Historical Association, 88, 153.
History, 11, 136-137, 152, 154, 187.
Hobbes, T., 138.
Hobhouse, 107.

Hobsbawm, E., 179, 190, 196-198.
holism, 17, 51-80.
Hoskins, W.G., 234-235.

Idealism, Idealist philosophy, 1, 8, 11,
    17, 51-80, 83-86, 104-109, 156-164,
    209-212, 236.
Ideal types, 169-170.
Iggers, G., 13.
imperial history, 67, 68-69, 136-137.
individualism, 14-17, 20-50, 98, 106,
    136, 152, 161, 204, 229.
Institute of Historical Research, 88.
intellectuals, 225.
intuitive theory of morals, 36-37, 79-80.
Ireland, 34-35.

Jann, R., 87.
Jerrold, D., 128.
Joad, 122.
John, E., 156, 185-187.
Jowett, 58.

Kant, 35, 79.
Keylor, 13.
Kiernan, V., 179, 195-196, 198.
Kingsley, C., 26-29, 31, 33, 36, 51, 59,
    60, 227.
Kolakowski, 22.

Labour Party, 134.
Langlois (and Seignobos), 97.
Lawrence, R.V., 95.
League of Nations, 111-112, 232.
Leathes, S. , 96.
Lecky, 34-38, 79.
Leff, G., 191-194, 198, 229, 240-242.
'Leicester school', 234-236.
Liberal Anglicans, 1-4, 6, 8, 12, 14, 20,
    33, 46, 66, 71, 78, 91-92.
logical positivism (logical empiricism),
    89, 133, 188-189.
L.S.E. (London School of Economics),
    168-170, 177.
Lucas. C.P., 136-147.
Lukes, S., *Individualism*, 14-17, 161.

Macaulay, 1, 4, 91, 169.
McDougall, 76-77, 108.
Macfarlane, 46, 229.
McIntyre, 205-206.
McKechnie, W.S., 74-75.
McLennan, 18, 178.

Maitland, F., 9, 12, 37, 68-69, 75
Malinowski, 170.
Mandelbaum, 22-23, 29.
Marshall, 59-60, 167.
Marx, Marxism, Marxists, 13, 16, 58,
    120, 122, 129-130, 133, 177-200,
    217-220.
Mathias, 239.
Maurice, F.D., 33, 39, 51, 59, 60, 66.
Mazzini, 58.
Mill, J.S., 15, 23, 24, 26, 27, 46.
Milman, 1, 35.
Modern Quarterly, The, 177, 182, 183.
moral judgment, 57, 148.
Morley, 30.
Muir, Ramsay, 106-107.
Müller, M., 44.

'naive realism', 18.
Namier, 110, 140-146, 212, 228.
Neale, J.E., 187.
Nettleship, 58.
New Left Review, 197.
Nietzsche, 8, 28, 119.
Nineteenth Century, The, 90.
nominalism, 17-18.

Oakeshott, M., 83, 86, 171-173,
    209-212, 228, 238.
Ogg, D., 127, 129.
Ornan, C., 133, 146, 180,
Oxford historians, Oxford University,
    31, 47, 72, 104-106, 126-128, 131.
Oxford Movement, 3.

Paris Peace Conference, 110-111.
PhD (DPhil), 88, 90.
philology, 44.
Pigou, 167-168.
Plumb, J.H., 232-233.
pluralism, 64-80.
Pocock, 209.
Pollard, A.F., 9, 11-12, 136, 152, 154.
Pollard, S., 229, 238-239
Popper, K., 142, 189, 212-216, 227.
Positivism, Positivists, 1, 4, 5, 11,
    21-41, 88-93, 122, 170-171, 173.
Postan, 132, 170-171, 211, 238.
Power, E., 112, 169-170.
Powicke, 112-13, 142-143, 156, 164-165,
    174-175.
professionalisation, 87-88
professionalism, 208.

Prothero, G., 68, 87, 96, 106, 110, 111.

Quetelet, A., 20-21.

racialism, 2, 43, 44-45, 47, 105.
Ranke, 3, 6, 33, 66.
Reformation (English), 45.
Ricardo, 58.
Rickert, 97.
Ritchie, D.G., 83-84, 87.
Robertson, J.M., 23, 30, 32.
Romanticism, Romantics, 2, 15.
Round, J.H., 10, 12, 90, 92.
Royal Historical Society, 88.
Ruggiero — see de Ruggiero
Ruskin, 58, 63.
Russell, B., 108.
Ryle, G., 185-186.

Schumpeter, 230.
Schwarz, 178.
science, 99-101, 164, 178, 179, 187-189.
science (history as), 26, 29-30, 83-101,
    152, 160-162, 173, 178, 179-182.
Scottish Universities, history at, 74.
Seeley, J.R., 10, 13, 33-34, 55, 66-68,
    109.
Seton-Watson, R.W., 110.
Sidgwick, H., 36-37, 59, 79-80.
Smith, Adam, 30, 58.
Smith, A.L., 63, 72-74, 105-106, 141.
Smith, Goldwin, 23, 25-26, 27, 31-32.
social Darwinism, 100, 114.
Social Register, The, 194-196.
sociology, 97-98, 217-220, 239-240.
Soffer, R., 98.
Spencer, H. , 37.
Spengler, 157-159, 223-224, 233.
Stanley, A.P., 1, 4, 38-39, 60, 66.
Stenton, F.M., 89-90.
Stephen, Fitzjames, 25-26.
Stone, C.G., 141.
Stone, L., 145-146.
Stubbs, 6, 9, 14, 20, 23, 31-32, 42-44,
    46, 63.
Sykes, N., 156, 165-166.

Tawney, R.H., 134-136, 169, 178, 182.
Taylor, A.J.P., 13,
Temperley, H., 109-110, 113, 115.
Tennyson, 99.
Thirlwall, 1.
Thompson, E.P., 178, 179, 190, 198-199.

Tolstoy, 41-42, 210, 214.
'Tory' history, 13.
Tout, T.F., 8, 11-12, 40, 93,
Toynbee, A., 58-59, 63.
Toynbee, A.J., 158, 205, 221, 223, 224, 233, 235.
Treitschke, 104-107, 109, 113.
Trevelyan, G.M., 9, 83, 101, 137, 232.
Trevor-Roper, H., 221-222, 228, 237.

Unwin, G., 64-66.
Usher, R.G., 94,
Utilitarianism, Utilitarians, 2, 15, 36.

Walsh, W.H., 224-226.
war (as a test), 56.
Ward, A.W., 96.

Webster, C., 109-113.
Wells, H.G., 128, 158, 233.
Whateley, 1, 35.
Whig interpretation, 2, 9-13, 14, 47, 64, 127-130, 146-148, 172, 177, 182, 205.
Whitehead, A.N., 99-100, 124, 161-162, 166.
Wilson, C., 187.
Woodward, E.L., 148, 232.
World War I, 56, 104-117, 119, 137.
Wormell, D., 33, 66.

York Powell, 96.
Youngson, A.J., 230-231.

Zionism, 141, 145.

Saying **SORRY**

makes everyone
feel better, you see.

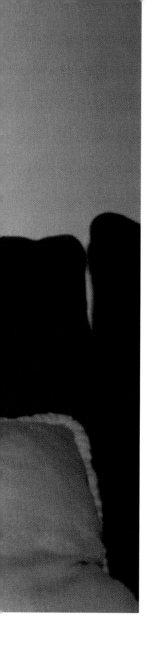

Remember to say
you're sorry—
just like me.

28

"I'm sorry" means,
"I'll try to do better," too.   27

I always say, "I'm sorry."
I really do.

or if I'm a little bit late for my class.

I give him a hug
and wipe his eyes.

I feel sorry for my brother whenever he cries.

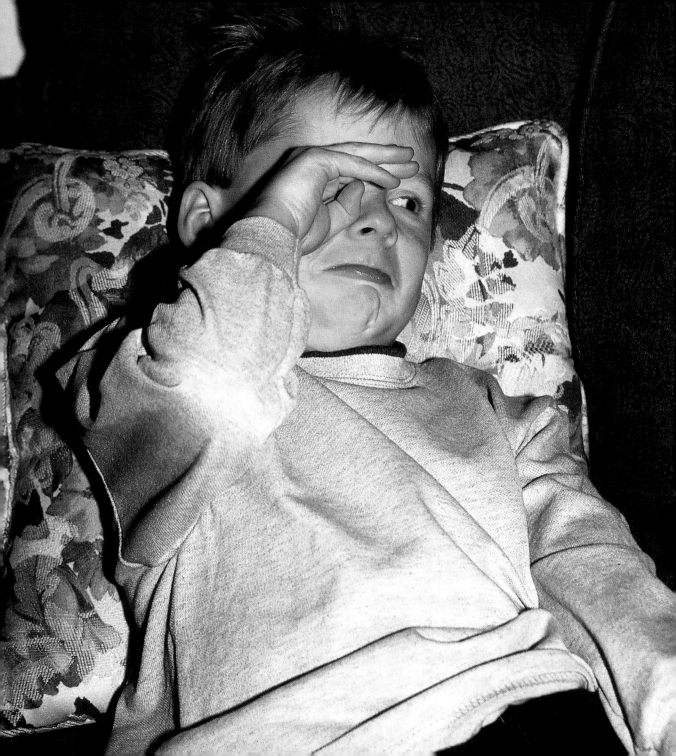

I feel sorry for people
when they are sick.
I say, "Sorry you're sick.
Get well quick."

I'm sorry to keep
you waiting.
Sorry to be so late.

I didn't make it.
It's past time for our date.

Published by The Child's World®, Inc.

Copyright © 2000 by The Child's World®, Inc.
All rights reserved. No part of this book may be
reproduced or utilized in any form or by any means
without written permission from the publisher.
Printed in the United States of America.

Design and Production:
The Creative Spark, San Juan Capistrano, CA

Photos: © 1998 David M. Budd Photography

Library of Congress Cataloging-in-Publication Data

Riley, Susan, 1946–
    I'm Sorry / by Susan Riley.
      p. cm. — (Thoughts and feelings)
    Includes bibliographical references (p.).
    Summary: Identifies occasions when one may "feel sorry," such as being
late, illness, and spilling milk.
    ISBN 1-56766-675-2 (alk. paper)
    1. Sadness Juvenile literature. 2. Regret Juvenile literature. [1. Conduct
of life.] I. Title. II. Series.
BF575.G7R55 1999
395.1'22—dc21
                                             99-22905
                                               CIP

Thoughts and Feelings

I'm Sorry

Written by Susan Riley
Photos by David M. Budd

The Child's World®, Inc.